COMMON CORE CURRICULUM MAPS

IN ENGLISH LANGUAGE ARTS

Grades 6–8

COMMON CORE

JOSSEY-BASS
A Wiley Imprint
www.josseybass.com

OTHER BOOKS IN THE COMMON CORE SERIES:

Common Core Curriculum Maps in English Language Arts, Grades K–5

Common Core Curriculum Maps in English Language Arts, Grades 9–12

Published by Jossey-Bass
A Wiley Imprint
989 Market Street, San Francisco, CA 94103–1741—www.josseybass.com

Readers should be aware that Internet websites offered as citations and/or sources for further information may have changed or disappeared between the time this was written and when it is read.

Limit of Liability/Disclaimer of Warranty: While the publisher and author have used their best efforts in preparing this book, they make no representations or warranties with respect to the accuracy or completeness of the contents of this book and specifically disclaim any implied warranties of merchantability or fitness for a particular purpose. No warranty may be created or extended by sales representatives or written sales materials. The advice and strategies contained herein may not be suitable for your situation. You should consult with a professional where appropriate. Neither the publisher nor author shall be liable for any loss of profit or any other commercial damages, including but not limited to special, incidental, consequential, or other damages.

Jossey-Bass books and products are available through most bookstores. To contact Jossey-Bass directly call our Customer Care Department within the U.S. at 800-956-7739, outside the U.S. at 317-572-3986, or fax 317-572-4002.

Jossey-Bass also publishes its books in a variety of electronic formats. Some content that appears in print may not be available in electronic books.

Library of Congress Cataloging-in-Publication Data
Common Core curriculum maps in English language arts, grades 6–8.—1st ed.
    p. cm. — (The Common Core series)
  Includes index.
 ISBN 978-1-118-10821-5 (pbk.)
 ISBN 978-1-1-181-4802-0 (ebk.)
 ISBN 978-1-1-181-4803-7 (ebk.)
 ISBN 978-1-1-181-4804-4 (ebk.)
 1. Language arts (Middle school)—Curricula—United States—States. 2. Language arts (Middle school)—Standards—United States—States. I. Common Core, Inc.
 LB1631.C656 2012
 372.6′044—dc23

                                                                                    2011029325

Printed in the United States of America
FIRST EDITION
PB Printing   10 9 8 7 6 5 4

CONTENTS

FOREWORD

Good Schools: The Salt of Society

Carol Jago

Three hundred years ago Cotton Mather preached, "A Good School deserves to be call'd the very Salt of the Town that hath it." Without a school "wherein the Youth may by able Masters be Taught the Things that are necessary to qualify them for future Serviceableness," a community will founder.[1] Mather's advice to townspeople in Puritan New England reflects one of the philosophical underpinnings of the Common Core Curriculum Maps in English Language Arts: Schools matter. Curriculum matters. Teachers matter.

In order to determine which things should be taught, we must of course first define what it means to be serviceable in a twenty-first-century democratic society. To ensure a capable workforce and build a strong economy, high levels of literacy and numeracy are obviously essential. But what about the need for students to develop empathy and thoughtfulness? It is short-sighted to equate the value of education with economic growth. Like salt, good schools with rich curricula enhance the community by adding depth—and piquancy. Like salt, they are a preservative, ensuring that a society's values endure.

Many of the benefits we've come to demand as our rights in a modern society depend upon high levels of employment, but if we shift the discussion of the purpose of school from job training to preparing America's children to lead a worthwhile life, the calculus changes. Is simply working nine-to-five for forty years what you most aspire to for your children? Or do you want them to have an education that invites exploration of essential questions, inspires challenges to the status quo, and somehow prepares them for what we cannot yet know? Most parents want both.

The conundrum for curriculum developers is to avoid becoming so caught up in preparing students to make a living—which starts with paying attention in kindergarten; earning good grades through elementary school, middle school, and high school; achieving competitive SAT and ACT scores; and winning a place in college or in the workplace—that we lose sight of educating students to enrich their lives.

In *Not for Profit: Why Democracy Needs the Humanities,* philosopher Martha Nussbaum warns that, "With the rush to profitability in the global market, values precious for the future of democracy, especially in an era of religious and economic anxiety, are in danger of getting lost."[2] I share her concern. The movement to reform education primarily in order to make the United States more globally competitive seems wrong-headed and even counterproductive. Maybe I lack a competitive spirit, but I have always

---

1. Cotton Mather, "The Education of Children," http://www.spurgeon.org/~phil/mather/edkids.htm.
2. Martha Nussbaum, *Not for Profit: Why Democracy Needs the Humanities* (Princeton: Princeton University Press, 2010), 6.

wanted more for my students than just coming in first. I want them to learn about and to think about the world—today's world and yesterday's. Nussbaum explains, "World history and economic understanding must be humanistic and critical if they are to be at all useful in forming intelligent global citizens, and they must be taught alongside the study of religion and of philosophical theories of justice. Only then will they supply a useful foundation for the public debates that we must have if we are to cooperate in solving major human problems."[3] One means of learning about the problems that have beset and continue to bedevil humanity is through the study of the humanities—literature and art, history and philosophy. This is the kind of education the Common Core Curriculum Maps offer. I believe it is the education that every generation of citizens needs.

Unit Three of the Grade One curriculum map, Life Lessons, offers young children opportunities to explore the kind of education Martha Nussbaum recommends. As they work through the unit, "Students read and listen to fables with morals. They learn about rules for life in a book of manners. Reading the life story of George Washington Carver, students learn about a man who had to overcome obstacles in life to make important contributions to science and agriculture. Students learn about Thomas Edison's work with electricity and the rules for its safe use. Descriptive words are the focus of a lesson centered on the artwork of Georgia O'Keeffe. Finally, the children write narratives focused on life lessons and create informative posters focused on electrical safety." This interdisciplinary approach integrates the study of science and builds students' background knowledge. In so doing, it strengthens their reading comprehension and develops their facility with reading informational texts—a key expectation of the Common Core State Standards. It also invites children to investigate Georgia O'Keeffe's paintings and build their cultural literacy.

Some readers of the Common Core Curriculum Maps may argue that their students won't read nineteenth-century novels, that twenty-first-century students raised on Twitter need a faster pace and different kinds of text. I say language arts classrooms may be the last place where young people can unplug themselves from the solipsism of Facebook postings and enter a milieu different from their own. "But my students won't do the homework reading I assign," teachers wail. It isn't as though students don't have the time. A 2010 study by the Kaiser Family Foundation reports that children aged eight to eighteen spend an average of seven and a half hours daily "consuming entertainment media."[4] And this does not include the hour and a half a day they spend texting friends. Today's students have the time to read; many of them simply choose not to.

To those who look at the suggested works for the high school Common Core Curriculum Maps and think, "Our students could never read those books," I urge perusal of the primary grade curriculum maps. If children were immersed in rich literature and nonfiction from the first days of kindergarten and engaged in classroom conversations that encouraged them to think deeply about what they read, then negotiating Ralph Ellison's *Invisible Man* in eleventh grade and Jane Austen's *Sense and Sensibility* in twelfth is certainly possible. Though such books pose textual challenges for young readers, as part of a continuum and under the tutelage of an "able Master," the work is achievable. In our effort to provide students with readings that they can relate to, we sometimes end up teaching works that students can read on their own at the expense of teaching more worthwhile texts that they most certainly need assistance negotiating.

We need to remind ourselves that curriculum should be aimed at what Lev Vygotsky calls students' zone of proximal development. Writing in 1962, Vygotsky said, "the only good kind of instruction is that which marches ahead of development and leads it."[5] Classroom texts should pose intellectual challenges for readers and invite them to stretch and grow. Students also need books that feed their personal interests and allow them to explore "the road not taken." Reading a broad range of books makes students stronger readers and, over time, stronger people. Rigor versus relevance doesn't need to be an

---

3. Ibid., 94.
4. Ulla G. Foehr, Victoria J. Rideout, and Donald F. Roberts, "Generation M²: Media in the Lives of 8- to 18-Year-Olds," (Menlo Park, CA: Kaiser Family Foundation, January 2010), http://www.kff.org/entmedia/8010.cfm.
5. Lev Vygotsky, *Thought and Language*, trans. Eugenia Hanfmann and Gertrude Vakar (Cambridge, MA: MIT Press, 1962), 104.

either-or proposition. With artful instruction by able masters, students can acquire the literacy skills they need—not only to meet the Common Core State Standards, but also to meet the challenges this brave new world is sure to deal them.

Reading literature also helps students explore hypothetical scenarios and consider the ramifications of what might prima facie seem to be a good or profitable idea. Consider the Common Core Curriculum Maps' final Grade Seven unit, Literature Reflects Life: Making Sense of Our World. Addressing Common Core Reading Standard RL.7.6, "Analyze how an author develops and contrasts the points of view of different characters or narrators in a text," the map recommends students read Robert Louis Stevenson's *The Strange Case of Dr. Jekyll and Mr. Hyde.* This nineteenth-century novella invites young readers to reflect upon their own conflicting natures and offers a cautionary tale regarding experimentation. When we consider how best to prepare tomorrow's doctors, scientists, programmers, and engineers for the twenty-first century, it seems to me that reading stories about investigations that go very wrong is quite a good idea.

Later in his sermon, Cotton Mather states that "the Devil cannot give a greater Blow to the Reformation among us, than by causing Schools to Languish under Discouragements." The Common Core Curriculum Maps offer hope to discouraged teachers. They offer a plan for developing young minds, a plan that is both rigorous and has never been more relevant. It may seem odd to be taking guidance from a seventeenth-century Puritan, but I know I couldn't say it better. "Where schools are not vigorously and Honourably Encouraged, whole Colonies will sink apace into a Degenerate and Contemptible Condition, and at last become horribly Barbarous. If you would not betray your Posterity into the very Circumstances of Savages, let Schools have more Encouragement." Amen.

WRITTEN BY TEACHERS, FOR TEACHERS

To My Fellow Teachers:

Participating in the development of these Maps has been an eye-opening and incredibly rewarding professional development experience for me. I was especially drawn to the project because I knew that the Maps would be offered *for free* to teachers around the country. Since my first years as a classroom teacher, I've witnessed the powerful results that come from a marriage between rich content and literacy instruction; I wanted the Maps to exhibit this component. As an administrator, I approached this project from the perspective of creating resources that provide enough support for you without taking away your creative freedom. As a mother, I've thought about what an impact these Maps could and will—I hope—have on the education my children receive.

The new Common Core State Standards Initiative presented my colleagues and me—now close friends—with an ideal opportunity for twenty-first-century collaboration: we live in three different states, yet developed these Maps together. After much trial and error regarding our approach, we decided to pair the best literary and informational texts we know into meaningful thematic units, allowing students to develop literacy in a humanities-rich environment. We hope that the closely related components of these Maps will give you confidence to use them in various permutations in your classroom. We also hope you will collaborate with your colleagues to refine and create new activities that will not only ensure the standards are taught and learned, but will also yield deeper levels of student work and satisfaction.

In the middle school Maps of this volume, we have worked to provide the perfect juxtaposition of substantive and challenging content with engaging and interesting instructional approaches for middle school students. We have made every effort to engage students in a variety of age-appropriate and social ways, encouraging them to take complex ideas and apply them to their daily experiences inside *and outside* of class.

Our own collaboration on these Maps has been intellectually gratifying and joyful, and we hope they provide you with a similarly rewarding experience. These Maps are our gift to you, and we sincerely hope you enjoy the journey of making them your own.

Cyndi Wells
Lead coach and fine arts facilitator, Charlottesville, Virginia
Lead writer, fourth through eighth grade,
Common Core Curriculum Maps in ELA

To My Fellow Teachers:

For years we have been deluged with reform initiatives from on high that claimed they would improve student achievement. Few have actually brought progress. I joined the Common Core team of teachers out of conviction that the Common Core State Standards (CCSS) would make a difference and have a positive impact on our work in the classroom. The standards provide a framework for composing a rich, well-planned curriculum that guides our instruction.

Classroom teachers know that imaginative planning is at the heart of any successful lesson. The seventy-six Sample Lesson Plans (SLP), one for each of the units, are instructional road maps. The purpose of each SLP is to demonstrate how to create the necessary link between the literary and informational texts and the CCSS. The SLPs vary in focus and content—from a novel or selection of poems to a play or informational text. Each has a clear topic, a set of objectives, and suggested activities, as well as helpful guides for differentiated instruction. Consider these plans as a place to start. Use them directly or as a model for developing your own lessons.

Writing the maps and the SLPs has been both intellectually rewarding and joyful to us as classroom teachers. I hope you find that working with these volumes becomes equally joyful and useful in your own classrooms.

Dr. Ruthie Stern
High school teacher, New York City
Lead writer, Sample Lesson Plans, Common Core Curriculum Maps in ELA

INTRODUCTION

Few educators or policymakers would have guessed, even a year or so ago, that nearly all states would jettison their standards and embrace new, largely uniform standards for the teaching of ELA and math. Fewer still would have expected all of this to happen as quickly as it has.

The rapid rise of the Common Core State Standards (CCSS) is an unprecedented event at the national level—and more importantly, at the school level, where its implications are profound. For educators in most states, the CCSS raise the bar for what students should know and be able to do.[1] If you are reading this, you are probably responsible for implementing the CCSS in your school, district, or state. You will find that the CCSS contain explicit guidance about the reading, writing, speaking, listening, and language skills students are expected to master. Almost any single standard in the CCSS illustrates this. Here's one of the reading standards from seventh grade:

> Determine two or more central ideas in a text and analyze their development over the course of the text; provide an objective summary of the text. (RI.7.2)

The CCSS call for the new standards to be taught within the context of a "content-rich curriculum." But the CCSS do not specify what content students need to master, as this fell outside the scope of the standards-setting project. Here is how this is explained in the introduction to the CCSS:

> [W]hile the Standards make references to some particular forms of content, including mythology, foundational U.S. documents, and Shakespeare, they do not—indeed, cannot—enumerate all or even most of the content that students should learn. The Standards must therefore be complemented by a well-developed, content-rich curriculum consistent with the expectations laid out in this document.[2]

Responsibility for developing such a curriculum falls to schools, districts, and states. Common Core's Curriculum Maps in ELA are designed to meet the needs of the teacher, principal, curriculum director, superintendent, or state official who is striving to develop, or to help teachers to develop, new ELA curricula aligned with the CCSS. The Maps can also serve as a resource for those endeavoring to conduct professional development related to the standards.

---

1. Sheila Byrd Carmichael, Gabrielle Martino, Kathleen Porter-Magee, and W. Stephen Wilson, "The State of State Standards—and the Common Core—in 2010" (Washington, DC: Thomas B. Fordham Institute, July 2010), 13.

2. *Common Core State Standards for English Language Arts & Literacy in History/Social Studies, Science, and Technical Subjects* (Washington, DC: Common Core State Standards Initiative), 6.

The Maps provide a coherent sequence of thematic curriculum units, roughly six per grade level, K – 12. The units connect the skills outlined in the CCSS in ELA with suggested works of literature and informational texts and provide activities teachers could use in their classrooms. You will also find suggested student objectives in each unit, along with lists of relevant terminology and links to high quality additional resources. *Every standard in the CCSS is covered in the Maps,* most more than once. Standards citations are included after each sample activity/assessment to indicate alignment. Each grade includes a "standards checklist" showing which standards are covered in which unit. And most of the works the CCSS lists as "exemplar texts" are included in the Maps.

Moreover, each unit in this print edition of the Maps features a Sample Lesson Plan, a road map showing how to use one or more of the suggested texts in that unit to meet specific standards. Each Sample Lesson Plan includes step-by-step guidance for classroom activities tied to the lesson, questions that engage students in a deeper analysis and appreciation of the texts, and even suggestions for differentiated instruction. Many of the Sample Lesson Plans, particularly in the earlier grades, also include detailed guidance for connecting ELA lessons to other subjects, including math, science, history, geography, music, and art.

An important feature of Common Core's curriculum Maps is their attention to building students' background knowledge of a diverse array of events, people, places, and ideas. Cognitive science has demonstrated that students read better if they know something about the subject they are studying.[3] With this in mind, Common Core incorporated into its Maps themes, texts, and activities that teach students about "The Great Big World," as one of the kindergarten Maps is called. The content cloud shown in Figure I.1 includes much of the key content knowledge in the Maps. The larger an event, name, or idea appears in the cloud, the more emphasis it receives in the Maps. As you examine this cloud, do keep in mind that the Maps contain much that is not included here.

Figure I.1

Common Core's Maps were written by teachers for teachers. More than three dozen public school teachers had a hand in drafting, writing, reviewing, or revising the Maps. Collectively, these teachers brought dozens of years of experience to the mapping project. Each of the lead writers is deeply knowledgeable about the CCSS; some even served as feedback providers to the standards' writers. These

---

3. Daniel T. Willingham, *Why Don't Students Like School? A Cognitive Scientist Answers Questions About How the Mind Works and What It Means for the Classroom* (San Francisco: Jossey-Bass, 2009).

teachers looked to model curricula, including the International Baccalaureate, and at excellent, content-specific standards, such as the Massachusetts English Language Arts Curriculum Frameworks, for suggestions of what topics and titles to include at each grade. Most importantly, the teachers drew on their own considerable experience of what students enjoy learning about, and infused the Maps with that knowledge.

The Maps also reflect the contributions and perspective of the many teachers who reviewed them. Twice, the American Federation of Teachers convened the same panel of teachers that reviewed the CCSS to review Common Core's Maps. The Milken Family Foundation connected us with a dozen winners of the Milken Educator Award. These teachers, nationally recognized for excellence in the classroom, provided invaluable input and insight. And the National Alliance of Black School Educators identified superintendents, teachers, and content area specialists from across the country who reviewed the Maps in draft form. A public review of our draft Maps, conducted in the fall of 2010, elicited numerous helpful comments.

And the Maps will continue to evolve and improve. The second online edition of the Maps is open to public comment twenty-four hours a day, seven days a week. Anyone is able to critique any aspect of the Maps—any essential question, any student objective, any text suggestion. Viewers can rate each unit Map as a whole, and many other Map elements, such as suggested works and sample activities. Comments on the Maps are open for public view. Also, teachers can submit sample lesson plans that will be reviewed by a committee of teachers who will decide which ones to add to the official Maps website. In these ways and more, Common Core's Curriculum Maps in ELA are living documents, expanding and improving over time as they absorb and reflect the experience and perspective of educators across the nation.

We are thrilled that, as of this writing, the website featuring the maps (www.commoncore.org) has attracted more than three million visitors and that six state departments of education have recommended the Maps for use by districts statewide. The publication of the Maps is a momentous step for the mapping project. If you find this volume of interest we hope you will follow our project as we develop more inspiring and instrumental Maps-related resources for America's educators.

September 2011

Lynne Munson
President and Executive Director, Common Core

HOW TO USE THE COMMON CORE CURRICULUM MAPS

Common Core's Curriculum Maps in ELA are brand-new curriculum materials, built around the Common Core State Standards (CCSS) in English Language Arts. The CCSS dictated both the goals and contours of our Maps. The "exemplar texts" listed in the CCSS figure significantly in our unit Maps, which break down each grade, K–12, into a series of themed units. Each unit pairs standards with suggested student objectives, texts, activities, and more.

The Maps are intended to serve as "road maps" for the school year, as aids for jump-starting the lesson planning process. As common planning tools, these Maps can facilitate school and district-wide collaboration. They also can become the backbone of rich, content-based professional development as teachers work together to create and then refine curricula for their particular schools and classrooms.

The units are designed to be taught in sequence (particularly in elementary school), but teachers could certainly modify the units if they need to be taught in a different order. We do not expect teachers to use every text, nor to do every sample activity or assessment. The suggested texts simply offer a range of rich and relevant materials from which teachers may choose. The suggested activities or assessments are neither prescriptive nor exhaustive. Teachers can select from among them, modify them to meet their students' needs, and/or use them as inspiration for creating their own activities.

Each unit Map contains the following elements:

Overview. This is a brief description of the unit. It explains the unit's theme and provides a summary of what students will learn. It explains the structure, progression, and various components of the unit. It may offer some guidance regarding the selection of texts. The unit descriptions illuminate the connections between the skills identified in the standards and the content of the suggested works.

Essential question. The "essential question" highlights the usefulness, the relevance, and the greater benefit of a unit. It is often the "so what?" question about material covered. It should be answerable, at least to some degree, by the end of the unit, but it should also have more than one possible answer. It should prompt intellectual exploration by generating other questions. Here's an example from eighth grade: "How does learning history through literature differ from learning through informational text?"

Focus standards. These standards are taken directly from the CCSS and have been identified as especially important for the unit. Other standards are covered in each unit as well, but the focus standards are the ones that the unit has been designed to address specifically.

Suggested student objectives. These are the specific student outcomes for the unit. They describe the transferable ELA content and skills that students should possess when the unit is completed. The objectives are often components of more broadly worded standards and sometimes address content and skills necessarily related to the standards. The lists are not exhaustive, and the objectives should not supplant the standards themselves. Rather, they are designed to help teachers "drill down" from the standards and augment as necessary, providing added focus and clarity for lesson planning purposes.

Suggested works. These are substantial lists of suggested literary and informational texts. In most cases (particularly in the middle and high school grades), this list contains more texts than a unit could cover; it is meant to offer a range of options to teachers. Several permutations of the list could meet the goals of the unit. The suggested texts draw heavily from the "exemplar texts" listed in the CCSS. Exemplars are works the CCSS identified as meeting the levels of complexity and rigor described in the standards. These texts are identified with an (E) after the title of an exemplar text. An (EA) indicates a work by an author who has another work cited as an exemplar text.

Art, music, and media. These sections list works of visual art, music, film, and other media that reflect the theme of the unit and that a teacher can use to extend students' knowledge in these areas. Each unit includes at least one sample activity involving the works listed under this heading. ELA teachers who choose to use this material may do so on their own, by team teaching with an art or music teacher, or perhaps by sharing the material with the art or music teacher, who could reinforce what students are learning during the ELA block in their classroom. The inclusion of these works in our ELA Maps is *not* intended to substitute for or infringe in any way upon instruction that students should receive in separate art and music classes.

Sample activities and assessments. These items have been written particularly for the unit, with specific standards and often with specific texts in mind. Each activity addresses at least one standard in the CCSS; the applicable standard(s) are cited in parentheses following the description of each activity. The suggested activities or assessments are not intended to be prescriptive, exhaustive, or sequential; they simply demonstrate how specific content can be used to help students learn the skills described in the standards. They are designed to generate evidence of student understanding and give teachers ideas for developing their own activities and assessments. Teachers should use, refine, and/or augment these activities as desired, in order to ensure that they will have addressed all the standards intended for the unit and, in the aggregate, for the year.

Reading foundations. Our kindergarten through second-grade Maps include a section titled Reading Foundations that provides a pacing guide of instructional goals for the teaching of the CCSS reading Foundational Skills. This guide complements our Maps and was prepared by reading expert Louisa Moats, who also helped develop the reading standards for the CCSS.

Additional resources. These are links to lesson plans, activities, related background information, author interviews, and other instructional materials for teachers from a variety of resources, including the National Endowment for the Humanities and ReadWriteThink. The standards that could be addressed by each additional resource are cited at the end of each description.

Terminology. These are concepts and terms that students will encounter—often for the first time—over the course of the unit. The list is not comprehensive; it is meant to highlight terms that either are particular to the unit, are introduced there, or that play a large role in the work or content of the unit. These terms and concepts are usually implied by the standards, but not always made explicit in them.

Making interdisciplinary connections. This is a section included only in our Maps for the elementary grades. Here we very broadly list the content areas the unit covers and then suggest opportunities for making interdisciplinary connections from the Common Core ELA Maps to other subjects, including history, civics, geography, and the arts. We hope this section will be particularly helpful for K–5 teachers, who typically teach all subjects.

Sample lesson plans. Each unit includes a supplementary document that outlines a possible sequence of lessons, using one or more suggested unit texts to meet focus standards. Many of the texts used in the sample lesson plans are also CCSS exemplar texts. These sample lessons include guidance for differentiated instruction.

Standards checklist. Each grade includes a standards checklist that indicates which standards are covered in which unit—providing teachers an overview of standards coverage for the entire school year.

Addressing all of the CCSS. The curriculum writers worked carefully to ensure that the content and skills in each unit would build on one another so that in the aggregate, all standards would be addressed in a coherent, logical way. They grouped standards that they could envision fitting together in one unit. For example, if a unit were focused on asking and answering questions in informational text, then standards for shared research and expository writing were included in that unit as well. *All standards are addressed at least once,* if not a number of times, in the activities and assessments sections.

Interpreting CCSS citations. Our citations for the standards follow the format established by the CCSS (found in the upper right-hand corners of the pages in the CCSS ELA document):

strand.grade.number

For example, the first Reading Literature (RL) standard in grade four would be cited as RL.4.1. You will find our citations in the front of each focus standard and at the end of each sample activity/assessment. Where standards clearly corresponded to lessons listed under Additional Resources, standards also have been cited.

Understanding unit themes. The unit themes grew organically out of the process of selecting which standards would be the focus of each unit and consulting the list of exemplar texts. The teachers who wrote the Maps intentionally chose themes that would resonate with students, as well as lend coherence to the skills and content addressed. Some of the themes introduced in the early elementary grades, such as courage, re-emerge in later years. We have done so in a deliberate attempt to invite students to wrestle with some of the "great ideas," a hallmark of a liberal education. We hope that as students progress through school, they will consider the themes at greater levels of depth.

Teaching reading. Under the Reading Foundations sections for the kindergarten through second-grade Maps (and embedded into the third- through fifth-grade Maps) is a pacing guide for reading instruction. This guide is aligned with the CCSS reading Foundational Skills. The guide paces instruction in reading foundations logically across the grades. Concepts of print, phonological awareness, phonics, and text reading fluency are all addressed and woven into a developmental progression that leads to word recognition and text reading. Accomplishment of these milestones can be achieved with daily practice and brief activities that would require thirty to forty minutes of instructional time per day. A sample of those activities is also provided. Explicit, sequential, and cumulative teaching of these skills in no way should detract from, substitute for, or prevent the teaching of the oral language, comprehension, and literature-focused instruction, also described in the units.

The curriculum Maps are not tailored for any specific reading instruction method or management technique. *It is up to local school districts and teachers to determine how reading will be taught.* The sample activities and assessments reflect a mix of teacher- and student-centered instruction, but emphasize eliciting evidence of student understanding through authentic assessments.

Selecting materials. Many of the texts listed as exemplars in the CCSS Appendix B are included in our Maps. These texts take priority in our units and indeed shape unit themes. Like the exemplar texts themselves, the additional texts suggested in our Maps include literary works and informational texts that have stood the test of time, as well as excellent contemporary titles. The suggested texts include novels, short stories, poetry, essays, speeches, memoirs, biographies, autobiographies, fables, folktales, and mythology. Teachers will find texts written by authors of wide-ranging diversity: young and old, living and dead, male and female, American and foreign.

In the early grades, the Maps prioritize students' exposure to traditional stories and poetry, Mother Goose rhymes, and award-winning fiction and nonfiction chosen for quality of writing and relevance to themes. They also emphasize concepts of print, phonological awareness, phonics, and text reading fluency. In upper elementary and middle school grades, students read a variety of fiction and nonfiction on science and history topics, as well as diverse selections of classic and contemporary literature. High school begins by establishing in ninth grade a common understanding of literary and informational genres, subgenres, and their characteristics. Grades ten through twelve each focus on a different literary tradition, both American and international. Along the way, the Maps highlight numerous points of connection with history, science, and the arts.

Much consideration has been given to readability. Whenever possible, we have used Lexile level ranges, as described in the CCSS Appendix A, as a guide. We realize that there still will be a range of texts within each grade span. We also recognize that simple texts may be read at upper grades with more nuanced analysis. For this reason, some texts appear in more than one grade. Texts that fall outside the CCSS-recommended grade span are noted.

At the elementary and middle school levels, the text availability and readability levels also were cross-checked with the Scholastic Reading Wizard Reading Levels section, Amazon.com, and the Lexile levels (as available) on the Barnes & Noble website.

Evaluating student work. Aside from the inclusion of a scoring rubric for high school seminars, the Maps do not provide sample student work or scoring rubrics. We do hope that the interactivity feature of the online edition of the Maps may allow teachers to submit these kinds of materials, if they so desire. We expect to develop such additional tools as teachers and curriculum developers use and customize the Maps, and as we conduct ongoing professional development.

Differentiating instruction. The sample lesson plans provide specific guidance for differentiated instruction for advanced and struggling students. As with student work and scoring rubrics, we expect to develop further guidance on differentiation as the Maps are implemented and customized.

Incorporating art, music, and media. While literature is of course a vital component of the standards, some standards in the CCSS address the arts as well. Because Common Core promotes the importance of all students studying the arts, we have highlighted places where ELA instruction could be enhanced by connecting a work of literature or an objective of the unit to art, music, or film. For example, students might compare a novel, story, or play to its film or musical rendition. Where a particular period of literature or the literature of a particular region or country is addressed, works of art from that period or country may also be examined. We suggest, for example, that students study self-portraiture when they are encountering memoirs. In each case, connections are made to the standards themselves.

Promoting student understanding through recitation and memorization. Recitation requires close reading and therefore nurtures deeper levels of students' understanding. Students also benefit from the satisfaction of making a poem or piece of prose one's own for life. In addition, many teachers observe that memorization and recitation help develop a student's experience and confidence in public speaking, which could help students marshal evidence and make effective arguments in other contexts. Keep in mind that our suggestions for memorization activities are not meant to be mandatory in every unit.

GRADE 6

Entering middle school students who were taught with the Common Core curriculum maps for K–5 have a strong background in mythology, folktales, and fables from around the world; classic and contemporary fiction and poetry; and literary nonfiction related to historical and select scientific topics. They are able to write short essays in which they articulate a central idea and support it with examples from texts. In sixth grade, students take their knowledge to new levels as they begin to explore deeper and subtler themes. While reading *Peter Pan* and its prequel versions at the start of sixth grade, students consider the question: What distinguishes childhood from adulthood? Later in the year, they study folklore; consider aspects of courage; read literature, first-hand narratives, and informational texts about heritage and immigration; learn about the elements of a mystery story; read about flying from literary, historical, and scientific perspectives; and more. Throughout the units, they study morphology and etymology, building their own dictionaries of words that they have investigated. Students write in a variety of genres, including responses to literature, reflective essays, and stories. They use graphic organizers to lay out their ideas and plan their essays. They participate in class discussion and art enrichment activities; practice reading literature expressively; and deliver presentations. By the end of sixth grade, they are ready to study literature with complex and challenging themes.

Standards Checklist for Grade Six

Standard	Unit 1	Unit 2	Unit 3	Unit 4	Unit 5	Unit 6	Standard	Unit 1	Unit 2	Unit 3	Unit 4	Unit 5	Unit 6
Reading—Literature							3d	A	A		A	A	
1	A	A	A	A			3e	A	A		A	A	
2		A		A	A	FA	4	A	A	A	A	A	
3	A	FA		A	A	A	5		A	FA		A	
4	A	A	A	A	A		6		A		FA	A	A
5		A			FA	A	7			FA	A		A
6	A		FA	A			Speaking and Listening						
7	FA	A			A		1		FA	FA	A	A	A	A
8 n/a							1a	FA	A	A	A	A	A
9		A	A	FA	A		1b	FA	A	A	A	A	A
10						A	1c	A	FA	A	A	A	A
Reading—Informational Text							1d	A	FA	A	A	A	A
1	FA						2		A	A	FA	A	A
2		A		FA		A	3		A	FA			
3			FA	A		A	4				A	FA	
4	A	FA		A	FA		5						FA
5				A	A		6	A	A	A	A	A	A
6				A		FA	Language						
7			A	A		FA	1	FA	A	A	A	A	FA
8			A	A			1a	FA	A	A	A	A	A
9			FA			A	1b	FA	A	A	A	A	A
10						A	1c	A	A	A	A	A	A
Writing							1d	A	A	A	A	A	A
1	A		FA	FA	A	A	1e	A	A	A	A	A	A
1a	A		A	A	A	A	2	A	A	A	A	A	A
1b	A		A	A	A	A	2a	A	A	A	A	A	A
1c	A		A	A	A	A	2b	A	A	A	A	A	A
1d	A		A	A	A	A	3	A	A	A	FA	A	A
1e	A		A	A	A	A	3a	A	A	A	A	A	A
2		A			FA	FA	3b	A	A	A	A	A	A
2a		A			A	A	4	A	FA	FA	A		A
2b		A			A	A	4a	A	FA	A	A	A	A
2c		A			A	A	4b	A	FA	A	A	A	A
2d		A			A	A	4c	A	A	FA	A	A	A
2e		A			A	A	4d	A	A	FA	A		A
2f		A			A	A	5				A	FA	A
3	FA	FA			A	A	5a				A	A	A
3a	A	A			A	A	5b				A	A	A
3b	A	A			A	A	5c				A	A	A
3c	A	A			A	A	6						A

F = Focus Standard; A = Activity/Assessment

I Won't Grow Up

This first six-week unit of sixth grade starts off the year with reflections on childhood—from literature and poetry to students' own experiences.

ESSENTIAL QUESTION

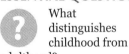 What distinguishes childhood from adulthood?

OVERVIEW

Students build on their knowledge of books read in fifth grade (see the Common Core Curriculum Maps for grades K–5) and explore the theme of growing up. Students read the original and prequel versions of *Peter Pan*. They have the opportunity to listen to one of the books on tape, compare and contrast the written and audio presentations, and extend this activity to watching the Broadway musical version. Students read biographies about and interviews with the respective authors of the various versions. After reading and discussing the elements of effective prequels, students write their own prequels to another well-known story in order to see just how challenging writing one can be. This unit ends with an informative/explanatory essay that addresses the essential question.

FOCUS STANDARDS

These Focus Standards have been selected for the unit from the Common Core State Standards.

RI.6.1: Cite textual evidence to support analysis of what the text says explicitly as well as inferences drawn from the text.

RL.6.7: Compare and contrast the experience of reading a story, poem, or drama to listening to or viewing an audio, video, or live version of the text, including contrasting what they "see" and "hear" when reading the text to what they perceive when they listen or watch.

W.6.3: Write narratives to develop real or imagined experiences or events using effective technique, relevant descriptive details, and well-structured event sequences.

SL.6.1: Engage effectively in a range of collaborative discussions (one-on-one, in groups, and teacher-led) with diverse partners on grade 6 topics, texts, and issues, building on others' ideas and expressing their own clearly.

SL.6.1(a): Come to discussions prepared, having read or studied required material; explicitly draw on that preparation by referring to evidence on the topic, text, or issue to probe and reflect on ideas under discussion.

SL.6.1(b): Follow rules for collegial discussions, set specific goals and deadlines, and define individual roles as needed.

L.6.1: Demonstrate command of the conventions of Standard English grammar and usage when writing or speaking.

L.6.1(a): Ensure that pronouns are in the proper case (subjective, objective, possessive).

L.6.1(b): Use intensive pronouns (e.g., *myself, ourselves*).

SUGGESTED STUDENT OBJECTIVES

- Read and compare an original text to its prequel (e.g., *Peter Pan* and *Peter and the Starcatchers*).
- Establish a plan for locating credible and reliable information when conducting research.
- Research the relationship between authors' lives and what they write about through reading author biographies, autobiographies, letters, and interviews; present findings to the class.
- Prepare for class discussions by taking notes on specific elements of texts read.
- Write a prequel for a story of choice that reflects appreciation for the selected work.
- Demonstrate understanding of texts by interpreting significant scenes for classmates.

SUGGESTED WORKS

(E) indicates a CCSS exemplar text; (EA) indicates a text from a writer with other works identified as exemplars.

LITERARY TEXTS

Stories

- "Eleven" (Sandra Cisneros) (E)
- *Peter Pan* (J. M. Barrie)
- *Peter and the Starcatchers* (Dave Barry, Ridley Pearson, and Greg Call)
- *Peter and the Shadow Thieves* (Dave Barry, Ridley Pearson, and Greg Call)
- *When I Was Your Age, Volume Two: Original Stories about Growing up* (Amy Ehrlich, ed.)
- *The Secret Knowledge of Grown-Ups* (David Wisniewski)
- *James and the Giant Peach* (Roald Dahl)
- *Charlie and the Chocolate Factory* (Roald Dahl)

Poetry

- "Past, Present, Future" (Emily Brontë)
- "A Birthday" (Christina Rossetti) (EA)

INFORMATIONAL TEXTS

Nonfiction

- *J. M. Barrie: The Magic Behind Peter Pan* (Susan Bivin Aller)
- *Boy: Tales of Childhood* (Roald Dahl) (EA)

Articles

- "Peter Pan's early years" (Bob Minzesheimer, *USA Today,* September 1, 2004)
- "Prequel to Peter Pan fills in the blanks with fun" (Sue Corbett, *Miami Herald,* no date)
- "Classic story flies in many forms" (A Peter Pan timeline)" (Bob Minzesheimer, *USA Today,* September 1, 2004)

ART, MUSIC, AND MEDIA

Music

- Moose Charlap and Carolyn Leigh, "I Won't Grow Up" (1954). *Note:* This song is from *Peter Pan,* the musical, and the version in which Cathy Rigby sings the part of Peter is recommended.

Film

- Glenn Casale and Gary Halvorson, dir., *Peter Pan* (2000)
- Marc Forster, dir., *Finding Neverland* (2004)
- Henry Selick, dir., *James and the Giant Peach* (1996)
- Mel Stuart, dir., *Willy Wonka and the Chocolate Factory* (1971)
- Tim Burton, dir., *Charlie and the Chocolate Factory* (2005)

Media

- *Peter Pan* (BBC Radio Presents) (Random House Audio)
- *Peter and the Starcatchers* (audiobook CD) (Brilliance Audio)
- *James and the Giant Peach* (audiobook CD) (Puffin Books)

SAMPLE ACTIVITIES AND ASSESSMENTS

1. LITERATURE RESPONSE

As you read the original and prequel versions of *Peter Pan*, take notes about the following in your journal:

- Setting
- List of characters and their traits
- The character's internal responses and external behaviors to events in the story
- The events that lead up to climax, and, ultimately, the character's development
- "I Won't Grow Up"—how do Peter Pan's actions reflect these famous words?

Be sure to write down the page numbers of relevant information, or mark your book with sticky notes, so you can go back and cite the text during class discussion. You will be given an opportunity to talk through your ideas with a partner prior to class discussion. (RL.6.1)

2. LITERATURE RESPONSE

Discuss the elements of setting (e.g., time, place, environment) with your classmates. Find examples of how time, place, and environment are used in Peter Pan. Write your ideas on a sticky note before sharing ideas as a class. After the class discussion, look back in the text to find specific examples of how J. M. Barrie described Neverland and even how he described the Darlings' home in England. Create a three-column chart in your journal (or as a table on the computer) to help organize your notes; use one column for each element of setting. (RL.6.1, RL.6.3)

3. LITERATURE RESPONSE

Create a character map of one of the characters from *Peter Pan*, citing specific examples from the text. As a class, we will compare and contrast similarities and differences in how the characters develop over the course of a story, and discuss how we learn from the behavior of literary characters—both through examples and "non-examples." (RL.6.1, RL.6.3)

4. CLASS DISCUSSION

In *Peter and the Starcatchers*, Dave Barry and Ridley Pearson took a well-known book, *Peter Pan,* and wrote about what happened before the events that took place in it. How do Barry and Pearson connect this story to the original? What elements and details do they retain, and which ones do they omit? Your teacher may ask you first to write your own response in your journal and share it with a partner prior to discussing as a class. Be sure to write down the page numbers of relevant information, or to mark your book with sticky notes, so you can cite the text during class discussion. (SL.6.1a,b, RL.6.1, RL.6.6)

5. NARRATIVE WRITING

Write a prequel to *Charlie and the Chocolate Factory* by Roald Dahl (or to another favorite book). What elements of the original are important to maintain in creating a prequel? What elements of setting (e.g., time, place, environment) will you include? Be sure to stay true to the original characters and open the prequel with an attention-getting scene, like the one in *Peter and the Starcatchers*. The well-developed prequel should hook the reader from the start. Edit your writing for pronouns, punctuation, and spelling. Your teacher may ask you to draw and scan an illustration to accompany it. (RL.6.3, W.6.3, W.6.4, L.6.1a,b, L.6.2a,b)

6. WRITING (ARGUMENT)

How is listening to *Peter Pan, Peter and the Starcatchers,* or *James and the Giant Peach* as an audiobook similar to and different from reading the book? Which do you prefer? Why? Write an argument to support your preference in your journal or post it on the classroom blog, and compare your response to those of your classmates. Discuss at least three reasons for your preference, citing evidence from the text. (RL.6.7, W.6.1, L.6.1a,b, L.6.2a,b)

7. DRAMATIZATION/FLUENCY

Choose a scene from one of the books that you find humorous or that touched you in some way. Work with classmates to present the scene as a dramatic reading. You may also record your presentation using a video camera to compare the difference in impact between seeing and hearing the words. (SL.6.6)

8. INFORMATIVE/EXPLANATORY WRITING

What did you learn about the authors from the biographies, autobiographies, letters, or interviews that you didn't know before? How much of the author's experience do you "see" in the text after learning more about him/her? Prior to drafting your essay, you should establish a plan for locating credible and reliable information. Your explanation should be a well-developed essay that includes three to four supporting details. Edit your writing for pronouns, punctuation, and spelling. (RI.6.1, L.6.1a,b, L.6.2a,b)

9. POETRY RESPONSE

How is the treatment of growing up similar and different in the poems and the prose we've read? Write your ideas in your journal prior to class discussion. (SL.6.6)

10. LITERATURE RESPONSE/MEDIA APPRECIATION

What does the phrase "I won't grow up" mean to you? Based on the lyrics from the musical version of *Peter Pan*, what does growing up mean to Peter? Does this song include all aspects of growing up? Your teacher may ask you to first write your own response in your journal and share it with a partner prior to discussing as a class. (SL.6.1a,b) (*Note:* Alternatively, you may watch the "I Won't Grow Up" scene from the movie or on YouTube and then discuss.) (RL.6.7)

11. WORD STUDY

Keep an index card file of words studied while reading *Peter Pan*. Keeping the words on index cards will help you when we sort words by prefix, suffix, root words, meaning, spelling feature, and so on. Can you select a word and find its root? How do prefixes and suffixes affect the part of speech and spelling? (*Note:* This will be an ongoing activity all year long.) (L.6.4a,b)

12. CLASS DISCUSSION (QUESTIONS THAT BUILD ON TEXTS READ IN GRADE FIVE)

Compare and contrast the character of Wendy Darling in *Peter Pan* with the character of Alice in *Alice's Adventures in Wonderland*. How are their experiences in a fantastic land similar? How are they different? How does the fact that these characters are female affect their fantastic experiences?

Eternal youth is a common theme between *Tuck Everlasting* and *Peter Pan*. Would you like to remain young forever? Why or why not? Cite specific passages or events from *Peter Pan* or *Tuck Everlasting* to support your claim. (SL.6.1a,b)

13. INFORMATIVE/EXPLANATORY WRITING

Write an informative/explanatory essay in response to the essential question (What distinguishes childhood from adulthood?). Choose at least three things learned from a character or an author and explain what you learned from them. Prepare the essay for publication by editing, especially for pronouns, punctuation, and spelling. Upload your essay to the classroom blog or a class wiki. Be prepared to make an audio recording of your essay and upload it as a podcast on the class web page for this unit. (W.6.9a,b, W.6.4, L.6.1a,b, L.6.2a,b)

14. GRAMMAR AND USAGE

Your teacher will teach mini-lessons on the individual language standards. For example, he/she will explain relative pronouns and adverbs to the class, and then you will practice some cloze activities as a class: (i.e., (1) I told you about the dog _____ [who, whose, whom, which, that] lives next door. (2) The stars were shining _____ [brightly, bright] in the night sky.) Select a piece of your own writing, circle the relative pronouns and adverbs, and ensure the correct words were used. (L.6.1a)

15. MECHANICS/GRAMMAR WALL

As a class, create a Mechanics/Grammar bulletin board where, throughout the year, you will add to a checklist of editing topics as they are taught through targeted mini-lessons (e.g., proper use of punctuation, capitalization). Once skills are taught in a mini-lesson and listed on the bulletin board, you are expected to edit your work for the elements before publication. (L.6.1, L.6.2, L.6.3)

16. MECHANICS

Your teacher will teach mini-lessons on the individual language standards. For example, as a class you will find examples of commas, parentheses, and dashes in books read in class. See if the class can generalize rules for when these are used. (See the following examples: (1) The 25th anniversary of our school (August 25, 2008) brought back memories for the retired teachers who worked there. (2) The 25th anniversary of our school—August 25, 2008—brought back memories for the retired teachers who worked there. (3) Sheila's youngest brother, Connor, will be visiting her in the hospital.) Then, you will choose a piece of your own writing and see if there is a place where information could be added—and decide if a comma, parentheses, or a dash is needed. Check your work with a partner. (L.6.2a)

17. VOCABULARY/WORD WALL

As a class, create a Vocabulary Word Wall bulletin board where, throughout the year, you will add and sort words as you learn them in each unit of study. (L.6.4)

ADDITIONAL RESOURCES

- *Literary Elements Map* (ReadWriteThink) (RL.6.3)
- *Lights, Camera, Action: Interviewing a Book Character* (ReadWriteThink) (RL.6.3)
- *Book Report Alternative: Creating a Childhood for a Character* (ReadWriteThink) (RL.6.3)
- *Action Is Character: Exploring Character Traits with Adjectives* (ReadWriteThink) (RL.6.1)
- *Internalization of Vocabulary Through the Use of a Word Map* (ReadWriteThink) (RL.6.4, RI.6.4)
- *Improve Comprehension: A Word Game Using Root Words and Affixes* (ReadWriteThink) (RL.7.4, RI.7.4)
- *Flip-a-Chip: Examining Affixes and Roots to Build Vocabulary* (ReadWriteThink) (RL.7.4, RI.7.4)
- *You Can't Spell the Word Prefix Without a Prefix* (ReadWriteThink) (RL7.4, RI7.4)
- *March Is Music in Our Schools Month* (ReadWriteThink) (SL.6.1)
- *Roald Dahl Was Born on This Day in 1916* (ReadWriteThink) (RL.6.7)
- Story map (ReadWriteThink)

TERMINOLOGY

Character development	Elements of setting: place, time, environment	Interviews
Character traits		Prequel

Grade Six, Unit One Sample Lesson Plan

"Eleven" by Sandra Cisneros

In this series of four lessons, students read "Eleven" by Sandra Cisneros, and they:

Examine Sandra Cisneros's "Eleven" and note its memoir qualities (RL.6.1, RL.6.2, RL.6.9)

Explore the literary art of fictionalizing memories (RL.6.6, L.6.6)

Reflect upon their memories (SL.6.1, W.6.3, W.6.4)

Summary

Lesson I: "Eleven"

Explicate "Eleven" (RL.6.1)

Analyze Cisneros's literary style (RL.6.6)

Explore the narrator's voice (RL.6.6)

Probe the narrator's conflict (RL.6.2)

Investigate the central theme of the story (RL.6.2)

Identify the literary genre, memoir (RL.6.9)

Note the memoir qualities in Cisneros's short story (RL.6.9)

Lesson III: Writing and Revising Memories

Revisit initial drafts of memoirs (W.6.3)

Rethink details (L.6.6)

Enhance descriptions (W.6.3, W.6.4)

Rewrite earlier drafts (W.6.3, W.6.5, L.6.1, L.6.2, L.6.3, W.6.10)

Lesson II: "Fictionalizing Memories"

Generate memories (SL.6.1)

Begin to reconstruct events that carry meaning (W.6.3)

Revisit the components of a story (RL.6.3, W.6.3)

Begin to translate mere memories into more memorable, meaningful moments (W.6.3, W.6.4, L.6.6)

Draft a memoir (W.6.3, W.6.4, W.6.10)

Lesson IV: Collecting Memories

Reflect upon one's memories (SL.6.1)

Emphasize the ability to make memorable moments more meaningful (RL.6.6)

Appreciate the stories of others (SL.6.1)

Lesson II: Fictionalizing Memories

Objectives

Generate memories (SL.6.1)

Begin to reconstruct events that carry meaning (W.6.3)

Revisit the components of a story (RL.6.3, W.6.3)

Begin to translate mere memories into more memorable, meaningful moments (W.6.3, W.6.4, L.6.6)

Draft a memoir (W.6.3, W.6.4, W.6.10)

Required Materials

☐ Childhood photos, artifacts of childhood, etc.

Procedures

1. Lead-In:
   Ask the students to take out their artifacts and lead a conversation in which they describe what they brought. The story "Eleven" is not about the red sweater; it is about growing up. Similarly, the purpose of the artifact is to help students relive memories.

2. Step by Step:
   a. Independently, the students will begin to take notes. This is a time for remembering details. For example, if the artifact is a picture, the students might think of the moment it was taken: Who else was around? Was he/she happy or sad? What was the occasion?
   b. Before the students begin to draft their memoirs, they should be reminded to consider the components that make stories, both fiction and nonfiction, exciting (narrative voice, conflict, characters, setting, and so on).
   c. Students will begin to draft their memoirs.

3. Closure:
   Since the writing activity will continue, summarize what has been accomplished so far, and what the students will do in the next lesson.

Differentiation

Advanced

- Students will collaboratively create interview questions on a shared online spreadsheet, based on teacher prompts, to help students for whom this assignment is difficult. Students will conduct interviews with a recording device such as a voice memo or video camera, asking probing questions to "pull" the story from the reluctant storyteller.

Struggling

- Students will talk about their artifact or photograph with a partner as a warm-up, participate in student interviews, and use the recorded interview to write the memoir draft. Students will write out main ideas from the recorded interview on index cards, sort them, and write their memoir draft focusing on three main components (narrative voice, characters, and setting).

- Students without artifacts and photographs will read "My Name," from *House on Mango Street* by Susan Cisneros, in a small group. Students will write a memoir based on their name.

Homework/Assessment
N/A

Grade 6 ▶ *Unit 2*

Folklore: A Blast from the Past

This six-week unit focuses on what folklore (myths, legends, tall, and pourquoi tales) reveals about world cultures—including our own.

ESSENTIAL QUESTION

? How is folklore simultaneously revealing and limiting?

OVERVIEW

Students explore myths and legends from a variety of sources: ancient Greek or Roman civilizations; Russian history; Viking, Eskimo, or Latin American cultures; or other cultures of the students' choice. In addition, students read informational text, listen to music, and examine art from the myth's or legend's country of origin. Class discussions focus on the fact that folklore provides a limited view of a culture and that it's important to research the country before making sweeping generalizations about it. The goal of this unit is not only for students to find commonalities across this genre, but to discover countries and cultures other than our own. The culminating project is an informative/explanatory essay in response to the essential question.

FOCUS STANDARDS

These Focus Standards have been selected for the unit from the Common Core State Standards.

RL.6.3: Describe how a particular story's or drama's plot unfolds in a series of episodes as well as how the characters respond or change as the plot moves toward a resolution.

RI.6.4: Determine the meaning of words and phrases as they are used in a text, including figurative, connotative, and technical meanings.

W.6.3: Write narratives to develop real or imagined experiences or events using effective technique, relevant descriptive details, and well-structured event sequences.

W.6.7: Conduct short research projects to answer a question, drawing on several sources and refocusing the inquiry when appropriate.

SL.6.1: Engage effectively in a range of collaborative discussions (one-on-one, in groups, and teacher-led) on grade 6 topics, texts, and issues, building on others' ideas and expressing their own clearly.

SL.6.1(c): Pose and respond to specific questions with elaboration and detail by making comments that contribute to the topic, text, or issue under discussion.

SL.6.1(d): Review the key ideas expressed and demonstrate understanding of multiple perspectives through reflection and paraphrasing.

L.6.4: Determine or clarify the meaning of unknown and multiple-meaning words and phrases based on grade 6 reading and content, choosing flexibly from a range of strategies.

L.6.4(a): Use context (e.g., the overall meaning of a sentence or paragraph; a word's position or function in a sentence) as a clue to the meaning of a word or phrase.

L.6.4(b): Use common, grade-appropriate Greek or Latin affixes and roots as clues to the meaning of a word (e.g., *audience, auditory, audible*).

SUGGESTED STUDENT OBJECTIVES

- Read, compare, and contrast myths, legends, and tall and pourquoi tales from a variety of countries/cultures.
- Compare and contrast one author's presentation of events with that of another.
- Compose your own myth, legend, tall tale, or pourquoi tale, exhibiting the form's essential characteristics.
- Compare and contrast the reading of a story (e.g., one of the *Just So Stories)* to an audio version.
- Conduct research on a country of choice and compare what you learn with what the country's folklore teaches you about that country's culture.

SUGGESTED WORKS

(E) indicates a CCSS exemplar text; (EA) indicates a text from a writer with other works identified as exemplars.

LITERARY TEXTS

Stories

- *Favorite Folktales from Around the World* (Jane Yolen)
- *The Firebird and Other Russian Fairy Tales* (Arthur Ransome)
- *Just So Stories* (Rudyard Kipling) (EA)
- *Cut from the Same Cloth: American Women of Myth, Legend, and Tall Tale* (Robert D. San Souci, Brian Pinkney, and Jane Yolen)
- *American Tall Tales* (Mary Pope Osborne and Michael McCurdy) (EA)
- *Talking Eggs* (Robert San Souci)

Greece/Ancient World

- *Black Ships Before Troy: The Story of the Iliad* (Rosemary Sutcliff) (E)
- *Heroes, Gods, and Monsters of the Greek Myths* (Bernard Evslin)
- *The Lightning Thief: Percy Jackson and the Olympians: Book 1* (Rick Riordan)
- *Women Warriors: Myths and Legends of Heroic Women* (Marianna Mayer and Heller Julek)

Rome

- *Roman Myths* (Geraldine McCaughrean and Emma Chichester Clark)

Viking

- *D'Aulaires' Book of Norse Myths* (Ingri D'Aulaire and Edgar Parin D'Aulaire)

Inuit-Eskimo

- *Tikta'Liktak: An Inuit-Eskimo Legend* (James A. Houston)

Latin America

- *Golden Tales: Myths, Legends, and Folktales from Latin America* (Lulu Delacre) (*Note:* This title also includes informational text.)

Poetry

- "Twelfth Song of Thunder" (Navajo, Traditional) (E)

INFORMATIONAL TEXTS

Nonfiction

Ancient World

- *The Usborne Internet-Linked Encyclopedia of World History* (Jane Bingham)

Greece

- *The Hero Schliemann: The Dreamer Who Dug for Troy* (Laura Amy Schlitz and Robert Byrd)
- *Greeks: Internet Linked* (Illustrated World History) (Susan Peach, Anne Millard, and Ian Jackson)
- *You Wouldn't Want to Be a Slave in Ancient Greece! A Life You'd Rather Not Have* (You Wouldn't Want to … Series) (Fiona MacDonald, David Salariya, and David Antram)

Rome

- *Romans: Internet Linked* (Illustrated World History) (Anthony Marks)
- *You Wouldn't Want to Live in Pompeii! A Volcanic Eruption You'd Rather Avoid* (You Wouldn't Want to … Series) (John Malam, David Salariya, and David Antram)
- *You Wouldn't Want to Be a Roman Soldier! Barbarians You'd Rather Not Meet* (You Wouldn't Want to … Series) (David Stewart and David Antram)

Vikings

- *First Facts about the Vikings* (Jacqueline Morley)
- *Vicious Vikings* (Horrible Histories TV Tie-in) (Terry Deary and Martin Brown)
- *You Wouldn't Want to Be a Viking Explorer! Voyages You'd Rather Not Make* (You Wouldn't Want to … Series) (Andrew Langley, David Salariya, and David Antram)

Inuit-Eskimo

- *The Inuit* (Watts Library) (Suzanne M. Williams)
- *Building an Igloo* (Ulli Steltzer)

Latin America

- *Golden Tales: Myths, Legends, and Folktales from Latin America* (Lulu Delacre)
- *Aztec, Inca, and Maya* (DK Eyewitness Books) (Elizabeth Baquedano and Barry Clarke)
- *Beneath the Stone: A Mexican Zapotec Tale* (Bernard Wolf)
- *The History Atlas of South America* (MacMillan Continental History Atlases) (Edwin Early, ed.)
- *First Americans: Story of Where They Came from and Who They Became* (Anthony F. Aveni and S. D. Nelson)

ART, MUSIC, AND MEDIA

Art

- *Winged Victory of Samothrace* (Greek, ca. 190 BCE)
- Marble portrait of the emperor Augustus (Roman, ca. 14–37 CE)
- Sutton Hoo Burial Helmet (Viking, early seventh century)
- Oseburg Burial Ship (Viking, 800 CE)
- Mural Painting at Teotihuacan (Latin American, ca. fourteenth to fifteenth century)
- Stelae from La Venta (Olmec, Latin America, ca. 1000–500 BCE)

Media

- *Just So Stories* (Rudyard Kipling) (audiobook CD) (HarperCollins)
- *The Lightning Thief: Percy Jackson and the Olympians: Book 1* (Rick Riordan and Jesse Bernstein) (Listening Library)

SAMPLE ACTIVITIES AND ASSESSMENTS

1. INTRODUCTORY ACTIVITY

Your teacher will start this unit by reading aloud a favorite folktale picture book, *Talking Eggs*, to review the elements of folktales, discuss folklore in general, and describe what he/she will expect from you in journal entries this year. (RL.5.1, SL.5.1, SL.5.3, W.5.4, W.5.8)

2. GRAPHIC ORGANIZER

As you read a variety of myths and legends, keep track of the following information in your journal or on a shared online spreadsheet:

- Characters
- Country of origin
- Problem (that can't be solved)
- Setting
- Title
- Hero (who comes to solve the problem or explains the mystery)
- Ending
- Characteristics unique to this country's folklore

Your teacher may ask you to share your responses with a partner before class discussion. Be sure to note the page numbers of relevant information or mark your book with sticky notes, so you can cite evidence from the text during class discussion. (RL.6.1, RL.6.2, RL.6.3)

3. CLASS DISCUSSION

Be prepared to compare and contrast two or more characters, settings, or events across stories, drawing on specific information from the stories that you and your classmates read. (SL.6.1, RL.6.2, RL.6.3)

4. CLASS DISCUSSION

How does *Black Ships Before Troy: The Story of the Iliad* by Rosemary Sutcliff provide insight into ancient Greek civilizations? Discuss insights into characters from this story, plot developments, and ancient Greek society in general. Your teacher may ask you to write your own responses in your journal and share them with a partner before class discussion. (RI.6.4, SL.6.1, RL.6.1)

5. LITERATURE RESPONSE

Outline how the plot of a myth, legend, tall tale, or pourquoi tale of choice unfolds in a series of episodes by creating a comic strip of key events. Be sure to include the characters and how they respond or change as the plot moves toward resolution. Make note of the page numbers to which each box refers so you can go back and cite the text during class discussion, if needed. You may want to use an online comic creation tool to publish your ideas. (RL.6.3)

6. CLASS DISCUSSION/VENN DIAGRAM

What are the similarities and differences you notice among myths, legends, tale tales, and pourquoi tales? Your teacher may ask you to write your own responses in your journal (or in an online template) and share them with a partner before class discussion. After class discussion, create a Venn diagram in your journal that outlines the similarities and differences among three of the types of folklore. (SL.6.1, RL.6.9)

7. NARRATIVE WRITING

Write your own myth or legend. As discussed in class, myths and legends were written to explain natural phenomena (often before scientific explanations were found). Follow the typical pattern (as in the following list), but also build on your insights from the graphic organizer in the first activity.

- Explanation of the setting
- The problem
- The failure to solve the problem
- The main character comes along
- He/she has a plan
- The solution is found
- Conclusion (usually a happy ending)

   Your well-developed myth or legend should clearly and logically include the characteristics of myths and legends (cited in the preceding list). Edit your writing for pronoun shifts and vagueness. Your teacher may ask you to draw and scan an illustration or to find relevant visuals from the Internet for publication on the class web page. (W.6.3, W.6.4, W.6.5, L.6.1, L.6.2a,b)

8. DRAMATIZATION/FLUENCY

Choose a scene from one of the myths or legends that you think are the most revealing about that culture. Work with classmates to present the scene as a dramatic reading. Record the readings using a video camera for future reference and to see how your fluency improves during the course of the year. (SL.6.6)

9. ART/CLASS DISCUSSION

Find art works that portray the characters or culture(s) about which you read. For instance, consider a Viking member of the Sutton Hoo ship or an Olmec sculptor creating a monumental work at La Venta. How does knowing the story behind the character give you a deeper insight into the artwork? What aesthetic or cultural considerations might have been on the artist's mind during the creation of such works? Your teacher may ask you to write your own responses in your journal and share them with a partner before class discussion. (SL.6.1, RL.6.3)

10. LITERATURE RESPONSE/MEDIA APPRECIATION

How is listening to *Just So Stories* as an audiobook similar to or different from reading the book? Which do you prefer? Why? Your teacher may ask you to write your own responses in your journal and share them with a partner before class discussion. Alternatively, you may respond to the prompt posted on the classroom blog by your teacher. (RL.6.7)

11. WORD STUDY

Keep an index card file of words studied while reading various myths, legends, tall tales, or pourquoi tales. Keeping the words on index cards will help you when we sort words by prefix, suffix, root words, meaning, spelling feature, and so on. Did you find words you recognize that are from the country/culture of the folklore read? How can word origins—*etymology*—affect our understanding of the words? (*Note:* This will be an ongoing activity all year long.) (L.6.4a,b, RI.6.4)

12. INFORMATIVE/EXPLANATORY WRITING AND MULTIMEDIA PRESENTATION

After reading folklore from a particular country, choose an informational text about the country/culture of origin to read. Talk with a partner about why it would be good to know more about the country or culture. Collaboratively formulate two to three questions to guide your research. Plan how you will conduct your research. Communicate your findings in an informative/explanatory essay in response to the essential question: How is folklore simultaneously revealing and limiting? Your writing should include at least two supporting details from each text. Edit your writing for pronoun shifts and vagueness. Your teacher may ask you to include relevant visuals found on the Internet. Your teacher may give you the option of adding a multimedia component to your research report, either by creating a digital slide presentation to highlight key points, or by reading your essay set to music and images from your country of choice. Present to the class. (RI.6.2, RI.6.4, W.6.2, W.6.4, W.6.7, W.9a,b, L.6.1, L.6.2a,b)

Optional reflection question: How does knowing information about the country of origin enhance your understanding of the folklore from that country? What information did you learn only from research? Discuss your responses with classmates in pairs, as a class discussion, and/or on the classroom blog.

13. GRAMMAR AND USAGE

Your teacher will teach mini-lessons on the individual language standards. For example, he/she will give some examples of sentences with vague references, and, as a class, you will make them specific.

- These should be solved. (example correction = Math problems 2 through 12 should be solved.)
- This is difficult when you are just beginning to learn it. (example correction = Spanish is difficult when you are just beginning to learn it.)
- Those are the best. (example correction = Ripe bananas are the best.)

Select a piece of your own writing; circle every use of *this, that, these,* and *those,* and make sure that the sentence is as clear and specific as it can be. (L.6.1d)

14. GRAMMAR/MECHANICS WALL

As a class, continue adding to the Mechanics/Grammar bulletin board started in Unit One. Remember—once skills are taught in a mini-lesson and listed on the bulletin board, you are expected to edit your work for these elements before publication. (L.6.1, L.6.2, L.6.3)

15. VOCABULARY/WORD WALL

As a class, continue adding to the Vocabulary Word Wall bulletin board where, throughout the year, you will add and sort words as you learn them in each unit of study. (L.6.4)

16. ART/CLASS DISCUSSION

View the *Winged Victory of Samothrace* in comparison to a wall painting of the Great Goddess at Teotihuacan. How are these two goddesses depicted? Are they portrayed similarly? What are some of the differences? Examine the images for evidence. What leads you to believe that these are goddesses that were worshipped? (SL.6.1, SL.6.2)

ADDITIONAL RESOURCES

- *Pourquoi Tales* (ReadWriteThink) (This site is geared towards grades 3–5, but may be adapted.)
- *Myth and Truth: The "First Thanksgiving"* (ReadWriteThink) (RL.6.2)
- *The Big Bad Wolf: Analyzing Point of View in Texts* (ReadWriteThink) (RL.6.3)
- *Plot Diagram* (ReadWriteThink) (RL.6.5)
- *Today Is St. Patrick's Day* (ReadWriteThink) (RL.6.4)

TERMINOLOGY

Culture	Folktale	Oral tradition
Etymology	Legend	Plot
Folklore	Myth	Pourquoi tale

Grade Six, Unit Two Sample Lesson Plan

"Twelfth Song of Thunder" Navajo Traditions

In this series of three lessons, students read "Twelfth Song of Thunder," a Navajo Tradition, and they:

Conduct online, museum, and library research on the Navajo Nation's history and its traditions of song and dance (RI.6.1, RI.6.7, W.6.7, W.6.8, SL.6.1c, SI.6.1d)

Document research findings (W.6.5, W.6.6, W.6.8)

Display findings (SL.6.1, SL.6.5, SL.6.6, L.6.2)

Summary

Lesson I: "Twelfth Song of Thunder"

Examine the rhythm of "Twelfth Song of Thunder" (SL.6.1)

Examine the use of repetitions (RL.6.4, SL.6.1)

Explore the purpose of the song (RL.6.2, RL.6.5, SL.6.1c, SL.6.1d)

Lesson II: Researching Navajo Traditions

Identify key sources for conducting research about the Navajo Nation (W.6.7, W.6.8)

Identify the geographical location of the Navajo Nation (W.6.7)

Chronicle key events of the Navajo Nation's history (RI.6.1, RI.6.7, W.6.7)

Explore the Navajo traditions of song and dance (SL.6.1c,d, W.6.7)

Lesson III: Document and Display Findings

Assemble facts gathered during research (W.6.10, SL.6.2)

Select a format for displaying the findings (W.6.5, W.6.6)

Document the findings (W.6.5, W.6.6, W.6.8)

Display findings (SL.6.1, SL.6.5, SL.6.6, L.6.2)

Lesson II: Researching Navajo Traditions

Objectives

Identify key sources for conducting research about the Navajo Nation (W.6.7, W.6.8)

Identify the geographical location of the Navajo Nation (W.6.7)

Chronicle key events of the Navajo Nation's history (RI.6.1, RI.6.7, W.6.7)

Explore the Navajo traditions of song and dance (SL.6.1c,d, W.6.7)

Required Materials

☐ Access to a library

☐ Access to the Internet

☐ Museum

(Teachers are encouraged, if possible, to take their students to local museums where exhibits portray Native American culture and traditions.)

Procedures

1. Lead-In:
If students visited a museum, ask them to share in small groups the data that they collected and identify the next steps in their research. If a museum visit was not possible, split students into groups and consider available resources for research, such as Discovery Education Streaming.

2. Step by Step:
   a. Students will assign group members to different stations:

   School library

   Internet (there are several Navajo Nation websites available)

   b. Students begin to collect and record data:

   Geographical

   Historical

   Cultural

3. Closure:
Students meet in their groups and briefly share results.

Differentiation

Advanced

- Students will research the Navajo Nation through the lens of geography, noting the important role that geography played in the development of Navajo history and culture. Students can evaluate and collect useful websites for their classmates to use for research and assemble them on the teacher's portal.

Struggling

- Work with students to create a graphic organizer on a shared online spreadsheet to help focus the research. Students can begin their research using the websites found by classmates (listed above). Give students the option of working in teams of two: one student as reader and the other as note-taker. Another option would be to allow students to use recording devices (such as a dictation application) to store interesting information as they read various sources and then to translate the information to print.

Homework/Assessment

Type research notes.

Grade 6 ▶ *Unit 3*

Embracing Heritage

In this eight-week unit, students continue to read stories and informational texts and discuss what they each reveal about our own country, the United States of America.

OVERVIEW

Remember, remember always that all of us, and you and I especially, are descended from immigrants and revolutionists.

FRANKLIN D. ROOSEVELT

ESSENTIAL QUESTION

? How does heritage define us individually and as a nation?

America is a nation of immigrants. This diversity has helped to make our country rich in ideas, traditions, and customs. Except for the Native Americans, every American came here from somewhere else—or is born of ancestors who did. People have come, and continue to come, to America to seek freedom and opportunity. Some did not come here voluntarily. And some immigrants encountered prejudice. To learn more about the role of immigration in American heritage, students read and discuss a variety of fictional and informational texts. To appreciate how we are shaped by the experiences we have and the people we encounter, students do a Generations Project, in which they consider perspectives from different generations within a family. The project also helps hone students' interview and research skills. In addition, students create semantic maps of the phrase "embracing heritage" in order to represent visually their understanding of this phrase. They write an informative/explanatory essay in response to the essential question: How does heritage define us individually and as a nation?

Note: This unit provides an example of how cross-curricular collaboration can naturally occur between English and other content areas. Students can read informational texts in history class, and compare those accounts to personal narratives and accounts about the immigrants' experience read in English class. Much discussion centers on the ways in which background information enhances understanding of literature (whether on immigration or any other history/science topic of teachers' choosing). This unit also demonstrates how the reading and writing standards provide instructional connectivity between learning in English and other content areas.

FOCUS STANDARDS

These Focus Standards have been selected for the unit from the Common Core State Standards.

RL.6.6: Explain how an author develops the point of view of the narrator in a text.

RI.6.3: Analyze in detail how a key individual, event, or idea is introduced, illustrated, and elaborated in a text (e.g., through examples or anecdotes).

RI.6.9: Compare and contrast one author's presentation of events with that of another (e.g., a memoir written by and a biography on the same person).

W.6.1: Write arguments to support claims with clear reasons and relevant evidence.

W.6.5: With some guidance and support from peers and adults, develop and strengthen writing as needed by planning, revising, editing, rewriting, or trying a new approach.

SL.6.3: Delineate a speaker's argument and specific claims, distinguishing claims that are supported by reasons and evidence from claims that are not.

L.6.4: Determine or clarify the meaning of unknown and multiple-meaning words and phrases based on grade 6 reading and content, choosing flexibly from a range of strategies.

L.6.4(c): Consult reference materials (e.g., dictionaries, glossaries, thesauruses), both print and digital, to find the pronunciation of a word or determine or clarify its precise meaning or its part of speech.

L.6.4(d): Verify the preliminary determination of the meaning of a word or phrase (e.g., by checking the inferred meaning in context or in a dictionary).

SUGGESTED STUDENT OBJECTIVES

- Define the word *heritage* and review the word *culture*.
- Explore U.S. immigrant experiences through historical fiction and nonfiction texts.
- Analyze multiple accounts of U.S. immigration from different points of view and describe important similarities and differences in the details they provide.
- Conduct interviews to gather information from human "primary sources" (e.g., with family members).
- Summarize information gleaned from interviews.
- Explain the importance of oral tradition.
- Conduct research on countries from which family members emigrated.
- Write arguments about the proposition that America is a "land of opportunity."
- Define related words and identify their parts of speech (e.g., *migrate, immigrate, emigrate,* etc.).

SUGGESTED WORKS

(E) indicates a CCSS exemplar text; (EA) indicates a text from a writer with other works identified as exemplars.

LITERARY TEXTS

Stories

- *One More River to Cross: The Stories of Twelve Black Americans* (Scholastic Biography) (Jim Haskins) (EA)
- *As Long As the Rivers Flow: The Stories of Nine Native Americans* (Scholastic Biography) (Paula Gunn Allen and Patricia Clark Smith)

- *Esperanza Rising* (Pam Munoz Ryan)
- *Project Mulberry* (Linda Sue Park)
- *Weedflower* (Cynthia Kadohata)
- *Escape from Saigon: How a Vietnam War Orphan Became an American Boy* (Andrea Warren)
- "On Discovering America" from *Survey Graphic Magazine* (Pearl S. Buck)
- *One Eye Laughing, the Other Eye Weeping: The Diary of Julie Weiss, Vienna, Austria, to New York, 1938* (Dear America Series) (Barry Denenberg)
- *Something About America* (Maria Testa)
- *Journey of the Sparrows* (Fran Leeper Buss)
- *Behind the Mountains* (First Person Fiction) (Edwidge Danticat)
- *An Indian in Cowboy Country: Stories from an Immigrant's Life* (Pradeep Anand)
- *When Jesse Came Across the Sea* (Amy Hest and P. J. Lynch)
- *Dreaming of America* (Eve Bunting)
- *The Christmas Tapestry* (Patricia Polacco)

INFORMATIONAL TEXTS
Nonfiction

- *Coming to America: The Story of Immigration* (Betsy Maestro and Susannah Ryan)
- *If Your Name Was Changed at Ellis Island* (If You[r] … Series) (Ellen Levine and Wayne Parmenter)
- *A History of US: Reconstructing America 1865–1890* (Book 7) (Joy Hakim) (EA)
- *How People Immigrate* (True Books) (Sarah De Capua)
- *Immigrant Kids* (Russell Freedman) (EA)
- *New Kids in Town: Oral Histories of Immigrant Teens* (Scholastic Biography) (Janet Bode)
- *First Crossing: Stories about Teen Immigrants* (Donald R. Gallo)
- *Through the Eyes of Your Ancestors: A Step-by-Step Guide to Uncovering Your Family's History* (Maureen Alice Taylor)
- *Do People Grow on Family Trees? Genealogy for Kids and Other Beginners: The Official Ellis Island Handbook* (Ira Wolfman and Michael Klein)

ART, MUSIC, AND MEDIA
Art

- Jacob Riis, various photographs
- Childe Hassam, *Village Scene* (1883–1885)
- Childe Hassam, *Winter in Union Square* (1889–1890)
- Childe Hassam, *Flags on Fifty-Seventh Street: The Winter of 1918* (1918)

Music and Lyrics

- "Coming to America" (Neil Diamond)

SAMPLE ACTIVITIES AND ASSESSMENTS

1. CLASS DISCUSSION

What is meant by the word *heritage*? Which elements of heritage does one look for when learning about a culture? Write your ideas down on a sticky note and "Give one, get one."

(*Note: Culture* was discussed and defined in Grade Five, but you may want to review it. Answers to the elements of heritage may include something that is passed down from previous generations, a tradition, our family members' culture, etc.) With your class, create a chart of elements to look for in texts read during this unit. We will continue to add to this list as we gain additional insights into heritage during this unit. Your teacher may ask you to create an online concept map using a web tool. (SL.6.1)

2. CLASS DISCUSSION

How do the stories from this unit provide insight into the experiences of immigrants? How are their stories alike? Different? Cite specific information from the texts to justify your responses. Do the stories turn out as you expected? Why or why not? Your teacher may ask you to write your own response in your journal and share it with a partner before class discussion. (SL.6.1, SL.6.3, RL.6.1)

3. LITERARY RESPONSE (AND/OR WRITING: ARGUMENT)

After reading one of the immigrant stories, respond in your journal to this James Baldwin quotation (from the character's point of view): "Know from whence you came. If you know whence you came, there are absolutely no limitations to where you can go." Be sure to cite specific examples from the text to justify your response. Post your response on the classroom blog and compare it to responses by your classmates. This activity can be expanded into a writing (argument) assignment. (RL.6.1, RL.6.6, L.6.1, L.6.2a,b)

4. RESEARCH/TRAVEL BROCHURE (AND/OR MULTIMEDIA PRESENTATION)

Conduct research on one of the countries you have read about in this unit (from which an immigrant left), drawing on several sources (e.g., print, digital, video, multimedia, etc.). You may have the opportunity to work collaboratively with a partner through the entire research process: sharing ideas; formulating research questions; planning the research; conducting the research; evaluating the credibility and relevance of the information; and, finally, synthesizing the information and reporting your findings in a report or brochure. Type a report or create a travel brochure. Be sure to follow the format provided by your teacher for citing the sources used in your research. For the travel brochure, what should visitors learn that would increase understanding of that country's heritage? Work with peers to get feedback and improve your report or brochure and publish using publishing software. An optional extension is to present your findings as a multimedia presentation (e.g., digital slides or video). (W.6.7, RI.6.7, RI.6.9)

5. GENEALOGY/MULTIMEDIA GENERATIONS PROJECT

As a way for you to personalize immigration stories, you are encouraged to learn about the countries from which your family emigrated. Prior to starting this project, plan with a classmate which aspects of their immigration you would like to research and why, how you plan to conduct and organize your research, and how you plan to search through sources efficiently for relevant information. Then, as a class, collaboratively generate meaningful interview questions that will generate the information you need. Interview three family members (or family friends) from different generations for this project, asking ten questions about significant aspects of their respective childhoods and life growing up. The purpose of this project is to get perspectives from different generations within one family to show how we are shaped by the experiences we have and by the people we encounter. Your essay/multimedia project should be logically ordered with at least three quotations from each family member interviewed. Edit your work for the grammar conventions studied so far this year (see Standards for more details) and upload it to your class web page to facilitate sharing with family members far away. Include photographs or other artifacts if desired. (RI.6.3, RI.6.7, L.6.1a,b,c,d; L.6.2a, L.6.2b)

6. CLASS DISCUSSION

Analyze various accounts of immigrant experiences, then identify and distinguish among facts, opinions, and reasoned judgments presented in the texts. How do these sources combine to give you a better picture of the immigrant experience than informational text or literature alone? Your teacher may ask you to write your response in your journal and share it with a partner before class discussion. Be sure to write down the page numbers of facts and opinions or mark your book with sticky notes so you can go back and cite the text during class discussion. (RI.6.3, RL.6.9, RI.6.8, SL.6.3)

7. WRITING (ARGUMENT)

People have been immigrating to the United States for more than two hundred years. Even today, there are people who immigrate to America. Do you think the reasons for current immigration are similar to or different from the reasons of those who immigrated two hundred years ago? Write your position on a sticky note and discuss your preliminary ideas with classmates. Plan with a classmate which aspects of past and current immigration patterns you would like to research and how you plan to conduct and organize your research, and how you plan to search through sources efficiently for relevant information. Then, draft your argument about whether the reasons are more similar or different between these two waves of immigration. Write a well-developed paper that includes an engaging opening statement of your position, at least three supporting details from two different sources, and a strong conclusion. Edit your writing for the grammar conventions studied so far this year. Your teacher may ask you to include relevant visuals found on the Internet. (W.6.1, W.6.4, W.6.5, RI.6.8, L.6.1, L.6.2a,b)

8. DRAMATIZATION/FLUENCY

Write a poem or a song for two voices about an immigrant's experience. The poem should be modeled after the poetry in *Joyful Noise: Poems for Two Voices* by Paul Fleischman (read in fifth grade), and the song modeled after Neil Diamond's lyrics in "Coming to America." The song or poem should accurately reflect historical information (or present-day information). Work with classmates to present the song or poem as a dramatic reading and record it with a video camera. (SL.6.6)

9. WORD STUDY

Keep an index card file of words studied while reading about immigrant experiences. Keeping the words on index cards will help you when we sort words by prefix, suffix, root words, meaning, country of origin, spelling feature, and more. Just as we can trace the path of our ancestors, we can trace the path of words. Choose some words and trace back from modern-day uses of the words to their historical origins (e.g., *culture, heritage, immigration, emigration, immigrant, endowment, lineage, racism, tolerance, legacy, ancestry,* etc.). (*Note:* This will be an ongoing activity all year long.) In addition, you will create an individual semantic map of the phrase "embracing heritage" in order to represent visually your understanding of this phrase. (RL.6.4, L.6.4)

10. INFORMATIVE/EXPLANATORY WRITING

Write an informative/explanatory essay in response to the essential question: How does heritage define us individually and as a nation? To prepare for the essay, make a T-chart that describes in one column what is common about immigrant experiences and in the other column what is different (drawing on your own research). Provide at least three ways of learning and cite examples from the texts to support your assertions. Be prepared to make an audio recording of your essay and upload it as a podcast to accompany your Genealogy/Multimedia Generations Project (discussed in Activity 5). Prepare it for upload to the classroom blog or a class wiki. (W.6.5, W.6.9a,b, L.6.1, L.6.2a,b)

11. MECHANICS/GRAMMAR WALL

As a class, continue adding to the Mechanics/Grammar bulletin board started in Unit One. Remember—once skills are taught in a mini-lesson and listed on the bulletin board, you are expected to edit your work for these elements before publication. (L.6.1, L.6.2, L.6.3)

12. VOCABULARY/WORD WALL

As a class, continue adding to the Vocabulary Word Wall bulletin board where, throughout the year, you will add and sort words as you learn them in each unit of study. (L.6.4)

13. ART/CLASS DISCUSSION

Riis and Hassam both depicted New York City during the same period, yet they chose strikingly different subject matter. Speculate on the reasons for this difference. (SL.6.1, SL.6.2)

14. ART/CLASS DISCUSSION

Riis was one of the first artists to use flash photography. How did the stillness that this technology required affect his choice of subject matter and the time of day in which he worked? (SL.6.1, SL.6.2)

15. ART/CLASS DISCUSSION

Why do you think Hassam chose the colors and patterns that he did? Do you believe this is what the scenes actually looked like? (SL.6.1, SL.6.2)

ADDITIONAL RESOURCES

- *Annie Moore Becomes the First Immigrant to Enter Ellis Island in 1892* (ReadWriteThink) (W.6.8)
- *Song and Poetry Analysis Tools* (Library of Congress) (RI.6.7)
- *Thinking About Songs as Historical Artifacts* (Library of Congress) (RI.6.8)
- *Thinking About Poems as Historical Artifacts* (Library of Congress) (RI.6.8)
- Gateway to Dreams: An Ellis Island/Immigration WebQuest for Upper Elementary Grades (Today's Teacher)
- Phillip Lopate, "Immigrant Fiction: Exploring an American Identity" (The Gilder Lehrman Institute of American History)
- Pearl S. Buck: "On Discovering America" Reading Questions (National Endowment for the Humanities)
- *The Peopling of America* (The Statue of Liberty–Ellis Island Foundation, Inc.)
- Lydia Lum, "Angel Island: Immigrant Journeys of Chinese-Americans" from *An Oral History of Chinese Immigrant Detainees*
- Immigration History Research Center (University of Minnesota)
- Photographs from Ellis Island (Library of Congress)
- *New Americans Series, Cultural Riches* (PBS)
- *Travel Brochures: Highlighting the Setting of a Story* (ReadWriteThink)
- *Create a Travel Brochure* (Scholastic)

TERMINOLOGY

Biography	Heritage	Lore	Realism
Epilogue	Legacy	Memoir	Traditional literature

Grade Six, Unit Three Sample Lesson Plan

Immigrant Kids by Russell Freedman

In this series of four lessons, students read *Immigrant Kids* by Russell Freedman, and they:

Explore the conditions that immigrants experienced, as described in *Immigrant Kids* (RI.6.1, RI.6.2, SL.6.1)

Conduct independent research (RI.6.1, RI.6.2, RI.6.7, W.6.7, W.6.8)

Examine why immigration to America continues (SL.6.1)

Summary

Lesson I: Immigrant Kids

Note the origins of the book (RI.6.1, RI.6.2)

Examine the immigrant experience, as portrayed in *Immigrant Kids* (RI.6.1, RI.6.2, SL.6.1)

Homes

Schools

Work

Consider why, despite the challenges depicted in *Immigrant Kids*, America is a nation that continues to attract immigrants (SL.6.1)

Lesson III: Preparing to Present

In groups, examine the material that has been researched (RI.6.2, RI.6.3, RI.6.7, SL.6.1c)

Identify areas where more information is needed (SL.6.1c, SL.6.4)

Consider ways to present the work (SL.6.1)

Prepare the material for presentation (W.6.2a,b,c,d,e; W.6.4, W.6.5, W.6.6, W.6.7, W.6.8)

Lay out material

Lesson II: Immigration Continues—A Research Project

Examine the world map

Identify the countries for research purposes

Conduct preliminary research in groups (RI.6.1, RI.6.2, RI.6.7, W.6.7, W.6.8)

Narrow the area of research (RI.6.1, RI.6.2, RI.6.7, W.6.7, W.6.8)

Assign specific roles

Continue to conduct research (RI.6.1, RI.6.2, RI.6.7)

Lesson IV: An Exhibit

Representatives of each of the groups introduce the project

Examine the exhibit

Take notes while "touring" the exhibit (RI.6.2, W.6.7)

Compose personal reflections (W.6.2, W.6.4)

Lesson III: Preparing to Present

Objectives

In groups, examine the material that has been researched (RI.6.2, RI.6.3, RI.6.7, SL.6.1c)

Identify areas where more information is needed (SL.6.1c, SL.6.4)

Consider ways to present the work (SL.6.1)

Prepare the material for presentation (W.6.2a,b,c,d,e; W.6.4, W.6.5, W.6.6, W.6.7, W.6.8)

Lay out material

Required Materials

☐ Research work
☐ Maps
☐ Markers
☐ Poster boards
☐ Glue

Procedures

1. Lead-In:
Students revisit the material that has been researched, assess what may still be missing, and conduct further research before preparing the material for presentation.

2. Step by Step:
   a. Groups conclude research.
   b. Groups prepare the material for presentation. The material includes maps, written passages, charts, and so on.
   c. At the conclusion of step b, groups move on to a presentation of the material.

3. Closure:
Students report on the progress of the groups.

Differentiation

Advanced

- In heterogeneous research groups, give students leadership opportunities and more difficult research assignments. Students will think of a question to extend the research and then answer that question. Encourage students to use a wider variety of sources in their research, both in-person and online. They should evaluate and justify which ones contribute to the depth of their research in an annotated bibliography. Students can design a class web page on which to archive all projects for presenting and viewing after this lesson is complete. Encourage students to go deeper into an aspect of research that interests them, and present it in a multimedia/creative format. Students can evaluate and collect useful websites for their classmates to use for research, and collect them on the teacher's web portal.

Struggling

- Prior to this lesson, work with students to create a graphic organizer for compiling research findings. Students can begin their research using the websites found by classmates (listed above). Assign more straightforward research to students in heterogeneous research groups. Offer them the opportunity to present in a multimedia/creative format. Perhaps create a digital template on a shared online spreadsheet for students to use. The template will help students ensure that they include all required information.

Homework/Assessment
N/A

Courageous Characters

In this six-week unit, students select a fictional story with a courageous character and pair it with related informational text from the same historical time period.

OVERVIEW

Students choose from stories about varied circumstances in which people acted with tremendous courage: in times of slavery, instances of shipwrecks, or during the days of unfair child labor practices. Students recognize that acts of courage may have lasting effects on others. In this unit, students have the opportunity to refine their definitions of courage by examining how characters—real and fictional—grow by overcoming obstacles. After reading about outwardly courageous people, students consider quiet acts of courage, and class discussions reveal the importance of those people who often remain unnoticed or behind the scenes. Students examine how language and vocabulary enhance the reader's experience, cite specific passages of text to justify their thoughts, and critically examine the artistic license often taken in historical fiction. In the culminating project for this unit, students write and publish their own stories of courageous characters.

FOCUS STANDARDS

These Focus Standards have been selected for the unit from the Common Core State Standards.

RL.6.9: Compare and contrast texts in different forms or genres (e.g., stories and poems; historical novels and fantasy stories) in terms of their approaches to similar themes and topics.

RI.6.2: Determine a central idea of a text and how it is conveyed through particular details; provide a summary of the text distinct from personal opinions and judgments.

W.6.1: Write arguments to support claims with clear reasons and relevant evidence.

W.6.6: Use technology, including the Internet, to produce and publish writing as well as to interact and collaborate with others; demonstrate sufficient command of keyboarding skills to type a minimum of three pages in a single sitting.

SL.6.2: Interpret information presented in diverse formats (e.g., visually, quantitatively, orally) and explain how it contributes to a topic, text, or issue under study.

L.6.3: Use knowledge of language and its conventions when writing, speaking, reading, or listening.

SUGGESTED STUDENT OBJECTIVES

- Define *courage*.
- Read a variety of literature and informational text about challenging historical events and memorable experiences.
- Compare and contrast stories with courageous characters.
- Explore the similarities and differences in authors' characterization techniques.
- Read informational text to understand the historical context for the setting of a story with courageous characters.
- Write an argument about a historical event studied.
- Define related words and identify their parts of speech (e.g., *courage, courageous, courageousness, conviction, convince*, etc.).

SUGGESTED WORKS

(E) indicates a CCSS exemplar text; (EA) indicates a text from a writer with other works identified as exemplars.

LITERARY TEXTS

Stories

- *The Power of Light: Eight Stories for Hanukkah* (Isaac Bashevis Singer and Irene Lieblich) (EA)
- *Fire from the Rock* (Sharon M. Draper)
- *War Comes to Willy Freeman* (James and Christopher Collier)
- *Sadako and the Thousand Paper Cranes* (Eleanor Coerr)

Slavery and Overcoming Slavery

- "The People Could Fly" from *The People Could Fly* (Virginia Hamilton and Leo and Diane Dillon) (E)
- *Free at Last! Stories and Songs of Emancipation* (Doreen Rappaport and Shane W. Evans)

Asia

- *The Tale of the Mandarin Ducks* (Katherine Paterson and Leo and Diane Dillon) (E)
- *Sign of the Chrysanthemum* (Katherine Paterson and Peter Landa) (EA)
- *Kira-Kira* (Cynthia Kadohata)
- *Red Scarf Girl: A Memoir of the Cultural Revolution* (Ji-Li Jiang)
- *Under the Blood-Red Sun* (Graham Salisbury)
- *Snow Falling in Spring: Coming of Age in China During the Cultural Revolution* (Moying Li)

Shipwrecks
- *SOS Titanic* (Eve Bunting)
- *Timothy of the Cay* (Theodore Taylor)
- *Shipwreck Season* (Donna Hill)

Child Labor
- *Uprising: Three Young Women Caught in the Fire That Changed America* (Margaret Peterson Haddix)
- *Lyddie* (Katherine Paterson) (EA)
- *Counting on Grace* (Elizabeth Winthrop)
- *The Circuit: Stories from the Life of a Migrant Child* (Francisco Jiménez)
- *Iqbal* (Francesco D'Adamo)

Poetry
- "If" (Rudyard Kipling) (EA)
- *Lives: Poems about Famous Americans* (Lee Bennett Hopkins and Leslie Staub)
- "Casabianca" (Felicia Dorothea Hemans)

INFORMATIONAL TEXTS
Nonfiction
- *Kids with Courage: True Stories About Young People Making a Difference* (Barbara A. Lewis)

Slavery and Overcoming Slavery
- *Harriet Tubman: Conductor on the Underground Railroad* (Ann Petry) (E)
- *Narrative of the Life of Frederick Douglass, An American Slave, Written by Himself* (Frederick Douglass) (E)
- *Rebels Against Slavery: American Slave Revolts* (Patricia C. McKissack and Frederick L. McKissack)
- *Leon's Story* (Leon Walter Tillage and Susan L. Roth)
- *Many Thousand Gone: African Americans from Slavery to Freedom* (Companion to *The People Could Fly*) (Virginia Hamilton, Leo Dillon, and Diane Dillon)
- *Up Before Daybreak: Cotton and People in America* (Deborah Hopkinson)

Asia
- *Samurai: Warlords of Japan* (High Interest Books) (Arlan Dean)
- *Life in Ancient Japan* (Peoples of the Ancient World) (Hazel Richardson)

Shipwrecks
- *A Night to Remember: A Classic Account of the Final Hours of the Titanic* (Walter Lord) (E)
- *You Wouldn't Want to Sail on the Titanic! One Voyage You'd Rather Not Make* (You Wouldn't Want to … Series) (David Evelyn Stewart, David Salariya, and David Antram)

- *Exploring the Titanic: How the Greatest Ship Ever Lost—Was Found* (Robert D. Ballard)
- *Shipwreck at the Bottom of the World: The Extraordinary True Story of Shackleton and the Endurance* (Jennifer Armstrong)

Child Labor

- *Kids On Strike!* (Susan Campbell Bartoletti)
- *Kids at Work: Lewis Hine and the Crusade Against Child Labor* (Russell Freedman and Lewis Hine) (EA)

ART, MUSIC, AND MEDIA

Art and Architecture

- Frederick Douglass Home (Washington, DC, ca. 1855)
- Lincoln Memorial (Washington, DC, 1912–1922)
- Washington Monument (Washington, DC, 1848–1888)
- Iwo Jima Memorial (Rosslyn, Virginia, 1954)
- Vietnam War Memorial (Washington, DC, 1982)

Music

- Traditional, possibly Wallis Willis, "Swing Low, Sweet Chariot"
- Traditional, "Nobody Knows the Trouble I've Seen"
- Traditional, "Cotton Mill Girls" (as sung by Michèle Welborne)

SAMPLE ACTIVITIES AND ASSESSMENTS

1. CLASS DISCUSSION

What is meant by the word *courage*? Look up the word in a dictionary (print or online) and write your ideas down on a sticky note. (*Note:* Answers may include the quality of mind or spirit that enables a person to face difficulty, danger, pain, or sorrow.) Let's create a class word map of the word *courage*. As you find examples of courage in texts read during this unit, write them on sticky notes and add them to our word map. Your teacher may ask you to create an online concept map with a web tool. (SL.6.1a,b,c,d)

2. LITERARY RESPONSE

While reading one of the stories about a courageous character, keep notes in your journal or on a shared online spreadsheet about the following:

- What obstacles does he/she overcome, and how does he/she do it?
- How does the protagonist respond to different events?
- What/who is the antagonist?
- Does the character grow over the course of the novel, or was he/she always courageous?
- What does the protagonist learn about him-/herself?

You may have the opportunity to share your ideas with a partner before class discussion. Be sure to write down the page numbers of relevant information or mark your text with sticky notes so you can go back and cite the text during class discussion. (RL.6.2, RL.6.3, RI.6.8)

3. CLASS DISCUSSION

How do the stories from this unit provide insight into the courageous characters? How are their stories alike? How are they different? Cite specific information from the text to justify your response. (RL.6.1, RL.6.9, SL.6.1)

4. LITERATURE RESPONSE

Create a Venn diagram in your journal of a courageous character compared with a noncourageous, or cowardly, character. The differences between courageous and cowardly characters may seem obvious, but are there ways in which these characters are similar? Discuss your insights with a partner or use an online template. (RL.6.1, RL.6.3, RL.6.6)

5. JOURNAL RESPONSE/START A BLOG

Does courage always require overt acts of bravery? What are other ways of thinking about courageous characters? Write your responses to the questions in your journal and share them with a partner. Then, work with classmates to create your own class blog about unrecognized courageous characters, either in literature or real life. (RI.6.8, W.6.4, W.6.9a,b)

6. DRAMATIZATION/FLUENCY

Choose an emotional passage from a story we've read that exemplifies a character's courage. Work with classmates to present it as a dramatic reading. After the reading, ask your classmates to point out language that enhanced meaning, conveyed style, and helped achieve a feeling of strong emotion. Record the reading using a video camera so you can evaluate your performance. (SL.6.6, RL.6.4, L.6.5a,b,c)

7. INFORMATIVE/EXPLANATORY WRITING

After reading one of the stories with a courageous character, write a well-developed paper about how the character had "the courage to follow his/her convictions." What were his/her convictions? What challenges arose when the character followed these convictions? Be sure to cite at least three specific examples from the text to justify your response. Edit your writing for the grammar conventions studied so far this year. Your teacher may ask you to post your essay on the classroom blog. (W.6.9a, RL.6.3, L.6.1, L.6.2a,b)

8. INFORMATIONAL TEXT RESPONSE

Read a variety of stories and interviews from the same time period (e.g., *Titanic* survivors, slaves, or children who worked during the Depression). How are their accounts similar? Different? Why would accounts of the same event vary? Trace and evaluate the specific claims in a text with a partner who read about the same topic, and decide if they are sound and if there is sufficient evidence to support the claims. Write responses in your journal, or upload them in response to the teacher prompt on the classroom blog, and share them with a partner who read about the time period. (RI.6.5, RI.6.6, RI.6.8, W.6.8, W.6.9a,b, SL.6.2)

9. FACT OR FICTION GRAPHIC ORGANIZER

Historical fiction gets its name because these stories are based on true events, but the author may modify events to make a good story. Read informational text about the historical setting of a story read and create a T-chart or Venn diagram in your journal (or in an online template) that outlines historical facts and historical fiction from the story. Cite specific information from the texts read in the format provided by your teacher or mark your book with sticky notes to justify your response. Check each others' work for instances of plagiarism, as this concept was introduced by your teacher during this unit. (RL.6.9, RI.6.2, RI.6.5, RI.6.6)

10. ORAL PRESENTATION

Choose a story from *The People Could Fly* to read, summarize, and present to the class. Part of the presentation should include the meaning of the story, the qualities of the courageous character, and how the dialect affects the story. Record your presentation using a video camera so you can evaluate your performance. (L.6.1e, L.6.3a,b, SL.6.6)

11. WRITING (ARGUMENT) (OPTION 1)

Survivors from the *Titanic* reported that musicians on the ship played music to keep the passengers calm as the crew loaded lifeboats. Do you think this was an act of courage? Why or why not? Write a well-developed paper that includes an engaging opening statement of your position, at least three clear reasons, and relevant evidence from texts read. Edit your writing for the grammar conventions studied so far this year. Upload your published essay to the classroom blog, where you can receive feedback on the strength of your argument from your classmates. (W.6.1, SL.6.4, RL.6.4, W.6.4, L.6.1a,b,c,d; L.6.2a,b)

12. WRITING (ARGUMENT) (OPTION 2)

The poem "Casabianca," by Felicia Dorothea Hemans, was based on a true incident. In your opinion, was she courageous or crazy? Write a well-developed paper that includes an engaging opening statement of your position, at least three clear reasons, and relevant evidence from texts read. Edit your writing for the grammar conventions studied so far this year. Upload your published essay to the classroom blog, where you can receive feedback on the strength of your argument from your classmates. (W.6.1, W.6.4, SL.6.4, L.6.1a,b,c,d; L.6.2a,b)

13. WORD STUDY

Keep an index card file of words studied while reading about courageous characters. Keeping the words on index cards will help you when we sort words by prefix, suffix, root words, meaning, country of origin, spelling feature, and more. Focus on words that help describe the overt and quiet courageousness of characters and historical figures (e.g., *bravery, conviction, oppression*, etc.). (*Note:* This continues an etymology activity from Unit Three and will be an ongoing activity all year long.) (RI.6.4, RL.6.4, L.6.4)

14. CLASS DISCUSSION

One reason for storytelling and song is to help people to get through experiences of sorrow and pain. Choose selections from this unit and talk with a partner about if and how the character from your story would find comfort in a creative form of expression. (SL.6.1, SL.6.4)

15. REFLECTIVE ESSAY

Write your own essay describing an exemplary courageous character. Include some graphics or visuals that demonstrate the setting (either historical or present-day), and publish it so that others can enjoy it. Write an introduction that answers the essential question: How are acts of courage revealed in writing? Edit your writing for the grammar conventions studied so far this year before sharing your work with your teacher. Prepare your essay for upload to the classroom blog or a class wiki. (W.6.3, W.6.4, W.6.6, L.6.1a,b,c,d; L.6.2a,b, SL.6.6)

16. ART/CLASS DISCUSSION

How do we memorialize courageous people and actions? Examine each of the memorials. In the case of the Lincoln Memorial and the Iwo Jima Memorial, consider how the figures are portrayed and presented. How does this approach compare to the Washington Monument and the Vietnam War Memorial, which do not include images of people? How do these approaches differ from preserving someone's home as a monument, as in the case of Frederick Douglass? (SL.6.1, SL.6.2)

17. MECHANICS/GRAMMAR WALL

As a class, continue adding to the Mechanics/Grammar bulletin board started in Unit One. Remember—once skills are taught in a mini-lesson and listed on the bulletin board, you are expected to edit your work for these elements before publication. (L.6.1, L.6.2, L.6.3)

18. VOCABULARY/WORD WALL

As a class, continue adding to the Vocabulary Word Wall bulletin board where, throughout the year, you will add and sort words as you learn them in each unit of study. (L.6.4)

ADDITIONAL RESOURCES

- *Choose Your Own Adventure: A Hypertext Writing Experience* (ReadWriteThink) (W.6.3)
- *Families in Bondage* (National Endowment for the Humanities) (RL.6.9)
- *Slave Narratives: Constructing U.S. History Through Analyzing Primary Sources* (National Endowment for the Humanities) (RI.6.7)
- *Underground Railroad: Escape from Slavery—An Interactive Unit on Scholastic.com* (RI.6.7)
- *Susan B. Anthony Voted on This Date in 1872, Leading to Her Arrest* (ReadWriteThink) (RI.6.3)
- *Heroes Around Us* (ReadWriteThink) (RL.6.2)
- *Titanic: The RMS Titanic Sank on This Day in 1912* (ReadWriteThink)
- *Spirituals* (National Endowment for the Humanities)
- *Africans in America* (PBS)
- *In Motion: The African American Migration Experience* (Schomburg Center for Research in Black Culture, The New York Public Library)
- Word map (ReadWriteThink)
- Venn diagram circles (ReadWriteThink)

TERMINOLOGY

Antagonist

Character development

Protagonist

Grade Six, Unit Four Sample Lesson Plan

"If" by Rudyard Kipling

In this series of four lessons, students read "If" by Rudyard Kipling, and they:

> Examine the theme of "If" (RL.6.1, RL.6.2, RL.6.5, SL.6.1c,d)
>
> Explore oral renditions of "If" (SL.6.2, RL.6.7)
>
> Compose new stanzas for "If" (W.6.4, W.6.5, W.6.10, L.6.1, L.6.2, L.6.3, L.6.6)
>
> Perform new stanzas (RL.6.10)

Summary

Lesson I: "If"

Annotate "If" for its use of repetitions (RL.6.4, SL.6.1)

Investigate the ideas in each of the four stanzas (RL.6.1, RL.6.2, RL.6.5, SL.6.1c,d)

Recite (aloud) "If" (RL.6.10)

Lesson III: Composing New Stanzas

In groups, probe the structure of the stanzas in "If" (RL.6.5)

Each group composes a new stanza for "If" (W.6.4, W.6.5, W.6.10, L.6.1, L.6.2, L.6.3, L.6.6)

Groups prepare to perform the new stanzas (RL.6.10)

Lesson II: Renditions of "If"

View several renditions of "If" (SL.6.2, RL.6.7)

Ponder the experience of viewing and listening to poetry (RL.6.7, W.6.9a)

Explore the presenters' interpretations of "If" (W.6.9a, SL.6.1, SL.6.2)

Lesson IV: Performing New Stanzas

Rehearse renditions of new stanzas in groups (RL.6.10)

Memorize and recite new stanzas (RL.6.10)

Reflect upon the experience (SL.6.1)

Lesson II: Renditions of "If"

Objectives

View several renditions of "If" (SL.6.2, RL.6.7)

Ponder the experience of viewing and listening to poetry (RL.6.7, W.6.9a)

Explore the presenters' interpretations of "If" (W.6.9a, SL.6.1, SL.6.2)

Required Materials

☐ Computers with Internet access

Procedures

1. Lead-In:

Introduce the students to oral renditions of "If." (Many renditions of "If" exist on online; decide how many performances the students should watch.) Below are a few suggestions:

- 1998 World Cup
- Harvey Keitel
- Dennis Hopper on the *Johnny Cash Show*

2. Step by Step:
   a. The students discuss their initial response to viewing and listening to poetry.
   b. Students highlight the different interpretations of each rendition.

3. Closure:

Watch a different rendition that students have not yet seen.

Differentiation

Advanced

- Create your own interpretation of "If" and record it using a video camera, not only to evaluate your performance, but also to share it with your classmates.
- Choose one of the following assignments or create your own:
  - Read a variety of Kipling's poems. Choose a poem that appeals to you and write a letter to Kipling about the poem.
  - Read about Kipling's life. Choose a time in his life that *may* have inspired the writing of "If" and write a persuasive paragraph justifying your answer.
  - Write an essay on the poem "If," describing a moment in your life when you related to the sentiments in the poem.

Struggling

- On three small sticky notes, ask students to write three words from "If" that are new to them or that are simply "fuzzy" in meaning. Place the sticky notes on a display board, creating a visual representation of the words. Ask students to use dictionaries to learn the meaning(s) of the word and the part(s) of speech and which meaning the author intended in the poem.
- Throughout the lesson series, take a few minutes each day to have students play charades or other games with the vocabulary.
- Students should choose their favorite version of "If" and be able to justify why it's their favorite. Work on a choral presentation for another class and possibly record it using a video camera.

Homework/Assessment

N/A

Grade 6 ▶ Unit 5

Figure It Out

In this four-week unit, students have the opportunity to read classic and contemporary mysteries, make sense of nonsense poems, and solve riddles and math problems.

OVERVIEW

Students delve deeply into language and vocabulary specific to mysteries and problem solving. They examine how understanding these words is key to uncovering connections made in texts. Students are asked to articulate their basis for predictions, describe why and when they revise those predictions, and share the strategies they use to solve a variety of problems. Divergent approaches to similar problems are encouraged, followed by analysis of why students chose a particular strategy. In the culminating activity for this unit, students write an informative/explanatory essay in response to the essential question.

ESSENTIAL QUESTION

? How do strategies for solving math problems compare with strategies for solving mysteries?

FOCUS STANDARDS

These Focus Standards have been selected for the unit from the Common Core State Standards.

RL.6.5: Analyze how a particular sentence, chapter, scene, or stanza fits into the overall structure of a text and contributes to the development of the theme, setting, or plot.

RI.6.4: Determine the meaning of words and phrases as they are used in a text, including figurative, connotative, and technical meanings.

W.6.2: Write informative/explanatory texts to examine a topic and convey ideas, concepts, and information through the selection, organization, and analysis of relevant content.

SL.6.4: Present claims and findings, sequencing ideas logically and using pertinent descriptions, facts, and details to accentuate main ideas or themes; use appropriate eye contact, adequate volume, and clear pronunciation.

L.6.5: Demonstrate understanding of figurative language, word relationships, and nuances in word meanings.

SUGGESTED STUDENT OBJECTIVES

- Discern which passages from texts contribute to the development of a text's plot, setting, and/or theme.
- Distinguish between explicit clues and inferences drawn from the text.
- Compare and contrast mystery stories by a variety of authors.
- Articulate strategies used when solving problems (i.e., highlighting key information) and when figuring out mysteries (i.e., refining predictions as each chapter is read).
- Compare and contrast the experience of reading a mystery with listening to or viewing an audio, video, or live version.

SUGGESTED WORKS

(E) indicates a CCSS exemplar text; (EA) indicates a text from a writer with other works identified as exemplars.

LITERARY TEXTS
Math Stories

- *The Westing Game* (Ellen Raskin)
- *G Is for Googol: A Math Alphabet Book* (David M. Schwartz and Marissa Moss)
- *Math Curse* (Jon Scieszka)
- *Toothpaste Millionaire* (Jean Merrill)

Classic Mysteries

- *The Mysterious Adventures of Sherlock Holmes* (Arthur Conan Doyle)
- *Three-Act Tragedy* (Agatha Christie)

Contemporary Mysteries

- *39 Clues* series (Rick Riordan)
- *The Mysterious Benedict Society* (Trenton Lee Stewart and Carson Ellis)
- *The Name of this Book Is Secret* (Secret Series) (Pseudonymous Bosch)
- *Chasing Vermeer* (Blue Balliet and Brett Helquist)

Poetry

- "Jabberwocky" (Lewis Carroll) (E)
- *Math Talk: Mathematical Ideas in Poems for Two Voices* (Theoni Pappas)
- *Poetry for Young People: Edward Lear* (Edward Lear, Edward Mendelson, and Laura Huliska-Beith)
- *Poetry for Young People: Edgar Allan Poe* (Edgar Allen Poe, Brod Bagert, and Carolynn Cobleigh)
- *39 Clues Book 1: The Maze of Bones* (Rick Riordan) (Scholastic Audio Books)

INFORMATIONAL TEXTS
Nonfiction
- *The Number Devil: A Mathematical Adventure* (Hans Magnus Enzensberger) (E)
- *Go Figure! A Totally Cool Book About Numbers* (Johnny Ball)
- *The $1.00 Word Riddle Book* (Marilyn Burns and Martha Weston)
- *Math-terpieces: The Art of Problem Solving* (Greg Tang and Greg Paprocki)
- *Grapes of Math: Mind-Stretching Math Riddles* (Greg Tang and Harry Briggs)

ART, MUSIC, AND MEDIA
Art
- Balthus, *The Mountain* (1936–1937)
- Balthus, *The Street* (1933–1935)
- Balthus, *The Living Room* (1942)
- Balthus, *Solitaire* (1943)
- Chris Van Allsburg, illustrations from *The Mysteries of Harris Burdick* (1984)

Media
- *The New Adventures of Sherlock Holmes* (Arthur Conan Doyle) (Anthony Boucher) (audiobook CD)
- *The Essential Agatha Christie Stories: Agatha Christie's Best Short Sleuths Crack Twenty-Two Famous Cases* (Agatha Christie) (BBC Audiobooks America)

SAMPLE ACTIVITIES AND ASSESSMENTS

1. CLASS DISCUSSION
How do you make sense of nonsense poems such as "Jabberwocky" by Lewis Carroll? How do you figure out what words mean when they don't really exist? How are clues provided in the text structure, repetition, or content of the poem? Your teacher may ask you to write your ideas down in your journal and share them with a partner before class discussion. (RL.6.4, SL.6.1)

Optional follow-up activity: Write your own nonsense poem and see if classmates can make sense of it.

2. "DEDUCTION OR INDUCTION?" T-CHART GRAPHIC ORGANIZER
As you discuss how you solve mysteries and math problems, classify your approach as *inductive* or *deductive*.

- When do you use inductive reasoning? When do you use deductive reasoning? Why?
- Which of the following problem-solving approaches use inductive reasoning and which use deductive reasoning?
  - Acting out the scenario
  - Role-playing

- Drawing a picture
- Making a list
- Working backwards
- Making educated guesses and checking how they work
- Drawing a web of facts, events, and characters
- What strategies do your characters use (e.g., Reynis, Kate, Sticky, and Constance from *The Mysterious Benedict Society*)?

Your teacher may ask you to write your response in your journal (or chart it in a shared online spreadsheet) and share it with a partner before each section of the class chart is filled in. Be sure to make notes of page numbers with relevant information so you can go back and cite the text during class discussion. (RL.6.5, RI.6.4)

3. CLASS DISCUSSION

Usually there is more than one way to solve a (math) problem. What have you learned about inductive and deductive reasoning? How does hearing your classmates articulate their thinking increase your understanding of problem solving? (SL.6.1, SL.6.4)

4. MATH CONNECTION

Ask your math teacher if you can solve the "Painted Cube Problem" in math class, or solve some math problems from *The $1.00 Word Riddle Book* by Marilyn Burns or found online. Write in your journal about the thought process used to solve these problems, or create a screenshot of your work online, and use this experience to add to your graphic organizer (in Activity 2). (RI.6.4, RI.6.5, W.6.4)

5. JUST THE FACTS GRAPHIC ORGANIZER

Since you and your classmates are reading different mysteries, keep track of this information in your journal or mark your book with sticky notes to facilitate class discussions about these points:

- Title and author of your mystery
- Each character's name, his/her traits, and his/her role in the mystery
- List of clues, including page numbers on which they are found
- Make and revise predictions (because mystery stories continually evolve, it is important to make predictions and return to them each time new evidence is found)
- Solution

Your teacher may ask you to write your response in your journal and share it with a partner before class discussion. The class can also create a shared online spreadsheet to facilitate the exchange of information. (RI.6.4, RI.6.5)

6. WRITING (ARGUMENT)

As a follow-up to the Just the Facts graphic organizer (in Activity 5), write an argument to respond to this question: Which character played the most pivotal role in the mystery read? Why? Write a well-developed paper that includes an engaging opening statement of your position, at least three clear reasons, and relevant evidence from the mystery read. Cite at least two significant passages, and explain how and why those passages contribute to the development of the plot. Edit your writing for varied sentence patterns and consistency in style and tone. You may upload your essay to the classroom blog. (W.6.1, W.6.4, L.6.1, L.6.2a,b, L.6.3a,b)

7. LITERATURE RESPONSE: *THE WESTING GAME*

The clues provided to the heirs in *The Westing Game* are mostly words from the song "America the Beautiful" taken out of order. When rearranged, they notice the missing parts spell out the name of an heir—but this is actually a red herring. Select your own song, change the order of the lyrics, delete some words or letters, and see if your classmates can solve *your* mystery. (RL.6.5, W.6.2)

Optional extension: Remix your own song using music recording software.

8. LITERATURE RESPONSE

Select a pivotal passage or scene from the mystery you are reading. How does this scene fit into the overall structure of the text? How does it contribute to your understanding of the plot? Write your thoughts down in your journal. Reevaluate your claim at the end of the book. Do you still think that passage was critical to the solution? Why or why not? Talk with a partner to justify your answer, and cite specific details from the text. (RL.6.5, W.6.2, SL.6.4)

9. WRITING (ARGUMENT)

How does listening to a mystery such as *The Mysterious Adventures of Sherlock Holmes* as an audiobook compare to reading the book? Which do you prefer? Why? Write an argument to explain your preference. Be sure to include at least three reasons for your preference and examples for each reason. Take the online poll on your classroom blog for this topic. If the class responses are equally divided, your teacher may ask you to upload your response on the classroom blog to get feedback from your classmates. (RL.6.7, W.6.1, L.6.1)

10. DRAMATIZATION/FLUENCY

Choose your favorite poem from this unit to memorize and/or recite to the class using appropriate eye contact, adequate volume, and clear pronunciation. Record your presentation using a video camera so you can evaluate your performance. (Alternatively, you can write your own poem based on a poem read in class.) After the reading, ask your classmates to point out figurative language, word relationships, and/or nuances in word meanings. (SL.6.1, L.6.5)

11. WORD STUDY

Keep an index card file of words studied while reading mysteries, riddles, and math problems (e.g., *alibi, evidence, sleuth, suspect, victim, witness, red herring, investigator, hunch, motive,* etc.). Keeping the words on index cards will help you when we sort words by prefix, suffix, root words, meaning, spelling feature, and so on. (*Note:* This will be an ongoing activity all year long.) (L.6.4a,b,c)

12. NARRATIVE WRITING

After reading and discussing mysteries in class, try to write your own mystery that incorporates the new vocabulary words learned in this unit. Talk your ideas through with a partner, but don't give away the ending! See how long you can keep your reader engaged without giving away the resolution. Your well-developed mystery should hook the reader with a mysterious opening sentence and have a logical sequence of events that is made clear in the concluding section. Edit your writing for varied sentence patterns and consistency in style and tone (see Standards for more details) before publishing your mystery on a class web page. (W.6.3, W.6.4, W.6.5, W.6.6, L.6.1, L.6.2a,b, L.6.3a,b)

13. ART/CLASS DISCUSSION

Compare the work of Balthus to the illustrations in *The Mysteries of Harris Burdick* by Chris Van Allsburg. What are the differences you notice between fine art (Balthus) and illustrations (Van Allsburg)? How are the looks of these two artists similar? How are they different? Illustrators are sometimes inspired by the work of fine artists. Might this have been the case here? (SL.6.1, SL.6.4)

14. ART/WRITING

Study the small details and imagery in Balthus's *The Street* and *The Mountain*. What is happening in these paintings? Imagine what might have occurred before and after each scene. Write a short story describing what you see, and what might happen next to these characters. (W.6.3, W.6.4, W.6.5)

15. INFORMATIVE/EXPLANATORY WRITING

In this unit, you have read mystery books, made sense of nonsense poems, and solved riddles and math problems. Write an informative/explanatory essay in response to the essential question: How do strategies for solving math problems compare with strategies for solving mysteries? Cite specific examples from texts read to justify your response. Edit your writing for varied sentence patterns and consistency in style and tone. Upload your essay to the classroom blog. (W.6.2, W.6.4, W.6.5, W.6.6, W.6.9a,b, L.6.1, L.6.2a,b, L.6.3a,b, SL.6.4)

16. MECHANICS/GRAMMAR WALL

As a class, continue adding to the Mechanics/Grammar bulletin board started in Unit One. Remember—once skills are taught in a mini-lesson and listed on the bulletin board, you are expected to edit your work for these elements before publication. (L.6.1, L.6.2, L.6.3)

17. LANGUAGE/STYLE

Read the opening pages from two books, such as *Math Curse* by Jon Scieszka and a book from the *39 Clues* series by Rick Riordan, by different authors in this unit. Describe both authors' styles. Are they formal or informal? How does each author's style compare to yours? Choose a piece of your own writing and compare it with a classmate's. Describe how your styles are similar and different. Read your work aloud, and listen for shifts in style. Working with a partner, revise your work as necessary so the style is consistent. (L.6.3b)

ADDITIONAL RESOURCES

- *Everyone Loves a Mystery: A Genre Study* (ReadWriteThink) (RL.6.4)
- *Mystery Cube* (ReadWriteThink) (RL.6.2)
- Edward Stratemeyer, *Creator of Book series, such as Nancy Drew, Was Born on This Day in 1862* (ReadWriteThink) (RL.6.3)
- *Celebrate Blues Legend Robert Johnson's Birthday* (ReadWriteThink) (L.6.3)
- *Becoming History Detectives Using Shakespeare's Secret* (ReadWriteThink) (RL.6.9)

- *History's Mysteries* (Education World) (W.6.1)
- *Chasing Vermeer: Picture the Process! Do You See What I See? and Patterns and Pentominoes* (Scholastic) (SL.6.6)
- *Ingredients of a Mystery* (Scholastic) (RL.6.3)
- *Puzz.com 1001 Best Puzzles* (Puzz.Com)

TERMINOLOGY

Alibi	Inference	Red herring	Witness
Deductive reasoning	Investigator	Sleuth	
Evidence	Mystery	Suspect	
Inductive reasoning	Problem solving	Victim	

Grade Six, Unit Five Sample Lesson Plan

The Number Devil: A Mathematical Adventure by Hans Magnus Enzensberger

In this series of four lessons, students read *The Number Devil: A Mathematical Adventure* by Hans Magnus Enzensberger, and they:

Examine Enzensberger's ways of introducing math in fictional form (RL.6.1, RL.6.2, RL.6.3, RI.6.2, RI.6.3, RI.6.8)

Emulate Enzensberger's style and write new mathematical adventures (SL.6.1, W.6.2, W.6.3, W.6.4, W.6.5)

Summary

Lesson I: Meet the Number Devil and Robert

Articulate the plot of the dream in "The First Night"

Identify the leading characters of the dream (RL.6.6)

Examine the setting of the dream (RL.6.3)

Identify the shape and function of the calculator in the chapter

Investigate the mathematical concepts of the dream (RI.6.2, RI.6.3, RI.6.8)

Lesson II: Eleven Nights—Eleven Dreams

(*Note*: In eleven groups)

Read the assigned dream

Discuss the plot of the dream

Note the evolution of the characters (RL.6.6)

Identify the setting (RL.6.3)

Explore the particular shape and function of the calculator

Investigate the mathematical concepts in the dream (RI.6.2, RI.6.3, RI.6.8)

Consult the Seek-and-Ye-Shall-Find List (see Additional Resources)

Lesson III: Eleven New Dreams

Revisit the assigned dream

Recollect the mathematical concepts

Exchange ideas for a new dream (SL.6.1.a,b,c,d)

Collaborate in the creation of a new mathematical adventure (W.6.2a, W.6.3.a,b, W.6.4, W.6.5)

Lesson IV: Eleven New Dreams Revealed

Share Robert's new dreams (SL.6.1)

Enjoy Robert's new adventures (SL.6.1)

Appreciate the new mathematical challenges

Lesson III: Eleven New Dreams

Objectives

Revisit the assigned dream

Recollect the mathematical concepts

Exchange ideas for a new dream (SL.6.1.a,b,c,d)

Collaborate in the creation of a new mathematical adventure (W.6.2.a, W.6.3.a,b, W.6.4, W.6.5)

Required Material

☐ Class sets of *The Number Devil: A Mathematical Adventure* by Hans Magnus Enzensberger

☐ Lined paper for writing

☐ Rulers

☐ Calculators

☐ Colored pencils and markers

☐ Drawing paper

Procedures

1. Lead-In:

In the groups that were established in Lesson II, students revisit the assigned dream and recollect its mathematical concepts.

2. Step by Step:

a. Each group exchanges ideas for a new dream and a new mathematical adventure for Robert. Each of the dreams must have several necessary components:

A plot

Two characters

A setting

A calculator

Mathematical concepts

Remind the students that all of the components above must work together.

b. Once the students have their story line, they must clearly articulate their mathematical adventure. They may use calculators, rulers, or any other tools that are available.

c. Students need to consider the illustrations that they will draw. The illustrations must reflect the specific setting of their story. Students must determine what the calculator will look like. They must also decide how to represent the mathematical concept that they explore.

d. With guidance, the students assign roles for writing and illustrating Robert's new adventures.

e. Collaboratively, the students write, revise, draw, and complete a new mathematical adventure.

3. Closure:

The closure for this work is in the next lesson, when each group shares its work with the rest of the class.

Differentiation

Advanced

- Intentionally assign students to a dream that contains a mathematical concept that is more difficult to explain.
- Encourage students to select a challenging concept for their new mathematical adventure.
- Encourage students to represent their mathematical adventure online. After writing the adventure, transform it into a screen capture or comic using a comic creation web tool.
- If the students are good editors, have them peer edit the dreams written by classmates.

Struggling

- Intentionally assign students to a dream that contains a mathematical concept that is easier to explain.
- Provide students with a list of easier mathematical concepts from which to choose. If students are stymied, provide the book *Math Curse*, by Jon Scieszka, as an additional support.
- Provide students with a graphic organizer to complete as they brainstorm their adventure (plot, two characters, setting, calculator, and mathematical concept).
- After partners talk through their mathematical adventure, write the first section with them before asking them to continue on their own.
- Allow students to represent their mathematical adventure online, transforming it into a screen capture, a comic using a comic creation web tool, or an online story.

Homework/Assessment

The above assignment will enable the teacher to assess the students':

- Comprehension of mathematical concepts
- Ability to articulate their understanding in an imaginative way
- Ability to work collaboratively with their peers

Grade 6 ▶ *Unit 6*

Winging It

In this final six-week unit of sixth grade, students read *Dragonwings* by Lawrence Yep, compare this novel to biographies of aviators, and read about the science and history of flight.

ESSENTIAL QUESTION

? How do literature and informational text reveal why people dream of flying?

OVERVIEW

Reading *Dragonwings* helps students recall class conversations that incorporate the themes from this year: flying (from *Peter Pan*), reading folklore, embracing heritage, courageous characters, and "figuring it out." *Dragonwings* is also an effective springboard for a conversation about people's dreams. The goal of this unit is for students to apply all their reading, writing, speaking, and listening strategies and skills learned up until this point in the year. The year culminates with a multimedia project on the science of flight, making connections to how people worked to make their dreams of flying come true.

FOCUS STANDARDS

These Focus Standards have been selected for the unit from the Common Core State Standards.

RL.6.2: Determine a theme or central idea of a text and how it is conveyed through particular details; provide a summary of the text distinct from personal opinions or judgments.

RI.6.6: Determine an author's point of view or purpose in a text and explain how it is conveyed in the text.

RI.6.7: Integrate information presented in different media or formats (e.g., visually, quantitatively) as well as in words to develop a coherent understanding of a topic or issue.

W.6.2: Write informative/explanatory texts to examine a topic and convey ideas, concepts, and information through the selection, organization, and analysis of relevant content.

SL.6.5: Include multimedia components (e.g., graphics, images, music, sound) to visual displays in presentations to clarify information.

L.6.1: Demonstrate command of the conventions of Standard English grammar and usage when writing or speaking.

SUGGESTED STUDENT OBJECTIVES

- Compare and contrast a variety of fictional and nonfictional texts about flight and dreams of flying.
- Identify the theme or themes in texts read and describe how the author develops them.
- Compare and contrast literature with biographies of aviators and videos of some of the first flights.
- Compare the experience of reading a text to watching it performed live.
- Perform an original skit for classmates about aviators and the science of flight.
- While conducting research for an informative/explanatory essay, compare the information from primary-source documents (videos) with the secondary sources read (e.g., biographies); include in your essay the sources most appropriate to support your thesis.

SUGGESTED WORKS

(E) indicates a CCSS exemplar text; (EA) indicates a text from a writer with other works identified as exemplars.

LITERARY TEXTS
Stories

- *Dragonwings* (Lawrence Yep) (E)
- *First to Fly: How Wilbur and Orville Wright Invented the Airplane* (Peter Busby)
- *Flight* (Robert Burleigh)

Picture Books (as an Introduction to the Unit)

- *A is for Airplane: An Aviation Alphabet* (Mary Ann McCabe Riehle, Fred Stillwell, and Rob Bolster)
- *The Airplane Alphabet Book* (Jerry Pallotta)

Poetry

- *I Am Phoenix: Poems for Two Voices* (Paul Fleischman)

INFORMATIONAL TEXTS
Nonfiction

- *Flying Free: America's First Black Aviators* (Philip S. Hart)
- *Fantastic Flights: One Hundred Years of Flying on the Edge* (Patrick O'Brien)
- *Black Eagles: African Americans in Aviation* (James Haskins)
- *Strange and Wonderful Aircraft* (Harvey Weiss)
- *The Simple Science of Flight: From Insects to Jumbo Jets* (Henk Tennekes)
- *Flight: Discover Science Through Facts and Fun* (Gerry Bailey)

Biographies

- *Sterling Biographies: The Wright Brothers: First in Flight* (Tara Dixon-Engel)
- *Wilbur and Orville Wright: Taking Flight* (Stephanie Sammartino McPherson and Joseph Sammartino Gardner)

- *The Wright Brothers: How They Invented the Airplane* (Russell Freedman)
- *Charles A. Lindbergh: A Human Hero* (James Cross Giblin)
- *William Boeing: Builder of Planes* (Community Builders) (Sharlene Nelson and Ted Nelson)
- *Amelia Earhart* (DK Biography) (Tanya Lee Stone)
- *Up in the Air: The Story of Bessie Coleman* (Philip S. Hart and Barbara O'Connor)

ART, MUSIC, AND MEDIA

Art

- Orville Wright, Wilbur Wright, and John T. Daniels, *First flight* (early twentieth century)
- Orville Wright and Wilbur Wright, *Wilbur gliding down steep slope of Big Kill Devil Hill* (early twentieth century)
- Orville Wright and Wilbur Wright, *Crumpled glider wrecked by the wind on Hill of the Wreck* (early twentieth century)
- Photographer unknown, *Charles Lindbergh, three-quarter length portrait, standing, left profile, working on engine of The Spirit of St. Louis* (early twentieth century)
- Attributed to Orville and/or Wilbur Wright, *Orville Wright, Major John F. Curry, and Colonel Charles Lindbergh, who came to pay Orville a personal call at Wright Field, Dayton, Ohio* (early twentieth century)

SAMPLE ACTIVITIES AND ASSESSMENTS

1. INTRODUCTORY ACTIVITY/CLASS DISCUSSION

Your teacher will read *A is for Airplane: An Aviation Alphabet* by Mary Ann McCabe Riehle and/or *The Airplane Alphabet Book* by Jerry Pallotta to the class. How can picture books give you background information about topics that may be new to you? Were you surprised by the amount of information within an alphabet book? Talk with a partner about the answers to these questions, then write your response in your journal. (RI.6.6, RI.6.7)

2. LITERATURE RESPONSE

As you read *Dragonwings*, keep a journal that specifies:

- The characteristics of Moon Shadow and Windrider that enable them to overcome obstacles
- The obstacles that they face
- Their internal responses and external behaviors to these obstacles
- The events that lead up to the climax and, ultimately, the characters' growth
- The theme of the book

After reading the novel, the class will create an alphabet book summary as a class, so keep a list of ideas for each letter in your journal. (W.6.9a, W.6.9b, RL.6.2, RL.6.3, RL.6.5, RL.6.10)

3. JOURNAL ENTRY/FIGURATIVE LANGUAGE

After reading Chapter Three (where Windrider recounts his dream of being the physician to the dragon king), mark the text with sticky notes in places where Yep uses imagery, alliteration, metaphors, similes, and personification. Share your ideas with a partner before the class discussion. As a follow-up, write about your own dreams using similar types of figurative language. (L.6.1, L.6.5)

4. GRAPHIC ORGANIZER/LITERARY RESPONSE

As a class, keep a chart of the aviators studied using the categories listed here, either on chart paper or on a shared online spreadsheet. At the end of the unit, this information will be used to make comparisons and generalizations about people who are passionate about aviation, either as a hobby or a career.

- Aviator's name
- Obstacles he/she faces
- Why he/she is famous
- What turning point in his/her life led him/her into aviation?
- What did you learn about this person that surprised you?

Your teacher may ask you to write your responses in your journal and share them with a partner before each section of the class chart is filled in. Be sure to make notes of page numbers with relevant information or mark your text with a sticky note so you can cite the text during class discussion. (W.6.7, W.6.8, W.6.9b, RI.6.6, RI.6.10)

5. CLASS DISCUSSION

Talk about the aviators studied. How are their stories alike? How are they different? What traits do they have in common? Cite specific information from the text read to justify your responses. Write a summary of the class discussion in your journal or on the classroom blog. (L.6.1, RI.6.9)

6. WRITING (ARGUMENT)

"Success is not a destination; it's a journey." Write an argument in response to this quotation from the perspective of the aviator you studied. Would he/she agree with this phrase? Why or why not? Your well-developed argument should include an engaging opening statement of your aviator's position, at least three clear reasons, and relevant evidence cited from the informational text read. Edit your writing for the grammar conventions studied so far this year. Be prepared to record yourself reading your essay as a podcast. (RI.6.7, RI.6.10, W.6.1, RL.6.10, L.6.1, L.6.2, L.6.3)

7. DRAMA, DRAMA, DRAMA

Work in small groups to create and present a short skit about the principles of flight and/or an aviator you learned about from experiments, simulations, videos, or multimedia sources in science class. Try to include the idioms about flying learned in this unit. Write the script paying careful attention to capitalization, punctuation, spelling, and word choice. Your classmates will compare your presentation with your written version and will discuss the differences between seeing it performed live and reading it. Record your performance using a video camera so you can evaluate your performance. (RI.6.7, RI.6.10, W.6.7, L.6.2a,b, RL.6.10)

8. POETRY PERFORMANCE

Choose your favorite poem from *I Am Phoenix: Poems for Two Voices* and present a dramatic reading to the class. (Alternatively, write your own poem for two voices about flight, and present it to the class with a classmate.) Record your performance using a video camera so you can evaluate your performance. (RL.6.2, SL.6.6)

9. INFORMATIVE/EXPLANATORY WRITING AND MULTIMEDIA PRESENTATION

Create an informative/explanatory multimedia essay or presentation in which you respond to the question: How do literature and informational text reveal why people dream of flying? Continue building on the research skills you have learned this year. Cite at least two specific details from two different sources from your research, including links to videos of flights or interviews with aviators. Compare the information from primary-source documents with the secondary sources read (biographies). Use a variety of words learned and studied throughout the year (from Word Study). Edit your writing for the grammar conventions studied so far this year prior to publication. This assessment will end with a class discussion in which you discuss what you have learned about the research process this year. (RI.6.7, RI.6.10, SL.6.5, L.6.1, L.6.2, L.6.3a,b, L.6.6, W.6.2, W.6.6, W.6.8, W.6.10, RL.6.10)

10. MECHANICS/GRAMMAR WALL

As a class, continue adding to the Mechanics/Grammar bulletin board started in Unit One. Remember—once skills are taught in a mini-lesson and listed on the bulletin board, you are expected to edit your work for these elements before publication. (L.6.1, L.6.2, L.6.3)

11. VOCABULARY/WORD WALL

As a class, continue adding to the Vocabulary Word Wall bulletin board where, throughout the year, you will add and sort words as you learn them in each unit of study. (L.6.4)

12. ART/CLASS DISCUSSION

As you reflect on the background on the Wright Brothers and Charles Lindbergh, describe what you see in the images. How do these images show their passion and ambition to achieve flight? What do the photos teach us about the process involved in such progress? Discuss the degree to which the photos focus on the people versus the planes. (SL.6.1, SL.6.2)

ADDITIONAL RESOURCES

- *The Wright Brothers Made Their Phenomenal Flight* (ReadWriteThink) (RI.6.7)
- *America on the Move* (National Museum of American History) (RI.6.7)
- *Charles Lindberg Began His Transatlantic Flight on May 20, 1927* (ReadWriteThink) (RI.6.2)
- *Women Aviators in World War II: "Fly Girls"* (National Endowment for the Humanities) (RI.6.3)
- *ABC Bookmaking Builds Vocabulary in the Content Areas* (ReadWriteThink) (L.6.4)
- *Aviation History Online Museum* (a website for researching the history of flight) (RI.6.3)
- *First Flight* (a website for researching flight and aviation) (RI.6.3)
- Lesson Plans for *Dragonwings* (WebEnglishTeacher.com)
- *Video Interview with Lawrence Yep* (Reading Rockets)
- *Wright Brothers Have Lift Off* (and other examples of first flights)

TERMINOLOGY

Figurative language	"Flying by the seat of your pants"	Imagery	simile, alliteration, onomatopoeia"
Idioms such as:		Literary techniques:	
"Fly in the face of"	"Flying colors"	"rhyme scheme,	Memoir
"Fly off the handle"	"When pigs fly"	meter, metaphor,	Personification

Grade Six, Unit Six Lesson Plan

Dragonwings by Laurence Yep

In this series of ten lessons, students read *Dragonwings* by Laurence Yep, and they:

- Examine the character of Windrider (RL.6.1, RL.6.3, RL.6.5, SL.6.1, SL.6.4)
- Illustrate scenes from the novel (RL.6.1, RL.6.3, RL.6.5, SL.6.5)
- Investigate the story of Fung Joe Guey (RI.6.7, RI.6.10, W.6.7, W.6.10)
- Explore Orville and Wilbur Wright's early flights (RI.6.7, RI.6.10, W.6.7, W.6.10)
- Produce an exhibit of early aviators (SL.6.4, SL.6.5, L.6.1)

Summary

Lessons I–V: Windrider

- Examine the significance of Chapter III, "The Dragon Man" (RL.6.1, SL.6.1, SL.6.4)
- Explore the relationship between Windrider and Orville Wright (RL.6.3)
- Trace the development of Dragonwings (RL.6.5)
- Note Windrider's vision (RL.6.5)
- Explore the inner strength of Windrider (RL.6.3)
- Illustrate select scenes from the novel (RL.6.1, RL.6.3, RL.6.5, SL.6.5)

Lessons VIII–IX: Orville and Wilbur Wright

- Conduct research into the lives of Orville and Wilbur Wright (RI.6.7, RI.6.10, W.6.7, W.6.10)
- Explore the accomplishments of Orville and Wilbur Wright (W.6.7)
- Document information about Orville and Wilbur Wright (W.6.2)

Lesson VI–VII: Fung Joe Guey

- Conduct research about the life of Fung Joe Guey (RI.6.7, RI.6.10, W.6.7, W.6.10)
- Explore the accomplishments of Fung Joe Guey (W.6.7)
- Document information about Fung Joe Guey (W.6.2)

Lesson X: Early American Aviators

- Assemble research information (SL.6.4, SL.6.5)
- Display findings on poster boards (SL.6.4, SL.6.5, L.6.1)
- Display illustrations of select scenes from *Dragonwings* (Lessons I–V) (SL.6.5)
- Survey findings (SL.6.2)
- Explore the connection between historical events and writing fiction (RL.6.9, W.6.9)

Lesson X: Early American Aviators

Objectives

Assemble research information (SL.6.4, SL.6.5)

Display findings on poster boards (SL.6.4, SL.6.5, L.6.1)

Display illustrations of select scenes from *Dragonwings* (Lessons I–V) (SL.6.5)

Survey findings (SL.6.2)

Explore the connection between historical events and writing fiction (RL.6.9, W.6.9)

Required Materials

☐ Poster boards

☐ Markers

☐ Glue

Procedures

1. Lead-In:
The students assemble all the material gathered about Fung Joe Guey and the Wright Brothers; they also assemble the illustrations they produced while reading *Dragonwings*.

2. Step by Step:
   a. Lead a class discussion to determine the way in which the material gathered will be displayed.
   b. In groups, students arrange the material on poster boards.

      They identify the most important facts and where to place them.

      They consider colors that are used; they also consider the size of the font.

      They add captions if necessary.

      They determine how to display their own illustrations.

   c. While students survey the display, they consider the final objective of the lesson. (You may choose to provide students with worksheets.)

3. Closure:
Lead a class discussion exploring the connection between historical events and writing fiction.

Differentiation

Advanced

- Students may choose to create a digital version of their poster board project, using a computer graphics program.
- Students may create a class web page where the presentations can be archived and shared. The electronic posters can be uploaded, or the tri-fold boards used can be photographed. Set up a blog where others can add comments.

Struggling

- Give students a guiding checklist as they do the research and an organizational design for the final product. Help students, as needed, with the creation and organization of the poster boards.
- Create a template on a shared online document for students who want to do an electronic presentation.

Homework/Assessment
N/A

GRADE 7

Students entering seventh grade have read literature from many standpoints: in connection with history, science, and the arts; in pursuit of answers to a question; in consideration of a theme or literary element; and as a way of gaining insight into human existence. In seventh grade, they continue reading texts from different angles. Students read literature from and about the Middle Ages in order to gain insight into character. They consider themes of perseverance and determination in a wide variety of fictional and historical texts. In one unit, Yeats's "Song of Wandering Aengus" leads into a study of the theme of survival in the wild; at the end of the unit, students return to the poem with new understanding. In another, students read science fiction. The units are not limited to their central themes; there are side topics and excursions into related subjects. As in sixth grade, students study morphology, etymology, and word history throughout the units, building their own dictionaries of words that they have investigated. Students write in a variety of genres, including responses to literature, reflective essays, and stories. In addition, they create multimedia presentations. Students also write research essays about an author whose work they have read and develop their skills of argumentation. They use graphic organizers to lay out their ideas and plan their essays. They participate in class discussion and learn more about art; practice reading literature expressively; and deliver presentations. By the end of seventh grade, they are ready to begin studying complex aspects of literature.

Standards Checklist for Grade Seven

Standard	Unit 1	Unit 2	Unit 3	Unit 4	Unit 5	Unit 6	Standard	Unit 1	Unit 2	Unit 3	Unit 4	Unit 5	Unit 6
Reading—Literature							3c	A		A	A	A	
1	FA	A		A	FA	A	3d	A		A	A	A	
2	FA		A	FA	A	A	3e	A		A	A	A	
3	A	FA		A	A		4			A	A	A	A
4	A	A	A	A	A		5				A	A	A
5	A	A	FA	A		A	6					A	A
6		A	A	A		FA	7		FA	A	A	A	
7		A	FA	A	A	A	Speaking and Listening						
8 n/a							1	F	FA	A	A	A	A
9	FA	A			A		1a	FA	A	A	A	A	A
10	A					A	1b	FA	A	A	A	A	A
Reading—Informational Text							1c		FA	A	A	A	A
1	FA	A			A		1d		FA	A	A	A	A
2	A	FA					2		A	FA			
3			FA				3			A	A	A	FA
4	A		A				4		A	A	FA	A	A
5				FA	A		5		A		A	FA	A
6	A		A		A		6	A	A	A	A		A
7			A		A		Language						
8				A	A		1	A	A	A	A	FA	A
9		A	FA		FA		1a	A	A	A	A	A	A
10	A				A		1b	A	A	A	A	A	A
Writing							1c	A	A	A	A	A	A
1	A	A	A	FA		FA	2	A	A	A	A	A	A
1a	A	A		A		A	2a	A	A	A	A	A	A
1b	A	A		A		A	2b	A	A	A	A	A	A
1c	A	A		A		A	3	A	A	A	A	A	FA
1d	A	A		A		A	3a	A	A	A	A	A	A
1e	A	A		A		A	4	FA	FA	A	A	A	A
2	A	A	FA		FA	A	4a	FA	A	A	A	A	A
2a		A	A		A		4b	A	FA	A	A	A	A
2b		A	A		A		4c	FA	A	A	A	A	A
2c		A	A		A		4d	A	FA	A	A	A	A
2d		A	A		A		5		A		FA		A
2e		A	A		A		5a		A		A		A
2f		A	A		A		5b		A		A		A
3	FA		A	A	A	A	5c		A		A	A	A
3a	A		A	A	A		6				FA		A
3b	A		A	A	A								

F = Focus Standard; A = Activity/Assessment

Grade 7 ▶ *Unit 1*

Characters with Character

This first six-week unit of seventh grade starts the year off with reflections on characters from literature and historical time periods.

OVERVIEW

Students build on their knowledge of the medieval time period, first introduced to them as fourth graders. (Note that basic informational and picture books are provided to build the necessary background knowledge for understanding of this unit.) Students have a variety of Middle Ages novels from which to choose. The novels are set in Byzantium, England, France, Korea, or Africa. While the historical time period is secondary to the focus on characterization, historical accuracies and creative license are considered. Students discuss how elements of a story interact, practice citing textual evidence, and formalize a process for determining word meanings. This unit ends with an informative/explanatory essay in response to the essential question.

FOCUS STANDARDS

These Focus Standards have been selected for the unit from the Common Core State Standards.

RL.7.1: Cite several pieces of textual evidence to support analysis of what the text says explicitly as well as inferences drawn from the text.

RL.7.2: Determine a theme or central idea of a text and analyze its development over the course of the text; provide an objective summary of the text.

RL.7.9: Compare and contrast a fictional portrayal of a time, place, or character and a historical account of the same period as a means of understanding how authors of fiction use or alter history.

RI.7.1: Cite several pieces of textual evidence to support analysis of what the text says explicitly as well as inferences drawn from the text.

W.7.3: Write narratives to develop real or imagined experiences or events using effective technique, relevant descriptive details, and well-structured event sequences.

SL.7.1: Engage effectively in a range of collaborative discussions (one-on-one, in groups, and teacher-led) with diverse partners on grade 7 topics, texts, and issues, building on others' ideas and expressing their own clearly.

SL.7.1(a): Come to discussions prepared, having read or researched material under study; explicitly draw on that preparation by referring to evidence on the topic, text, or issue to probe and reflect on ideas under discussion.

SL.7.1(b): Follow rules for collegial discussions, track progress toward specific goals and deadlines, and define individual roles as needed.

L.7.4: Determine or clarify the meaning of unknown and multiple-meaning words and phrases based on grade 7 reading and content, choosing flexibly from a range of strategies.

L.7.4(a): Use context (e.g., the overall meaning of a sentence or paragraph; a word's position or function in a sentence) as a clue to the meaning of a word or phrase.

L.7.4(c): Consult general and specialized reference materials (e.g., dictionaries, glossaries, thesauruses), both print and digital, to find the pronunciation of a word or determine or clarify its precise meaning or its part of speech.

SUGGESTED STUDENT OBJECTIVES

- Describe the relationship between characterization techniques and the development of theme in a story.
- Cite textual evidence, especially as it relates to characterization.
- Explain the importance of balancing historical accuracy with "creative license" when writing historical fiction; evaluate the ways in which authors achieve that balance.
- Explain the historical context of a story and how authors make historical fiction believable.
- Compare and contrast characters and settings across stories from different countries about the Middle Ages.
- Write "Character with Character" narratives that use effective technique, relevant descriptive details, and well-structured event sequences.
- Perform a monologue for classmates.

SUGGESTED WORKS

(E) indicates a CCSS exemplar text; (EA) indicates a text from a writer with other works identified as exemplars.

LITERARY TEXTS

Stories

Medieval Europe

- *Favorite Medieval Tales* (Mary Pope Osborne)
- *Good Masters! Sweet Ladies! Voices from a Medieval Village* (Laura Amy Schlitz)
- *The World of King Arthur and His Court: People, Places, Legend, and Lore* (Kevin Crossley-Holland)

- *Anna of Byzantium* (Tracy Barrett)
- *Castle Diary: The Journal of Tobias Burgess* (Richard Platt and Chris Riddell)
- *The Seeing Stone* (Arthur Trilogy, Book One) (Kevin Crossley-Holland)
- *Crispin: The Cross of Lead* (Avi)
- *Old English Riddles: From the Exeter Book* (Michael Alexander)
- *Adam of the Road* (Elizabeth Janet Gray)
- *The Midwife's Apprentice* (Karen Cushman)

Medieval Korea

- *A Single Shard* (Linda Sue Park)

Medieval Africa

- *Sundiata: Lion King of Mali* (David Wisniewski)
- *Traveling Man: The Journey of Ibn Battuta 1325–1354* (James Rumford)
- *Sundiata: An Epic of Old Mali* (Djibril Tamsir Niane)

INFORMATIONAL TEXTS

Nonfiction

Medieval Europe

- *Cathedral: The Story of Its Construction* (David Macaulay) (E)
- *The Medieval World* (Philip Steele)
- *Manners and Customs in the Middle Ages* (Marsha Groves)
- *Joan of Arc* (Diane Stanley)
- *Personal Recollections of Joan of Arc* (Mark Twain)
- *Outrageous Women of the Middle Ages* (Vicki Leon)
- *The Horrible, Miserable Middle Ages: The Disgusting Details About Life During Medieval Times* (Fact Finders: Disgusting History Series) (Kathy Allen)
- *The Middle Ages: An Illustrated History* (Oxford Illustrated Histories) (Barbara Hanawalt)
- *How Would You Survive in the Middle Ages* (How Would You Survive … Series) (Fiona MacDonald, David Salariya, and Mark Peppe)

Medieval Africa

- *The Royal Kingdoms of Ghana, Mali, and Songhay: Life in Medieval Africa* (Patricia and Frederick McKissack)

ART, MUSIC, AND MEDIA

Art

Armor

- *Child's Suit of Armor*, French or German (sixteenth century) (Walters Art Museum)

Byzantine Art

- Mosaics at Hagia Sophia, Istanbul, Turkey (562–1204)
- Mosaics at Chora Church, Istanbul, Turkey (1315–1321)

Islamic Art

- Textile art of the Caucasus, Persia
- The Islamic Art Collection at the Los Angeles County Museum of Art

Western European Medieval Art

- Giotto, *Madonna di Ognissanti,* 1306–1310
- Simone Martini and Lippo Memmi, *Annunciation* (1330)
- Attributed to Jean de Touyl, *Reliquary Shrine* (fourteenth century)

Gothic Art and Architecture

- Chartres Cathedral, Chartres, France
- Notre Dame de Paris, Paris, France
- Westminster Abbey, London, England

Illuminated Manuscripts

- Herman, Paul, and Jean de Limbourg, *The Belles Heures of Jean de France, Duc de Berry* (1405–1408/1409)

Music

- Gregorian chants and madrigals

SAMPLE ACTIVITES AND ASSESSMENTS

1. INTRODUCTORY ACTIVITY (FOR THE YEAR)

You will be reading a variety of literature and informational texts this year and perhaps some genres that you haven't encountered before. On a shared online spreadsheet, your teacher will give you a list of twenty genres (such as adventure, historical fiction, comedy, ancient history, science fiction, fantasy, etc.) from which to select titles and to which you may add new titles. Be sure to select titles, and topics, of enduring interest. One of your goals by the end of the year is to read books from at least three genres that are new to you. (RL.7.10, RI.7.10)

2. INFORMATIONAL TEXT RESPONSES

After reading *Cathedral: The Story of Its Construction* by David Macaulay, outline the major steps involved in constructing a cathedral by creating a comic strip or digital slide presentation of key events. Be mindful of important details. Be sure to note the page numbers that each box refers to so you can go back and cite the text during class discussion. Make a list of new vocabulary words that you learned from this book and that you encounter in other (fictional) texts. Your teacher may ask you to take notes in your journal of key events and share them with a partner before creating your comic strip or slide presentation. Be sure to note page numbers with relevant information or mark your text with sticky notes so you can cite the text, if needed. Practice the citation format introduced by your teacher. (RI.7.1, RI.7.2, RI.7.4, RI.7.6)

3. GRAPHIC ORGANIZER

As you read one of the novels that take place in the Middle Ages, take notes in your journal about how the characters are affected by the time period in which they lived. Be sure to make notes of page numbers with relevant information or mark your text with a sticky note so you can cite the text during class discussion. As an optional extension, create a movie about a character's experience.

- Where was that person's place in the feudal system?
- What was his or her economic status?
- Where did the character live, and why?
- What did the character's parents do, and what does this mean for the character?
- What was that character's context? What was happening in the world?
- What was a typical day like for this person?

Your teacher may give you the opportunity to share your notes with a partner who read the same text, prior to class discussion. (RL.7.1, RL.7.3, RL.7.9)

4. CLASS DISCUSSION

Compare and contrast characters and plots from the various novels read and discuss how authors accurately portray or alter history. After class discussion, create a Venn diagram in your journal—or use an online template that outlines the similarities and differences among three of the characters discussed. (SL.7.1a,b, RL.7.9)

5. WRITING (ARGUMENT)

While reading *A Single Shard,* think about where Tree-ear gets courage for his dangerous mission. First write a response to this question in your journal: "Are characters born brave, or is courage developed by facing fears?" Then compose a well-developed paper that includes an engaging opening statement, at least three clear reasons for your answer, and relevant evidence cited from the text read. Edit your writing for phrases and clauses, as well as commas separating coordinate adjectives. Your teacher may ask you to upload your essay to the classroom blog. (RL.7.1, RL.7.9, W.7.1, L.7.1a, L.7.2a)

6. WRITING (ARGUMENT)

While reading *The Midwife's Apprentice,* think about how a nameless girl becomes a memorable character. Think about the techniques the author uses to develop this memorable character. Then compose a well-developed paper in response to the following question: "Do good characterization techniques help convey the theme of a story?" Include an engaging opening statement, at least three clear reasons for your answer, and relevant evidence cited from the informational text read. Edit your writing for phrases and clauses, as well as commas separating coordinate adjectives. Your teacher may ask you to upload your essay to the classroom blog. (RL.7.1, RL.7.2, RL.7.3, W.7.1, L.7.1a, L.7.2a)

7. NARRATIVE WRITING

Write your own well-developed "Character with Character" story. It can take place during the Middle Ages or in another time period of your choosing. Incorporate elements and techniques learned in this unit. Your characterization techniques should help develop the theme of the story. You will have the opportunity to talk with a partner prior to writing the first draft, and again at the end, to revise and strengthen your story. Edit your writing for phrases and clauses, as well as commas separating coordinate adjectives. Feel free to add visual aids or illustrations to your story once it is complete. Be prepared to publish your story on the class web page. (RL.7.2, W.7.3, L.7.1a, L.7.2a)

8. CLASS DISCUSSION

How does the epic poem *Sundiata: An Epic of Old Mali* capture the mystery of a medieval African king? Find evidence from the text to explain your position. Write your ideas in your journal prior to a class discussion. (SL.7.1a,b, RL.7.2)

9. DRAMATIZATION/FLUENCY

Choose a monologue or dialogue from *Good Masters! Sweet Ladies! Voices from a Medieval Village* by Laura Amy Schlitz that has a strong character. Memorize and/or recite the monologue, or work with a classmate to present the dialogue as a dramatic reading and record it using a video camera so you can evaluate your performance. (SL.7.6)

10. ART/CLASS DISCUSSION

Discuss as a class how art can provide insight into a historical time period. Show the Chora Church mosaics alongside the Hagia Sophia mosaics. Both sets of mosaics were created to endow the viewer with a sense of religion's role in everyday life—since they could neither read nor write, many viewers relied on visual images. What do you see happening in these images? What events may be occurring? Do these mosaics provide a sense of power? Who is the dominant figure? What message would religious leaders want their viewers to take away? (SL.7.1a,b)

11. ART/WRITING

View Giotto's *Madonna* and Martini's *Annunciation*. Write a descriptive response to the following questions: How are colors, lines, and textures used to create a sense of majesty? Who is the central figure in both works, and how do you know? What does examining these two panel paintings teach us about the medieval style of art? Consider the flatness of the bodies, the exquisite drapery, and the use of color. What affects you the most? Which of these two pieces do you think is more beautiful? (W.7.2)

12. WORD STUDY

Where do words come from? How does knowing their origin help us not only to spell the words, but also understand their meaning? This is why we study etymology. Create a personal dictionary of terms found, learned, and used throughout this unit (i.e., *chivalry, feudalism, medieval, secular, serf, vassal,* etc.). This dictionary will be used all year long to explore the semantics (meanings) of words and their origins, especially those with Greek and Latin roots. (L.7.4a,c)

13. INFORMATIVE/EXPLANATORY WRITING

Write a written response to this question based on the novels read and discussed in class: "What makes characters in historical fiction believable?" Cite specific details from texts read. After your teacher reviews your first draft, work with a partner to strengthen your writing and edit for phrases and clauses, as well as commas separating coordinate adjectives. Be prepared to record your essay and upload it as a podcast on the class web page for this unit. (RL.7.9, W.7.9a,b, L.7.1a, L.7.2a)

14. GRAMMAR AND USAGE

Your teacher will teach mini-lessons on the individual language standards. For example, he/she will explain the function of phrases and clauses to the class. Find five phrases and five clauses in a book you are reading in class and explain their function. Select a piece of your own writing, underline and label phrases and clauses, and ensure that there are no misplaced or "dangling" modifiers. (L.7.1b)

15. MECHANICS/GRAMMAR WALL

As a class, create a Mechanics/Grammar bulletin board where, throughout the year, you will add to a checklist of editing topics as they are taught through targeted mini-lessons. Once skills are taught in a mini-lesson and listed on the bulletin board, you are expected to edit your work for the elements before publication. (L.7.1, L.7.2, L.7.3)

16. MECHANICS

Your teacher will teach mini-lessons on the individual language standards. For example, as a class you will talk about the strategy of using *and* to determine whether or not a comma is needed between two adjectives of equal importance. If the word *and* makes sense between two adjectives, then a comma is needed. Your teacher will give you examples of sentences (without commas), and you will determine whether a comma is needed or not and why. For example:

- The winding bumpy road led to a beautiful picnic spot. (needs a comma)
- The broken rear view mirror needed repair. (no comma)

Then, you will choose a piece of your own writing, underline words that could use more description, and add adjectives—some with and some without commas. Check your work with a partner. (L.7.2a)

17. VOCABULARY/WORD WALL

As a class, create a Vocabulary Word Wall bulletin board where, throughout the year, you will add and sort words as you learn them in each unit of study. (L.7.4)

ADDITIONAL RESOURCES

- *Internalization of Vocabulary Through the Use of a Word Map* (ReadWriteThink) (RL.7.4, RI.7.4)
- *Improve Comprehension: A Word Game Using Root Words and Affixes* (ReadWriteThink) (RL.7.4, RI.7.4)
- *Flip-a-Chip: Examining Affixes and Roots to Build Vocabulary* (ReadWriteThink) (RL.7.4, RI.7.4)
- *You Can't Spell the Word Prefix Without a Prefix* (ReadWriteThink) (RL.7.4, RI.7.4).
- *Analyzing and Comparing Medieval and Modern Ballads* (ReadWriteThink) (This lesson is geared toward grades 9–12, but may be adapted.) (RL.7.5)
- *Multiple Texts: Multiple Opportunities for Teaching and Learning* (ReadWriteThink) (RL.7.2)
- *Glimpses of Medieval Life* (The British Library)
- *Middle Ages* (Tolt Middle School, Carnation, WA)
- *Medieval Islamic Cultures* (San Francisco Unified School District, San Francisco, CA)
- *Middle Ages for Kids* (Kidipede: History and Science for Middle School Kids)
- *Building Big* (PBS)

TERMINOLOGY

Characterization	Monologue	Protagonist
Dialogue	Plot	Setting (historical)

Grade Seven, Unit One Sample Lesson Plan

Good Masters! Sweet Ladies! Voices from a Medieval Village by *Laura Amy Schlitz*

In this series of five lessons, students read *Good Masters! Sweet Ladies! Voices from a Medieval Village* by Laura Amy Schlitz, and they:

Revisit the characters of the medieval village (RL.7.3, RL.7.6, RL.7.9)

Prepare dramatic interpretations of *Good Masters! Sweet Ladies!* (SL.7.6)

Perform dramatic interpretations of *Good Masters! Sweet Ladies!* (SL.7.4, SL.7.6)

Summary

Lesson I: Good Masters! Sweet Ladies!

(*Note:* The assumption here is that the students have already read *Good Masters! Sweet Ladies!*)

Explore the "Foreword" of *Good Masters! Sweet Ladies! Voices from a Medieval Village* (RL.7.2, SL.7.6, L.7.6)

Note the original intent of the author (RL.7.2, SL.7.2)

Recall details about the characters in the village (RL.7.1, SL.7.6)

Select characters to portray (RL.7.3, SL.7.1)

Lesson II/III: Prepare Dramatic Interpretations of *Good Masters! Sweet Ladies!*

Note specific details about the assigned character (RL.7.1, SL.7.1, L.7.6)

Identify jobs for group work (SL.7.1)

Assign jobs to group members (SL.7.1)

Perform assigned tasks

Rehearse dramatic interpretation of the selected character (SL.7.4, SL.7.6)

Lesson IV/V: View Dramatic Interpretations of *Good Masters! Sweet Ladies!*

Prepare to perform dramatic interpretations of the characters from the medieval village (RL.7, SL.7.1, SL.7.6)

Perform dramatic interpretations of the characters from the medieval village (SL.7.4, SL.7.6)

View performances (SL.7.1d)

Explore reactions to the performances (RL.7.7, SL.7.1, SL.7.6)

Lessons II/III: Prepare Dramatic Interpretations of *Good Masters! Sweet Ladies!*

Objectives

Note specific details about the assigned character (RL.7.1, SL.7.1, L.7.6)

Identify jobs for group work (SL.7.1)

Assign jobs to group members (SL.7.1)

Perform assigned tasks

Rehearse dramatic interpretation of the selected character (SL.7.4, SL.7.6)

Required Materials

☐ *Good Masters! Sweet Ladies! Voices from a Medieval Village* by Laura Amy Schlitz

☐ Material for costumes

☐ Props

Procedures

1. Lead-In:

   Divide the class into small groups. Assign a character (the characters were identified in Lesson I) from the village to each group.

2. Step by Step:

   a. Group members recall details about their character. They also conduct further research concerning these details. For example, what would Will the Plowboy wear? How were medieval farmers dressed? What kind of stage props will they need?

   b. Once each group identifies specific details relevant to their character, they list the jobs necessary for producing the performance.
   A few examples:

   An actor to portray Will

   An actor to portray the mother, if her character is added

   Stage manager who is in charge of stage setting and props

   c. Group members are assigned specific roles.

   d. Group members begin to carry out their assignments.

   e. Group rehearses the dramatic presentations of its character.

3. Closure:

   Groups identify final tasks to be completed prior to their performances.

Differentiation

Advanced

- Allow students to do a real and a parodied interpretation of their character. For example, what would they need to change about Will if he were in a modern-day setting? What could remain the same? In writing, students summarize the elements of their parody prior to performing.
- Allow students to add new characters to the story, with the caveat that these characters have to be historically accurate.
- Give students an opportunity to bookmark the most helpful websites for other classmates to conduct their research. Collect the websites on a web portal.
- Record the performances with a video camera and allow students to create movies of the characters to post on a class web page or wiki. Ask classmates for feedback about their performance.

Struggling

- Provide a graphic organizer or sticky notes that students can use to record details about their character.
- Provide a graphic organizer with some prompting questions for students to record their research.
- Allow students to begin their research using the websites chosen by classmates (listed above).
- Record students with a video camera as they practice the dramatic reading, so they can evaluate their performance in order to improve.

Homework/Assessment

N/A

Grade 7 ▶ *Unit 2*

Perseverance

This second six-week unit of seventh grade builds upon the study of character by examining those who persevered in a variety of challenging circumstances.

OVERVIEW

Students read an array of novels—one about an orphan in the midst of the Civil War, another about a girl on a whaling ship in 1835, still another about a Latino teen working at the time of Cesar Chavez. They also read informational texts—about Helen Keller, Geronimo, or Martin Luther King Jr., to name a few. Students continue to reflect on the impact that historical events have on people, but also delve more deeply into the internal and external conflicts that characters experience and the qualities they possess that help them overcome challenges. Students continue to hone skills learned in the first unit about how characters develop and compare their development to the development of ideas in an informational text. This unit ends with an informative/explanatory essay in response to the essential question: How do individuals, real and fictional, use words and actions to demonstrate perseverance?

ESSENTIAL QUESTION

? How do individuals, real and fictional, use words and actions to demonstrate perseverance?

FOCUS STANDARDS

These Focus Standards have been selected for the unit from the Common Core State Standards.

RL.7.3: Analyze how particular elements of a story or drama interact (e.g., how setting shapes the characters or plot).

RI.7.2: Determine two or more central ideas in a text and analyze their development over the course of the text; provide an objective summary of the text.

W.7.7: Conduct short research projects from multiple print and digital sources, using search terms effectively; assess the credibility and accuracy of each source; and quote or paraphrase the data and conclusions of others while avoiding plagiarism and following a standard format for citation.

SL.7.1: Engage effectively in a range of collaborative discussions (one-on-one, in groups, and teacher-led) with diverse partners on grade 7 topics, texts, and issues, building on others' ideas and expressing their own clearly.

SL.7.1(c): Pose questions that elicit elaboration and respond to others' questions and comments with relevant observations and ideas that bring the discussion back on topic as needed.

SL.7.1(d): Acknowledge new information expressed by others and, when warranted, modify their own views.

L.7.4: Determine or clarify the meaning of unknown and multiple-meaning words and phrases based on grade 7 reading and content, choosing flexibly from a range of strategies.

L.7.4(b): Use common, grade-appropriate Greek or Latin affixes and roots as clues to the meaning of a word (e.g., *belligerent, bellicose, rebel*).

L.7.4(d): Verify the preliminary determination of the meaning of a word or phrase (e.g., by checking the inferred meaning in context or in a dictionary).

SUGGESTED STUDENT OBJECTIVES

- Define *perseverance.*
- Read and discuss fictional and informational texts featuring real people or characters that demonstrate perseverance.
- Analyze how the setting (historical context) of a story or biography affects character development.
- Explain authors' use of literary techniques such as diction and imagery.
- Compare and contrast the play *The Miracle Worker* to film and other print versions.
- Conduct research on a person of interest who demonstrated perseverance, such as Martin Luther King Jr. or Geronimo.
- Create a persuasive multimedia presentation.
- Write a bio-poem and memorize and/or recite it for the class.

SUGGESTED WORKS

(E) indicates a CCSS exemplar text; (EA) indicates a text from a writer with other works identified as exemplars.

LITERARY TEXTS

Stories

- *The Mostly True Adventures of Homer P. Figg* (Rodman Philbrick)
- *The Voyage of Patience Goodspeed* (Heather Vogel Frederick)
- *Jesse* (Gary Soto)
- *Lizzie Bright and the Buckminster Boy* (Gary D. Schmidt)
- *I Rode a Horse of Milk White Jade* (Diane Lee Wilson)
- *Treasure Island* (Robert Louis Stevenson)
- *Ties That Bind, Ties That Break* (Lensey Namioka)
- *The Miracle Worker (and Related Readings)* (William Gibson)

Poetry

- "Oranges" (Gary Soto) (E)

Drama

- *The Miracle Worker: A Play* (William Gibson)

INFORMATIONAL TEXTS

Biographies

- *Dare to Dream! 25 Extraordinary Lives* (Sandra McLeod Humphrey)
- *African American Firsts: Famous Little-Known and Unsung Triumphs of Blacks in America* (Joan Potter)
- *The World at Her Fingertips: The Story of Helen Keller* (Joan Dash)
- *Geronimo* (Joseph Bruchac)
- *The Civil Rights Movement in America* (Cornerstones of Freedom Series, Second Series) (Elaine Landau)
- *Dare to Dream: Coretta Scott King and the Civil Rights Movement* (Angela Shelf Medearis)

Photobiographies

- *Inventing the Future: A Photobiography of Thomas Alva Edison* (Marfe Ferguson Delano)
- *Helen Keller: A Photographic Story of a Life* (Leslie Garrett)
- *Helen's Eyes: A Photobiography of Annie Sullivan, Helen Keller's Teacher* (Marfe Ferguson Delano)

Graphical Autobiography

- *Persepolis: The Story of a Childhood* (Marjane Satrapi)

ART, MUSIC, AND MEDIA

Art

- N. C. Wyeth, *All day he hung round the cove, or upon the cliffs, with a brass telescope* (1911)
- N. C. Wyeth, *For all the world, I was led like a dancing bear* (1911)
- N. C. Wyeth, *Then, climbing on the roof, he had with his own hand bent and run up the colors* (1911)
- N. C. Wyeth, *Treasure Island*, title page illustration (1911)

Film

- Arthur Penn, dir., *The Miracle Worker* (1962)

SAMPLE ACTIVITIES AND ASSESSMENTS

1. CLASS DISCUSSION

What is meant by the word *perseverance*? Look up the word in a dictionary and write your ideas down on a sticky note. Your teacher will give you the opportunity to "Give one, get one" in order to go beyond the dictionary definition. Create a class word map of the word *perseverance*. As you find examples of perseverance in texts read during this unit, write them on sticky notes and add them to our chart. While working on this unit, your teacher may ask you to create an online concept map. (SL.7.1)

2. NOTE TAKING

As you read one of the novels or biographies about people or characters with perseverance, take notes in your journal or on a shared online document about how the individuals are affected by the time period in which they lived. Be sure to note page numbers with relevant information or mark your text with sticky notes so you can go back and cite the text during class discussion.

- During what historical time period does the novel/biography take place?
- Where did the person or character live, and why?
- What was that individual's historical context?
- What role, if any, does the person or character's family play in his/her outlook on life?
- What obstacle(s) does the individual overcome? How?

   Prior to class discussion, your teacher may give you the opportunity to share your notes and/or collaborate on a shared online document with a partner who read the same text. (RL.7.1, RL.7.3, RL.7.9)

3. CLASS DISCUSSION

Compare and contrast characters from the various novels and biographies read. What similarities exist between fictional characters and real people? Can you generalize about the types of experiences that build perseverance? What destroys perseverance? After class discussion, create a Venn diagram in your journal, or in an online template, that outlines the potentially positive and negative experiences. (SL.7.1, RL.7.9)

4. INFORMATIONAL TEXT RESPONSE

While reading *Dare to Dream! 25 Extraordinary Lives* by Sandra McLeod Humphrey, think about how everyone has a different limit to which they can be pushed while overcoming the challenges and obstacles they face. Write a response to this question in your journal: How do expectations affect what one can accomplish? Justify your answer with specific information from the text. Your teacher may ask you to post your response to this prompt on the classroom blog so you and your classmates can comment on each other's thoughts. (RI.7.1)

5. DRAMATIZATION/FLUENCY

Study the photobiography *Helen's Eyes: A Photobiography of Annie Sullivan, Helen Keller's Teacher,* by Marfe Ferguson Delano, noting how the pictures relate Annie Sullivan's life, including her time as Helen Keller's teacher. Then read *The Miracle Worker: A Play* by William Gibson in small groups or as a class. Practice speaking the lines prior to reading the play aloud. Discuss how the play form contributes to its meaning in a different way than the photobiography. In addition, discuss how the author develops the point of view of different characters. (RL.7.5, RL.7.6, RI.7.9, SL.7.1, SL.7.6)

6. MEDIA APPRECIATION/CLASS DISCUSSION

Discuss the similarities and differences among reading about Annie Sullivan, seeing the film version of *The Miracle Worker,* and reading the play. Do reading and watching all three versions give you a better picture of Helen Keller and Annie Sullivan than if you only read or saw one text? Write your ideas in your journal. Then, share your ideas with a partner prior to discussing as a class. (RL.7.5, RL.7.7)

7. RESEARCH AND WRITING (ARGUMENT) AND MULTIMEDIA PRESENTATION

Research a famous person (such as Martin Luther King Jr., Geronimo, or another person of your choosing) who persevered in spite of significant challenges. Use a wide range of credible print and electronic, primary, and secondary resources for your research. See if you can find a video clip online of him or her speaking. Write and present your multimedia report to the class, making a case for why the person you chose is a striking example of determination and perseverance in the face of difficult circumstances. Edit your work for sentence variety and spelling. (W.7.1, W.7.7, RI.7.2, SL.7.2, SL.7.5, L.7.1a,b, L.7.2a,b)

8. LITERATURE RESPONSE

Historical fiction such as *The Mostly True Adventures of Homer P. Figg* by Rodman Philbrick is based on true events. Write a response to this question in your journal: How does the author's style (i.e., word choice) affect the believability of the main character? Justify your answer with specific details from the text. (RL.7.3, RL.7.9)

9. CLASS DISCUSSION

Based on the book *Inventing the Future: A Photobiography of Thomas Alva Edison* by Marfe Ferguson Delano, Edison appears to view failures as successes. How can a failure be construed as a success? Write your ideas in your journal prior to class discussion. Then, discuss as a class, citing information from texts read. Follow the class discussion by posting your thoughts on the classroom blog so you and your classmates can continue this conversation. (RI.7.1, RI.7.2)

10. NARRATIVE WRITING/RECITATION

Write a bio-poem about an individual, real or fictional, who demonstrates the essence of perseverance. Memorize and/or recite the poem for the class. Record your recitation using a video camera so you can evaluate your performance. (SL.7.6, RL.7.4)

11. INFORMATIVE/EXPLANATORY WRITING

Compare the prose and poetry of Gary Soto. How do the form, diction, and imagery in "Oranges" compare to the form, diction, and imagery in *Jesse*? Write your initial ideas in your journal and then share ideas with a partner. Revise your writing to include additional ideas based on your discussion, if desired. Then write a well-developed paper, citing at least three specific examples from two different texts read. Edit your writing for sentence variety and spelling. Upload your paper to the classroom blog. (RL.7.5, W.7.2, W.7.9a, L.7.1a,b, L.7.2a,b)

12. WORD STUDY

[Continuing activity from Unit One.] Where do words come from? How does knowing their origin help us not only to spell the words, but also to understand their meanings? Add words found, learned, and used throughout this unit to your personal dictionary, including synonyms for *perseverance* (e.g., *determination, constancy, relentlessness, obstinacy, tenacity, steadfastness, stalwartness, drive, willpower,* etc.). This dictionary will be used all year long to explore the semantics (meanings) of words and their origins, especially those with Greek and Latin roots. (L.7.4)

13. INFORMATIVE/EXPLANATORY WRITING

Reflecting on the novels and biographies read and discussed in class, write an informative/explanatory essay in response to the essential question: How do individuals, real and fictional, use words and actions to demonstrate perseverance? Cite specific details from texts read. After your teacher reviews your first draft, work with a partner to edit and strengthen your writing, especially for sentence variety and spelling. Be prepared to record your final essay and upload it as a podcast or as the narrative to accompany a movie on the class web page for this unit. (W.7.9a,b, L7.1a,b, L7.2a,b)

14. VOCABULARY/WORD WALL

As a class, continue adding to the Vocabulary Word Wall bulletin board where, throughout the year, you will add and sort words as you learn them in each unit of study. (L.7.4)

15. ART/CLASS DISCUSSION

View the works by N. C. Wyeth, which were drawn to illustrate *Treasure Island*. How do these illustrations add to or alter your understanding of the text? Can these images stand alone as a work of art or do they require the text in order to be fully appreciated and understood? What does examining these works teach us about the difference between fine art and illustration? (SL.7.2, SL.7.4, SL.7.5)

ADDITIONAL RESOURCES

- *Drama Map* (ReadWriteThink) (RL.7.5)
- *Young Adult Literature About the Middle East: A Cultural Response Perspective* (ReadWriteThink) (RL.7.6)
- *She Did What? Revising for Connotation* (ReadWriteThink) (L.7.5)
- *Exploring Author's Voice Using Jane Addams's Award-Winning Books* (ReadWriteThink) (L.7.3)
- *Additional Poems by Gary Soto* (The Poetry Foundation)

TERMINOLOGY

Biography	Imagery
Character's conflict: external and internal	Graphical autobiography
	Photobiography
Diction	Tone

Grade Seven, Unit Two Sample Lesson Plan

"Oranges" and "Black Hair" by Gary Soto

In this series of five lessons, students read "Oranges" and "Black Hair" by Gary Soto, and they:

- Examine Gary Soto's autobiographical poems (RL.7.1, RI.7.2, RI.7.3, RL.7.5, SL.7.1, SL.7.4)
- Explore their own stories (RL.7.6, SL.7.6, W.7.7)
- Express their memories in poetic form (W.7.3, SL.7.6, L.6.6)

Summary

Lesson I: "Oranges"

Annotate the poem (for the objectives listed below) (RL.7.1, L.7.5)

Retell the story of the poem (RL.7.2, SL.7.1, SL.7.4, L.7.6)

Note its details (RL.7.1, RL.7.3, SL.7.1, L.7.5, L.7.6)

Explore the significance of the words:

"When I looked up, The lady's eyes met mine, And held them, knowing Very well what it was all About."

(RL.7.4, SL.7.1, SL.7.4, L.7.5, SL.7.6)

Explore the image of "fire" in the final line of the poem (RL.7.4, SL.7.1, SL.7.4, L.7.5, SL.7.6)

Lesson II: "Black Hair"

Annotate the poem (for the objectives listed below) (RL.7.1, L.7.5)

Retell the story of the poem (RL.7.2, SL.7.1, SL.7.4, L.7.6)

Examine the allusion to Hector Moreno (RL.7.4. SL.7.1, L.7.5)

Note the speaker's relationship with his family (RL.7.6, SL.7.1, L.7.6)

Probe specific lines that depict the speaker's point of view (RL.7.1, RL.7.6, SL.7.1, L.7.5, L.7.6)

Explore the tone of the poem (SL.7.1, L.7.5, L.7.6)

Relate the poem's title to its content (RL.7.1, RL.7.2, SL.7.1)

Lesson III: Memories and Compositions

Recall details of "Oranges" and "Black Hair" (RL.7.1, RL.7.3, SL.7.1, SL.7.4, L.7.6)

List ideas for personal poems (W.7.5)

Select a single idea (W.7.5)

Record as many details as possible (W.7.5)

Relate memories to a setting (W.7.5, L.7.5)

Relate memories to the senses (L.7.3)

Begin to group words (L.7.5b)

Begin to compose drafts of poems (W.7.3, W.7.5)

Lesson IV: Compositions and Revisions

Revisit drafts of poems (W.7.5, SL.7.1, L.7.6)

Note possible needs for revisions (L.7.3, L.7.6)

    Content/details

    Form of the poem (stanzas)

    Allusions

    Repetitions

    Metaphors/simile

    Symbol

Revise poems (W.7.5, SL.7.1, L.7.5, L.7.6)

Lesson V: Sharing Memories

Publish the poems (W.7.5)

Explore the poetry of classmates (SL.7.1c, SL.7.1d, L.7.5)

Critically consider the influence of reading poetry on the writing of poetry (SL.7.1, SL.7.4)

Lesson III: Memories and Compositions

Objectives

Recall details of "Oranges" and "Black Hair" (RL.7.1, RL.7.3, SL.7.1, SL.7.4, L.7.6)

List ideas for personal poems (W.7.5)

Select a single idea (W.7.5)

Record as many details as possible (W.7.5)

Relate memories to a setting (W.7.5, L.7.5)

Relate memories to the senses (L.7.3)

Begin to group words (L.7.5b)

Begin to compose drafts of poems (W.7.3, W.7.5)

Required Materials

☐ Class sets of "Oranges" by Gary Soto

☐ Class sets of "Black Hair" by Gary Soto

☐ Writing journals or loose-leaf paper

Procedures

1. Lead-In:

   Revisit the previously annotated (Lessons I & II) poems "Oranges" and "Black Hair" by Gary Soto.

2. Step by Step:

   a. In journals or on loose-leaf paper, students list memories for writing poems.

   b. Students revisit their list and consider which memory is the most vivid.

   c. Once the specific memory is selected, students begin to record as many details of the event as they can recollect. Remind the students to consider the setting of the event, the people who were present, the smells, and the sounds.

   d. Students revisit their notes and, based on the content, they make an initial decision about how many stanzas they will write. Remind the students that Gary Soto chose to write "Oranges" in two stanzas and "Black Hair" in three.

   e. Using their notes, students begin to group words.

   f. Students form stanzas from the grouped words and begin to add words, move words around, revise, read, and reread the poem.

A demonstration at each step may be useful; here is an example:

a. watermelon seeds

   corn on the beach

   mushrooms

   pine nuts

b. The topic I choose is mushrooms.

c. Here are the notes:

   "When I was a little girl, we used to collect mushrooms in the forest. The forest was full of pine trees. I remember the deep green color. I also remember that the leaves were not really like leaves, but spiky. That is why they call them needles. There were mushrooms only after the rain, so there was always a smell of rain. The mushrooms were always near the trees, and sometimes they hid under old pine leaves. My father taught me which ones were the good mushrooms. The top was brown and the bottom was like a yellow sponge. He also showed me how to pull the mushroom from the bottom so that I would not break it. And when you find the mushrooms, they are in a group, like a family. Back home, my mother showed me how to clean the mushrooms. We removed the yellow sponge. I used a spoon and kind of scooped the sponge. Then my mother sliced the mushrooms and she fried them with onions. She turned them around and around in the frying pan while we were all watching, and smelling, and getting hungry. Then she put them on toast. They were ready. Kind of slippery. So good."

d. I am likely to write two stanzas (below is an example of the first stanza) — one in the forest and one at home.

e. entering the forest

   green pine trees

   leaves like needles

wet smell of rain
hidden mushrooms
under which pile of old needles
move the needles
here they are
a group
a family of mushrooms
a father, a mother, two children
my father laughs
and shows me how to pick to mushrooms
careful, do not break them

f. We enter the forest,
I look up at the
Tall green trees,
And my dad says:
"Pine trees,
They hide the mushrooms."
"They have funny leaves," I say,
"Like needles.'
I kneel and gently
Move some wet needles.
My knees are now wet.
My hand touches something soft –
A family of mushrooms.
"I found them!"
My dad says:
"Gently, pick from the bottom,
Gently."
I am gentle.
I cradle the mushrooms
And I pull –
The father mushroom,
The mother one,
And two little ones.
And we look some more . . .

[Note that a dialogue between the speaker and her father is added here.
These are the types of revisions that the teacher can point out to her students.]

3. Closure:

    Student volunteers may choose to read drafts of their poems.

Differentiation

Advanced

- Select a "feeling" versus an "event" memory to describe.
- Create a concept web, or some other visual, to accompany the poem.
- Try to write poems in two different styles (for example, a haiku and free verse) and evaluate which is the more effective form and why.

Struggling

- Ask students to bring in a picture of an event to help with describing.
- Prior to writing, allow students to share their ideas with a partner in order to organize their thoughts. Alternatively, allow them to talk about the picture into a voice recorder, then transcribe their thoughts.
- Give students a pre-created template for organizing their thoughts around their memory. (For example, a web on a shared spreadsheet.)
- Encourage students to write their memories on index cards to facilitate sorting and organizing into stanzas.
- Allow students to mimic the structure of Gary Soto's work, using their own ideas.

Homework/Assessment

N/A

Grade 7 ▶ *Unit 3*

Courage in Life and in Literature

This third eight-week unit of seventh grade delves more deeply into character analysis, focusing on determined and courageous people in both informational texts and literature.

OVERVIEW

Students read, study, and discuss *Anne Frank: The Diary of a Young Girl.* Students choose another biography, such as *The Journal of Scott Pendleton Collins,* or a fictional work to explore how courage is projected through these works. Students see how and where these stories fit within informational texts on World War II. They also compare the ways in which Frank's diary is similar to and different from the play version of her story. Students focus their reading on in-depth analyses of interactions among individuals, events, and ideas in a variety of texts, comparing the ways in which different authors shape similar stories. This unit ends with an informative/explanatory essay in response to the essential question.

    Note: This unit provides an example of how cross-curricular collaboration can naturally occur between English and other classes. Students can read informational text in history class and scientific texts in science class, and then compare those accounts to personal narratives and accounts about life during World War II read in English class. Much discussion can center upon the way background information enhances understanding of literature (for example, whether on World War II, the Nazis, or any other history or science topic of the teacher's choosing). This unit also demonstrates how the reading and writing standards provide instructional connectivity between learning in English and other areas.

ESSENTIAL QUESTION

? How can reading about the courage of real people inform our understanding of determined literary characters?

FOCUS STANDARDS

These Focus Standards have been selected for the unit from the Common Core State Standards.

RL.7.5: Analyze how a drama's or poem's form or structure (e.g., soliloquy, sonnet) contributes to its meaning.

RL.7.7: Compare and contrast a written story, drama, or poem to its audio, filmed, staged, or multimedia version, analyzing the effects of techniques unique to each medium (e.g., lighting, sound, color, or camera focus and angles in a film).

RI.7.3: Analyze the interactions between individuals, events, and ideas in a text (e.g., how ideas influence individuals or events, or how individuals influence ideas or events).

RI.7.9: Analyze how two or more authors writing about the same topic shape their presentations of key information by emphasizing different evidence or advancing different interpretations of facts.

W.7.2: Write informative/explanatory texts to examine a topic and convey ideas, concepts, and information through the selection, organization, and analysis of relevant content.

SL.7.2: Analyze the main ideas and supporting details presented in diverse media and formats (e.g., visually, quantitatively, orally) and explain how the ideas clarify a topic, text, or issue under study.

L.7.6: Acquire and use accurately grade-appropriate general academic and domain-specific words and phrases; gather vocabulary knowledge when considering a word or phrase important to comprehension or expression.

SUGGESTED STUDENT OBJECTIVES

- Define *courage*.
- Read and discuss fictional and informational texts about people, real and fictional, that face conflict.
- Explain how knowing the historical context of a story may enhance your understanding of a story.
- Analyze two accounts of the same event and describe important similarities and differences in the details they provide.
- Explain how an author's style can help convey the theme of their stories, poems, or speeches.
- Compare and contrast *Anne Frank: The Diary of a Young Girl* to dramatic interpretations for stage and screen.

SUGGESTED WORKS

(E) indicates a CCSS exemplar text; (EA) indicates a text from a writer with other works identified as exemplars.

LITERARY TEXTS

Stories
- *I Am David* (Anne Holm)
- *Milkweed* (Jerry Spinelli)
- *The Devil's Arithmetic* (Jane Yolen)
- *When Hitler Stole Pink Rabbit* (Judith Kerr)
- *Number the Stars* (Lois Lowry)
- *Summer of My German Soldier* (Bette Greene)
- *Daniel's Story* (Carol Matas)
- *A Pocket Full of Seeds* (Marilyn Sachs)

being taken away. Enter your "takeaway" thoughts from this research and class conversation on the classroom blog so you can continue the conversation electronically. (RI.7.3, RI.7.6, W.7.2, W.7.7, W.7.8, SL.7.1, SL.7.2)

10. CLASS DISCUSSION AND WRITING (ARGUMENT)

You have read about Anne Frank and her life within the confines of an attic during World War II. How does knowing the historical context of the diary add to your appreciation of Anne's writing? Why? Write your ideas in your journal and share with a classmate prior to class discussion. After the class discussion, write a speech in which you explain your viewpoint and present it to the class. Use figurative language and select words carefully for maximum impact. Record your presentation using a video camera so you can evaluate your performance. Post the presentation on the class blog to get feedback from others outside of your classroom. (RI.7.3, RL.7.2, RL.7.6, W.7.4, SL.7.6)

11. DRAMATIZATION/FLUENCY (OPTION 1)

Write a dramatic interpretation of Anne Frank's (or someone else's) experience with conflict during the Holocaust; you may focus on interpersonal conflict, intrapersonal conflict, conflict between self and society, or another type of conflict. Your interpretation should incorporate the dramatic elements studied during the drama unit and accurately reflect the information learned in history class. Edit your writing for phrases and clauses, modifiers, and precise language. Record your presentation using a video camera so you can evaluate your performance. (W.7.3, W.7.4, RI.7.3, L.7.1, L.7.2a,b, L.7.3a)

12. DRAMATIZATION/FLUENCY (OPTION 2)

Choose a poem from *War and the Pity of War* or a diary entry from one of the books read; memorize the poem or passage and present it to the class. How does the text you chose reflect the courage of characters during the horrors of war? (SL.7.6, RL.7.2)

13. MEDIA APPRECIATION

Discuss the similarities and differences between Anne's biography and the play and film interpretations of her story. What parts were true to the original? What parts were changed? Why do you think the elements that changed were changed? Does it add or detract from the dramatic effect of Anne's story? Why or why not? Write your ideas in your journal or complete a two-circle or three-circle Venn diagram using online templates. Share with a classmate prior to class discussion. (RL.7.5, RL.7.7)

14. MEDIA APPRECIATION

Watch the HBO documentary *Paper Clips*, which is about a project started by middle school students to remember the people affected by the Holocaust. How does the format contribute to the meaning or impact? As a class, discuss why it is important to learn from history and pass that learning from generation to generation. (RL.7.5, RL.7.7, SL.7.2)

15. WORD STUDY

[Continuing activity from the first two units.] Just as we can trace the path of our ancestors—some back to World War II—we can trace the path of words. Choose some words learned this year in content classes, and trace back from modern-day uses of the words to their historical origins (i.e., *tyranny, assimilation, displacement, genocide, Gestapo, propaganda, internment, smuggle,* etc.). Add these to your personal dictionary. (L.7.4, L.7.6, RI.7.4)

Poetry

- *War and the Pity of War* (Neil Philip and Michael McCurdy)

Drama

- *The Diary of Anne Frank: A Play* (Frances Goodrich and Albert Hackett) (E)
- *101 Monologues for Middle School Actors: Including Duologues and Triologues* (Rebecca Young)

INFORMATIONAL TEXTS

Nonfiction

- *A History of US: War, Peace, and All that Jazz* (Joy Hakim) (E)
- *Ghost Soldiers: The Epic Account of World War II's Greatest Rescue Mission* (Hampton Sides)
- *True Stories of D-Day (True Adventure Stories)* (Henry Brook)
- *Dear Miss Breed: True Stories of the Japanese American Incarceration During World War II and a Librarian Who Made a Difference* (Joanne Oppenheim)
- *Hiroshima* (John Hersey)
- *Fighting For Honor: Japanese Americans and World War II* (Michael L. Cooper)
- *Never to Forget: The Jews of the Holocaust* (Milton Meltzer)
- *Six Million Paper Clips: The Making of a Children's Holocaust Memorial* (Peter W. Schroeder and Dagmar Schroeder-Hildebrand)
- *Atomic Structure and Chemical Reactions: Middle Grades and High School* (Nevin Katz)
- *The Making of the Atomic Bomb* (Richard Rhodes)

Biographies

- *Anne Frank: The Diary of a Young Girl* (Anne Frank)
- *Anne Frank: Beyond the Diary: A Photographic Remembrance* (Ruud van der Rol and Rian Verhoeven)
- *The Journal of Scott Pendleton Collins: A World War II Soldier, Normandy, France, 1944* (Walter Dean Myers)
- *Night* (Elie Wiesel)
- *Zlata's Diary: A Child's Life in Wartime Sarajevo* (Zlata Filipovic)
- *I Have Lived a Thousand Years: Growing Up in the Holocaust* (Livia Bitton-Jackson)

Memoir

- *A Friend Called Anne: One Girl's Story of War, Peace, and a Unique Friendship with Anne Frank* (Jacqueline van Maarsen)
- *Four Perfect Pebbles* (Lila Perl)
- *Children of Willesden Lane: Beyond the Kindertransport—A Memoir of Music, Love, and Survival* (Mona Golabek)

Speeches

- "Blood, Toil, Tears, and Sweat: Address to Parliament on May 13th, 1940" (Winston Churchill) (E)
- "Declaration of War on Japan" (Franklin D. Roosevelt)

ART, MUSIC, AND MEDIA

Film

- George Stevens, dir., *The Diary of Anne Frank* (Screenplay by Frances Goodrich and Albert Hackett) (1959)
- Robert Dornhelm, dir., *Anne Frank: The Whole Story* (2001)
- Elliot Berlin and Joe Fab, dir., *Paper Clips* (HBO documentary) (2004)
- Peter Jones, dir., *Bataan Rescue: The Most Daring Rescue Mission of World War II* (PBS documentary) (2005)

SAMPLE ACTIVITIES AND ASSESSMENTS

1. CLASS DISCUSSION

What is meant by the word *courage*? Look up the word in a dictionary and write your ideas down on a sticky note. Your teacher will give you the opportunity to "Give one, get one" in order to understand the word's *denotation* and its various *connotations*. Create a class word map of the word *courage*. As you find examples of courage in texts read during this unit, write them on sticky notes and add them to the chart or online concept map. (SL.7.1)

2. LITERATURE RESPONSE

In *Anne Frank: The Diary of a Young Girl,* Anne writes vividly about her experiences. What is it about the language she uses that offers insights into her character, especially her courage? Write a response to this question in your journal: What makes Anne Frank a person to whom I can relate? Justify your answer with specific examples of the language from the text and type your response on the classroom blog so you and your classmates can compare essays. (RL.7.4, RL.7.5, RL.7.6)

3. NOTE TAKING ON CHARACTERIZATION

As you read one of the fictional stories to compare it to *Anne Frank: The Diary of a Young Girl,* take notes in your journal or on a shared online document about how the characters' experiences are similar to and different from Anne Frank's. Be sure to note page numbers with relevant information or mark your text with sticky notes so you can cite the text during class discussion.

- Where did the character live?
- What was that character's context? What was happening in the world?
- What was a typical day like for this person?
- How is the character's experience similar to Anne Frank's?
- How is the character's experience different from Anne Frank's?
- What are some of the author's characterization techniques?

Prior to class discussion, your teacher may give you the opportunity to share your notes (and/o collaborate on shared online spreadsheet) with a partner who read the same text. (RL.7.2, RL.7.6)

4. CLASS DISCUSSION

Compare and contrast characters from the various novels read. Can you generalize about ways that authors create courageous characters? After class discussion, create a Venn diagram or other type of chart online or in your journal that outlines the similarities and differences among three of the characters discussed. (SL.7.1, RL.7.2, RL.7.5, RL.7.6)

5. INFORMATIVE/EXPLANATORY WRITING

As you read one of the fictional stories to compare it to *Anne Frank: The Diary of a Young Girl,* take notes in your journal about how the characters' experiences are similar to and different from Anne Frank's. Be sure to note page numbers with relevant information or mark your text with sticky notes so you can cite the text during class discussion. When done, write a well-developed paper, citing at least three to four specific examples. Edit your writing for phrases and clauses, modifiers, and precise language. Your teacher may ask you to upload your essay on the classroom blog. (W.7.2a,b,c,d,e; W.7.4, L.7.1a,b,c; L.7.2a,b, L.7.3a)

6. INFORMATIVE/EXPLANATORY WRITING

Analyze various accounts of World War II events from a variety of print and digital, primary, and secondary resources. In your journal (or a spreadsheet or text document), identify and distinguish among the facts, opinions, and reasoned judgments presented by different people. Include an analysis of the interactions among individuals, events, and ideas, drawing on various accounts from different authors. Include new vocabulary words learned during this unit. Edit your writing for phrases and clauses, modifiers, and precise language. You may even choose to prepare your essay as a podcast and present it to the class. (W.7.2, W.7.4, RI.7.3, RI.7.6, RI.7.9, L.7.1a,b,c; L.7.2a,b, L.7.3a, L.7.6, SL.7.4)

7. INFORMATIVE/EXPLANATORY WRITING

In an informative/explanatory essay or speech, describe how Churchill's use of repetition and/or rhetorical questions advances the theme of courage. Cite at least two examples from the text to support your thesis. (RI.7.2, W.7.2, W.7.9)

8. SPEECH ANALYSIS

Compare the speeches by Winston Churchill and Franklin D. Roosevelt. How are the styles and themes similar and different? In what ways does style contribute to the theme of each speech? Write your ideas on a T-chart or Venn diagram in your journal or online and share with a partner prior to class discussion. Cite specific examples of style, such as diction and the use of figurative language. (SL.7.3, RI.7.6, RI.7.7, RI.7.9)

9. RESEARCH

Many rights were taken away from the Jewish people during the Holocaust. Choose one of these rights to research in detail, following the research process through to the presentation of findings, either as an essay or other presentation. When you are done, write a note card about how the right you researched was taken away and include the date. As a class, create a bulletin board or spreadsheet of the note cards in order to share what you have learned with each other. Make sure that the events are arranged in correct chronological order. Discuss how people reacted with perseverance and courage at their rights

16. INFORMATIVE/EXPLANATORY WRITING

Reflecting on the novels read and discussed in class, write an informative/explanatory essay in response to the essential question: How can reading about the courage of real people inform our understanding of courageous literary characters? Cite specific details from texts read, not only from English class, but also from history class. After your teacher reviews your first draft, work with a partner to strengthen and edit your writing for phrases and clauses, modifiers, and precise language. Be prepared to summarize your thoughts on two digital slides that include visuals. All slides will be combined into a single presentation for posting on the class web page. (W.7.2, W.7.4, W.7.9a,b, L.7.1, L.7.2a,b, L.7.3a)

17. GRAMMAR AND USAGE

Your teacher will teach mini-lessons on the individual language standards. For example, he/she will teach the class about misplaced modifiers by putting sentences on the board, and asking you to describe why they are incorrect, and then correct them. For example:

- Slithering through the wet grass, we watched the garden snake. (*Correction:* We watched the garden snake slithering through the wet grass.)
- When he was three years old, Jerry's uncle showed him how to fly a kite. (*Correction:* When Jerry was three years old, his uncle showed him how to fly a kite.)
- The boys were spoken to sharply about loitering in the principal's office. (*Correction:* While in the principal's office, the boys were spoken to sharply about loitering.)

    Select a piece of your own writing and check for any misplaced or dangling modifiers. Correct them. (L.7.1c)

18. MECHANICS/GRAMMAR WALL

As a class, continue adding to the Mechanics/Grammar bulletin board started in Unit One. Remember—once skills are taught in a mini-lesson and listed on the bulletin board, you are expected to edit your work for these elements before publication. (L.7.1, L.7.2, L.7.3)

19. USAGE

Your teacher will give you some sentences containing redundancies, and you will try to simplify the sentences without affecting the meaning. For example (strikethrough shows the redundant phrase):

- ~~As far as I'm concerned~~, there is no need for further discussion of the topic.
- Grass has overgrown in areas because ~~of the fact that~~ we stopped mowing our lawn.
- ~~In my opinion,~~ this dress code policy ought to be revoked.
- "I am so mad," I said ~~angrily~~.

    Next, choose a piece of your own writing and read it aloud to a classmate. He/she should help you listen for any redundant words or phrases that could be eliminated. (L.7.3a)

20. VOCABULARY/WORD WALL

As a class, continue adding to the Vocabulary Word Wall bulletin board where, throughout the year, you will add and sort words as you learn them in each unit of study. (L.7.4)

ADDITIONAL RESOURCES

- *Anne Frank: One of Hundreds of Thousands* (National Endowment for the Humanities) (RI.7.9)
- *Teacher's Guide to Bataan Rescue: The Most Daring Rescue of World War II* (PBS)
- *Elie Wiesel was Born on September 30, 1928* (ReadWriteThink) (RI.7.6)
- *Walter Dean Myers, Author of the Printz Award–Winning Novel Monster, was Born in 1937* (ReadWriteThink) (RL.7.7)
- *Investigating the Holocaust: A Collaborative Inquiry Project* (ReadWriteThink) (RI.7.9)
- *Language Arts and Social Studies—It's the Connections that Matter Most!* (Ohio Resource Center for Mathematics, Science, and Reading)
- *Teacher's Guide to the Holocaust* (Florida Holocaust Museum)
- *Great Speeches Collection* (The History Place)

TERMINOLOGY

Connotation	Dialogue	Documentary	Screenplay
Denotation	Diction	Point of view	

Grade Seven, Unit Three Sample Lesson Plan

The Diary of Anne Frank: A Play by Frances Goodrich and Albert Hackett

Anne Frank Beyond the Diary: A Photographic Remembrance by Ruud Van Rol and Rian Verhoven

In this interdisciplinary series of eight lessons, students read *The Diary of Anne Frank: A Play* by Frances Goodrich and Albert Hackett, and *Anne Frank Beyond the Diary: A Photographic Remembrance* by Ruud Van Rol and Rian Verhoven, and they:

Examine the historical background to the life and death of Anne Frank (RI.7.2, RI.7.5, RI.7.6)

Evaluate the dramatic presentation of Anne Frank's life (RL.7.2, RL.7.3, RL.7.5)

Examine Anne Frank's personality (RL7.2, SL.7.1)

Consider why Anne Frank's legacy endures (SL.7.1)

Summary

Lesson I: Meet Anne Frank	Lesson II: Entering the Secret Annex (Act I)
Study the map of Europe and locate Germany and Holland (informational text)	Identify the purpose of dramatizing Anne Frank's story (RL.7.3, RL.7.5)
Meet Anne Frank (RI.7.6)	Imagine the early days in the annex (pp. 9–17) (RL.7.3)
Appreciate the need to contextualize the story of Anne Frank (informational text) (RI.7.5, RI.7.6)	Visualize the secret annex (RL.7.3)
	Explore the characters in the annex (RL.7.3)
Explore the meaning and scope of anti-Semitism and Nazism (RI.7.2)	Investigate the role of Miep Gies (include informational text) (RL.7.2, RL.7.3, RL.7.5)
	Listen to Anne's voice (select diary entry) (RL.7.2)

Lesson III: Life in the Annex (Act I)

Explore the dramatic impact of Hitler's voice (p. 17) (RL.7.3, RL.7.5)

Juxtapose Hitler's voice with Anne's words: "It's the silence that frightens me most" (p. 17) (RL.7.1, RL.7.2, RL.7.3, RL.7.5, SL.7.1)

Investigate the daily routine and tensions in the annex (RL.7.2)

Examine the dramatic impact of the closing moment of Act I (RL.7.3, RL.7.5, SL.7.1)

Listen to Anne's voice (select diary entry) (RL.7.2)

Lesson IV: Enduring and Longing (Act II)

Note the passage of time in the annex (RL.7.1, RL.7.2)

Examine the link that Miep Gies provides to the outside world (RL.7.2, RL.7.3, RL.7.5)

Explore the nature of Anne's longing (p. 48) (RL.7.5, SL.7.1)

Explore the relationship between Anne and Peter (RL.7.2)

Listen to Anne's voice (select diary entry) (RL.7.2)

Lesson V: Captured (Act II)

Contextualize Miep's news about the invasion of Europe by the Allies (informational text) (RL.7.2, RL.7.3, RL.7.5)

Investigate the significance of Anne's words: "I'd never turn away from who I am. I couldn't. Don't you know you'll always be Jewish … in your soul" (p. 60) (RL.7.2, SL.7.1)

Revisit *Anne Frank Beyond the Diary* and contextualize the play's conclusion (RL.7.2, SL.7.1)

Lesson VI: Dramatizing Moments in the Annex

Select passages for performance (RL.7.5)

Assign roles

Dramatize select moments in the annex (in groups) (RL.7.5)

Lesson VII: Dramatizing Moments in the Annex

Actively observe groups' representations of life in the secret annex (RL.7.5, RL.7.6)

(Individually) assess the impact of these representations (RL.7.5, RL.7.6)

Appreciate the limits of dramatizing the life and death of Anne Frank (SL.7.1)

Lesson VIII: "Give," and "Why?" by Anne Frank (from *Tales from the Secret Annex*)

Explore Anne's complex personality as it is portrayed in "Give," and "Why?" (RL.7.2, SL.7.1)

Think about Anne's ability to hold on to her humanity while in hiding (SL.7.1a, SL.7.1b, SL.7.1c)

Examine the enduring legacy of Anne Frank (SL.7.1)

Poetry

- *War and the Pity of War* (Neil Philip and Michael McCurdy)

Drama

- *The Diary of Anne Frank: A Play* (Frances Goodrich and Albert Hackett) (E)
- *101 Monologues for Middle School Actors: Including Duologues and Triologues* (Rebecca Young)

INFORMATIONAL TEXTS

Nonfiction

- *A History of US: War, Peace, and All that Jazz* (Joy Hakim) (E)
- *Ghost Soldiers: The Epic Account of World War II's Greatest Rescue Mission* (Hampton Sides)
- *True Stories of D-Day (True Adventure Stories)* (Henry Brook)
- *Dear Miss Breed: True Stories of the Japanese American Incarceration During World War II and a Librarian Who Made a Difference* (Joanne Oppenheim)
- *Hiroshima* (John Hersey)
- *Fighting For Honor: Japanese Americans and World War II* (Michael L. Cooper)
- *Never to Forget: The Jews of the Holocaust* (Milton Meltzer)
- *Six Million Paper Clips: The Making of a Children's Holocaust Memorial* (Peter W. Schroeder and Dagmar Schroeder-Hildebrand)
- *Atomic Structure and Chemical Reactions: Middle Grades and High School* (Nevin Katz)
- *The Making of the Atomic Bomb* (Richard Rhodes)

Biographies

- *Anne Frank: The Diary of a Young Girl* (Anne Frank)
- *Anne Frank: Beyond the Diary: A Photographic Remembrance* (Ruud van der Rol and Rian Verhoeven)
- *The Journal of Scott Pendleton Collins: A World War II Soldier, Normandy, France, 1944* (Walter Dean Myers)
- *Night* (Elie Wiesel)
- *Zlata's Diary: A Child's Life in Wartime Sarajevo* (Zlata Filipovic)
- *I Have Lived a Thousand Years: Growing Up in the Holocaust* (Livia Bitton-Jackson)

Memoir

- *A Friend Called Anne: One Girl's Story of War, Peace, and a Unique Friendship with Anne Frank* (Jacqueline van Maarsen)
- *Four Perfect Pebbles* (Lila Perl)
- *Children of Willesden Lane: Beyond the Kindertransport—A Memoir of Music, Love, and Survival* (Mona Golabek)

Speeches

- "Blood, Toil, Tears, and Sweat: Address to Parliament on May 13th, 1940" (Winston Churchill) (E)
- "Declaration of War on Japan" (Franklin D. Roosevelt)

ART, MUSIC, AND MEDIA

Film

- George Stevens, dir., *The Diary of Anne Frank* (Screenplay by Frances Goodrich and Albert Hackett) (1959)
- Robert Dornhelm, dir., *Anne Frank: The Whole Story* (2001)
- Elliot Berlin and Joe Fab, dir., *Paper Clips* (HBO documentary) (2004)
- Peter Jones, dir., *Bataan Rescue: The Most Daring Rescue Mission of World War II* (PBS documentary) (2005)

SAMPLE ACTIVITIES AND ASSESSMENTS

1. CLASS DISCUSSION

What is meant by the word *courage*? Look up the word in a dictionary and write your ideas down on a sticky note. Your teacher will give you the opportunity to "Give one, get one" in order to understand the word's *denotation* and its various *connotations*. Create a class word map of the word *courage*. As you find examples of courage in texts read during this unit, write them on sticky notes and add them to the chart or online concept map. (SL.7.1)

2. LITERATURE RESPONSE

In *Anne Frank: The Diary of a Young Girl*, Anne writes vividly about her experiences. What is it about the language she uses that offers insights into her character, especially her courage? Write a response to this question in your journal: What makes Anne Frank a person to whom I can relate? Justify your answer with specific examples of the language from the text and type your response on the classroom blog so you and your classmates can compare essays. (RL.7.4, RL.7.5, RL.7.6)

3. NOTE TAKING ON CHARACTERIZATION

As you read one of the fictional stories to compare it to *Anne Frank: The Diary of a Young Girl*, take notes in your journal or on a shared online document about how the characters' experiences are similar to and different from Anne Frank's. Be sure to note page numbers with relevant information or mark your text with sticky notes so you can cite the text during class discussion.

- Where did the character live?
- What was that character's context? What was happening in the world?
- What was a typical day like for this person?
- How is the character's experience similar to Anne Frank's?
- How is the character's experience different from Anne Frank's?
- What are some of the author's characterization techniques?

Prior to class discussion, your teacher may give you the opportunity to share your notes (and/or collaborate on shared online spreadsheet) with a partner who read the same text. (RL.7.2, RL.7.6)

4. CLASS DISCUSSION

Compare and contrast characters from the various novels read. Can you generalize about ways that authors create courageous characters? After class discussion, create a Venn diagram or other type of chart online or in your journal that outlines the similarities and differences among three of the characters discussed. (SL.7.1, RL.7.2, RL.7.5, RL.7.6)

5. INFORMATIVE/EXPLANATORY WRITING

As you read one of the fictional stories to compare it to *Anne Frank: The Diary of a Young Girl,* take notes in your journal about how the characters' experiences are similar to and different from Anne Frank's. Be sure to note page numbers with relevant information or mark your text with sticky notes so you can cite the text during class discussion. When done, write a well-developed paper, citing at least three to four specific examples. Edit your writing for phrases and clauses, modifiers, and precise language. Your teacher may ask you to upload your essay on the classroom blog. (W.7.2a,b,c,d,e; W.7.4, L.7.1a,b,c; L.7.2a,b, L.7.3a)

6. INFORMATIVE/EXPLANATORY WRITING

Analyze various accounts of World War II events from a variety of print and digital, primary, and secondary resources. In your journal (or a spreadsheet or text document), identify and distinguish among the facts, opinions, and reasoned judgments presented by different people. Include an analysis of the interactions among individuals, events, and ideas, drawing on various accounts from different authors. Include new vocabulary words learned during this unit. Edit your writing for phrases and clauses, modifiers, and precise language. You may even choose to prepare your essay as a podcast and present it to the class. (W.7.2, W.7.4, RI.7.3, RI.7.6, RI.7.9, L.7.1a,b,c; L.7.2a,b, L.7.3a, L.7.6, SL.7.4)

7. INFORMATIVE/EXPLANATORY WRITING

In an informative/explanatory essay or speech, describe how Churchill's use of repetition and/or rhetorical questions advances the theme of courage. Cite at least two examples from the text to support your thesis. (RI.7.2, W.7.2, W.7.9)

8. SPEECH ANALYSIS

Compare the speeches by Winston Churchill and Franklin D. Roosevelt. How are the styles and themes similar and different? In what ways does style contribute to the theme of each speech? Write your ideas on a T-chart or Venn diagram in your journal or online and share with a partner prior to class discussion. Cite specific examples of style, such as diction and the use of figurative language. (SL.7.3, RI.7.6, RI.7.7, RI.7.9)

9. RESEARCH

Many rights were taken away from the Jewish people during the Holocaust. Choose one of these rights to research in detail, following the research process through to the presentation of findings, either as an essay or other presentation. When you are done, write a note card about how the right you researched was taken away and include the date. As a class, create a bulletin board or spreadsheet of the note cards in order to share what you have learned with each other. Make sure that the events are arranged in correct chronological order. Discuss how people reacted with perseverance and courage at their rights being taken away. Enter your "takeaway" thoughts from this research and class conversation on the classroom blog so you can continue the conversation electronically. (RI.7.3, RI.7.6, W.7.2, W.7.7, W.7.8, SL.7.1, SL.7.2)

10. CLASS DISCUSSION AND WRITING (ARGUMENT)

You have read about Anne Frank and her life within the confines of an attic during World War II. How does knowing the historical context of the diary add to your appreciation of Anne's writing? Why? Write your ideas in your journal and share with a classmate prior to class discussion. After the class discussion, write a speech in which you explain your viewpoint and present it to the class. Use figurative language and select words carefully for maximum impact. Record your presentation using a video camera so you can evaluate your performance. Post the presentation on the class blog to get feedback from others outside of your classroom. (RI.7.3, RL.7.2, RL.7.6, W.7.4, SL.7.6)

11. DRAMATIZATION/FLUENCY (OPTION 1)

Write a dramatic interpretation of Anne Frank's (or someone else's) experience with conflict during the Holocaust; you may focus on interpersonal conflict, intrapersonal conflict, conflict between self and society, or another type of conflict. Your interpretation should incorporate the dramatic elements studied during the drama unit and accurately reflect the information learned in history class. Edit your writing for phrases and clauses, modifiers, and precise language. Record your presentation using a video camera so you can evaluate your performance. (W.7.3, W.7.4, RI.7.3, L.7.1, L.7.2a,b, L.7.3a)

12. DRAMATIZATION/FLUENCY (OPTION 2)

Choose a poem from *War and the Pity of War* or a diary entry from one of the books read; memorize the poem or passage and present it to the class. How does the text you chose reflect the courage of characters during the horrors of war? (SL.7.6, RL.7.2)

13. MEDIA APPRECIATION

Discuss the similarities and differences between Anne's biography and the play and film interpretations of her story. What parts were true to the original? What parts were changed? Why do you think the elements that changed were changed? Does it add or detract from the dramatic effect of Anne's story? Why or why not? Write your ideas in your journal or complete a two-circle or three-circle Venn diagram using online templates. Share with a classmate prior to class discussion. (RL.7.5, RL.7.7)

14. MEDIA APPRECIATION

Watch the HBO documentary *Paper Clips*, which is about a project started by middle school students to remember the people affected by the Holocaust. How does the format contribute to the meaning or impact? As a class, discuss why it is important to learn from history and pass that learning from generation to generation. (RL.7.5, RL.7.7, SL.7.2)

15. WORD STUDY

[Continuing activity from the first two units.] Just as we can trace the path of our ancestors—some back to World War II—we can trace the path of words. Choose some words learned this year in content classes, and trace back from modern-day uses of the words to their historical origins (i.e., *tyranny, assimilation, displacement, genocide, Gestapo, propaganda, internment, smuggle,* etc.). Add these to your personal dictionary. (L.7.4, L.7.6, RI.7.4)

16. INFORMATIVE/EXPLANATORY WRITING

Reflecting on the novels read and discussed in class, write an informative/explanatory essay in response to the essential question: How can reading about the courage of real people inform our understanding of courageous literary characters? Cite specific details from texts read, not only from English class, but also from history class. After your teacher reviews your first draft, work with a partner to strengthen and edit your writing for phrases and clauses, modifiers, and precise language. Be prepared to summarize your thoughts on two digital slides that include visuals. All slides will be combined into a single presentation for posting on the class web page. (W.7.2, W.7.4, W.7.9a,b, L.7.1, L.7.2a,b, L.7.3a)

17. GRAMMAR AND USAGE

Your teacher will teach mini-lessons on the individual language standards. For example, he/she will teach the class about misplaced modifiers by putting sentences on the board, and asking you to describe why they are incorrect, and then correct them. For example:

- Slithering through the wet grass, we watched the garden snake. (*Correction:* We watched the garden snake slithering through the wet grass.)
- When he was three years old, Jerry's uncle showed him how to fly a kite. (*Correction:* When Jerry was three years old, his uncle showed him how to fly a kite.)
- The boys were spoken to sharply about loitering in the principal's office. (*Correction:* While in the principal's office, the boys were spoken to sharply about loitering.)

Select a piece of your own writing and check for any misplaced or dangling modifiers. Correct them. (L.7.1c)

18. MECHANICS/GRAMMAR WALL

As a class, continue adding to the Mechanics/Grammar bulletin board started in Unit One. Remember— once skills are taught in a mini-lesson and listed on the bulletin board, you are expected to edit your work for these elements before publication. (L.7.1, L.7.2, L.7.3)

19. USAGE

Your teacher will give you some sentences containing redundancies, and you will try to simplify the sentences without affecting the meaning. For example (strikethrough shows the redundant phrase):

- ~~As far as I'm concerned,~~ there is no need for further discussion of the topic.
- Grass has overgrown in areas because ~~of the fact that~~ we stopped mowing our lawn.
- ~~In my opinion,~~ this dress code policy ought to be revoked.
- "I am so mad," I said ~~angrily~~.

Next, choose a piece of your own writing and read it aloud to a classmate. He/she should help you listen for any redundant words or phrases that could be eliminated. (L.7.3a)

20. VOCABULARY/WORD WALL

As a class, continue adding to the Vocabulary Word Wall bulletin board where, throughout the year, you will add and sort words as you learn them in each unit of study. (L.7.4)

ADDITIONAL RESOURCES

- *Anne Frank: One of Hundreds of Thousands* (National Endowment for the Humanities) (RI.7.9)
- *Teacher's Guide to Bataan Rescue: The Most Daring Rescue of World War II* (PBS)
- *Elie Wiesel was Born on September 30, 1928* (ReadWriteThink) (RI.7.6)
- *Walter Dean Myers, Author of the Printz Award–Winning Novel Monster, was Born in 1937* (ReadWriteThink) (RL.7.7)
- *Investigating the Holocaust: A Collaborative Inquiry Project* (ReadWriteThink) (RI.7.9)
- *Language Arts and Social Studies—It's the Connections that Matter Most!* (Ohio Resource Center for Mathematics, Science, and Reading)
- *Teacher's Guide to the Holocaust* (Florida Holocaust Museum)
- *Great Speeches Collection* (The History Place)

TERMINOLOGY

Connotation	Dialogue	Documentary	Screenplay
Denotation	Diction	Point of view	

Lesson III: Life in the Annex (Act I)

Explore the dramatic impact of Hitler's voice (p. 17) (RL.7.3, RL.7.5)

Juxtapose Hitler's voice with Anne's words: "It's the silence that frightens me most" (p. 17) (RL.7.1, RL.7.2, RL.7.3, RL.7.5, SL.7.1)

Investigate the daily routine and tensions in the annex (RL.7.2)

Examine the dramatic impact of the closing moment of Act I (RL.7.3, RL.7.5, SL.7.1)

Listen to Anne's voice (select diary entry) (RL.7.2)

Lesson IV: Enduring and Longing (Act II)

Note the passage of time in the annex (RL.7.1, RL.7.2)

Examine the link that Miep Gies provides to the outside world (RL.7.2, RL.7.3, RL.7.5)

Explore the nature of Anne's longing (p. 48) (RL.7.5, SL.7.1)

Explore the relationship between Anne and Peter (RL.7.2)

Listen to Anne's voice (select diary entry) (RL.7.2)

Lesson V: Captured (Act II)

Contextualize Miep's news about the invasion of Europe by the Allies (informational text) (RL.7.2, RL.7.3, RL.7.5)

Investigate the significance of Anne's words: "I'd never turn away from who I am. I couldn't. Don't you know you'll always be Jewish ... in your soul" (p. 60) (RL.7.2, SL.7.1)

Revisit *Anne Frank Beyond the Diary* and contextualize the play's conclusion (RL.7.2, SL.7.1)

Lesson VI: Dramatizing Moments in the Annex

Select passages for performance (RL.7.5)

Assign roles

Dramatize select moments in the annex (in groups) (RL.7.5)

Lesson VII: Dramatizing Moments in the Annex

Actively observe groups' representations of life in the secret annex (RL.7.5, RL.7.6)

(Individually) assess the impact of these representations (RL.7.5, RL.7.6)

Appreciate the limits of dramatizing the life and death of Anne Frank (SL.7.1)

Lesson VIII: "Give," and "Why?" by Anne Frank (from *Tales from the Secret Annex*)

Explore Anne's complex personality as it is portrayed in "Give," and "Why?" (RL.7.2, SL.7.1)

Think about Anne's ability to hold on to her humanity while in hiding (SL.7.1a, SL.7.1b, SL.7.1c)

Examine the enduring legacy of Anne Frank (SL.7.1)

Grade Seven, Unit Three Sample Lesson Plan

The Diary of Anne Frank: A Play by Frances Goodrich and Albert Hackett

Anne Frank Beyond the Diary: A Photographic Remembrance by Ruud Van Rol and Rian Verhoven

In this interdisciplinary series of eight lessons, students read *The Diary of Anne Frank: A Play* by Frances Goodrich and Albert Hackett, and *Anne Frank Beyond the Diary: A Photographic Remembrance* by Ruud Van Rol and Rian Verhoven, and they:

> Examine the historical background to the life and death of Anne Frank (RI.7.2, RI.7.5, RI.7.6)
>
> Evaluate the dramatic presentation of Anne Frank's life (RL.7.2, RL.7.3, RL.7.5)
>
> Examine Anne Frank's personality (RL7.2, SL.7.1)
>
> Consider why Anne Frank's legacy endures (SL.7.1)

Summary

Lesson I: Meet Anne Frank

Study the map of Europe and locate Germany and Holland (informational text)

Meet Anne Frank (RI.7.6)

Appreciate the need to contextualize the story of Anne Frank (informational text) (RI.7.5, RI.7.6)

Explore the meaning and scope of anti-Semitism and Nazism (RI.7.2)

Lesson II: Entering the Secret Annex (Act I)

Identify the purpose of dramatizing Anne Frank's story (RL.7.3, RL.7.5)

Imagine the early days in the annex (pp. 9–17) (RL.7.3)

Visualize the secret annex (RL.7.3)

Explore the characters in the annex (RL.7.3)

Investigate the role of Miep Gies (include informational text) (RL.7.2, RL.7.3, RL.7.5)

Listen to Anne's voice (select diary entry) (RL.7.2)

Lesson I: Meet Anne Frank

Objectives

Study the map of Europe and locate Germany and Holland

Meet Anne Frank (RI.7.6)

Appreciate the need to contextualize the story of Anne Frank (RI.7.5, RI.7.6)

Explore the meaning and scope of anti-Semitism and Nazism (RI.7.2)

Required Materials

- [ ] A large map of 1939 Europe
- [ ] A large map of 1944 Europe under German occupation
- [ ] *Anne Frank Beyond the Diary: A Photographic Remembrance*, by Ruud Van Rol and Rian Verhoven. (Class sets are recommended, but a single text will do. Change the lesson format if only one text is available; the objectives will remain the same.)
- [ ] Chart paper
- [ ] Markers

Procedures

1. Lead-In:
   a. Students study the two large maps that are on the board. Direct them first to notice the map of Europe in 1939, before the beginning of World War II.
   b. Students then examine a 1944 map of Europe under German occupation.

2. Step by Step:
Part I
   a. The discussion begins after all students have located Germany on both maps.
   b. Direct the class discussion as students consider the differences between the two maps.
   c. Students identify the countries that were occupied by Nazi Germany during World War II. Volunteers point to and name the countries that were occupied.

Part II
   a. Distribute *Anne Frank Beyond the Diary: A Photographic Remembrance* by Ruud Van Rol and Rian Verhoven.
   b. Read Anna Quindlen's "Introduction" aloud. (Students take turns reading in pairs or trios.)
   c. Identify key ideas that Quindlen highlights.
   d. Read "The Best Birthday Present" together. (Students take turns reading.)
   e. Students are now aware that Anne received her diary on June 12, 1942, days before going into hiding.
   f. Students turn to the Chronology on page 108; the chronology of events provides historical context to Anne's life.

Part III

1. a. In small groups, students read assigned pages from the book:

   "From Frankfurt to Amsterdam"

   "Hitler Comes to Power"

   "Fleeing to Another Country"

   "The Netherlands Is Occupied, the Persecution Begins"

   "Deportation of Dutch Jews"

   "Going into Hiding"

   "Daily Life"

   "The Diary Is Left Behind"

   "The Murder of Millions"

   b. Once students have read their assigned sections, the groups decide on key points to share with the rest of the class and write them on the chart paper provided. Display the charts around the classroom in the order of their appearance in the book. (Alternatively, students can compile key points set up by the sections above on the classroom blog or a shared spreadsheet.)

   c. Once back in their seats, each group introduces the rest of the class to their selection of the key ideas. Project the ideas from the computer (class blog or spreadsheet) to the interactive whiteboard.

   d. Students must copy all the information provided into their notebooks, or print out the class-assembled document.

3. Closure:
   Teacher-directed activity: Students need to understand the concept and practice of anti-Semitism in order to come a step closer to comprehending the events of World War II. Use informational texts and offer a brief lecture on the history of anti-Semitism and the emergence of Nazism in Germany. Countless sources provide this information.

Differentiation

Advanced

- Pre-assess (all) students for their knowledge of World War II. If students already know the content of the lesson/book, choose another related text from this unit for students to compare/contrast with.

- Allow students to set up a shared online spreadsheet for the class where students can collaboratively outline *The Photographic Remembrance.*

- Allow students to find and select images that reveal the key points from the readings for their classmates to discuss.

Struggling

- Pre-assess (all) students for their knowledge of World War II. Consider pre-teaching key ideas to students on the day prior (for example, give them the maps from the Lead-In section to study as a jumpstart).

- Have key ideas from the relevant chapters of the book pre-printed on index cards or paper. Students read through the ideas, and then highlight the ones they hear being read aloud.
- Consider pairing stronger and weaker readers, so the weaker readers can hear the chapter read aloud fluently.
- Have the chapters that will be read aloud available on audio recording so students who aren't fluent grade-level readers can listen and follow along.
- To build background knowledge of the World War II time period, select Discovery Education clips or select images for students to preview/review and discuss.

Homework/Assessment

Using the notes that they have taken in class, students outline *Anne Frank Beyond the Diary: A Photographic Remembrance*, by Ruud Van Rol and Rian Verhoven. This assignment helps students recap the lesson. It also provides an assessment of the class activities and the students' individual work.

Grade 7 ▶ *Unit 4*

Survival in the Wild

This four-week unit of seventh grade continues the close examination of characters and examines how setting plays a role in their development.

ESSENTIAL QUESTION

? What similarities and differences exist among characters who survive in the wild?

OVERVIEW

Students read "The Song of Wandering Aengus" by William Butler Yeats and use it as a springboard for discussions of characters' pursuits of the unknown. Students analyze the development of the theme of survival across various texts, evaluate nonfiction text structures, and present their analyses to their classmates. Students compare and contrast character experiences across novels, as well as the points of view in narration, and are encouraged to research the authors behind the stories, many of whom are wilderness survivors themselves. This unit ends with a review of Yeats's poem in order to see how this unit led to deeper understanding of the work. In addition, students are asked to write an informative/explanatory essay in response to the essential question.

FOCUS STANDARDS

These Focus Standards have been selected for the unit from the Common Core State Standards.

RL.7.2: Determine a theme or central idea of a text and analyze its development over the course of the text; provide an objective summary of the text.

RI.7.5: Analyze the structure an author uses to organize a text, including how the major sections contribute to the whole and to the development of the ideas.

W.7.1: Write arguments to support claims with clear reasons and relevant evidence.

SL.7.4: Present claims and findings, emphasizing salient points in a focused, coherent manner with pertinent descriptions, facts, details, and examples; use appropriate eye contact, adequate volume, and clear pronunciation.

L.7.5: Demonstrate understanding of figurative language, word relationships, and nuances in word meanings.

SUGGESTED STUDENT OBJECTIVES

- Analyze the development of characters and themes in texts about survival.
- Discuss how the authors' use of literary techniques in narration, such as flashback and point of view, engage the reader.
- Write an argument about the importance of reading original versions of stories, such as *The Call of the Wild*.
- Conduct research on authors who write about survival in the wild and present findings to the class.
- Compare and contrast *The Call of the Wild* in written form to the film version.
- Take comprehensible notes on important content, ideas, and details in texts (e.g., about character development).
- Write a survival-in-the-wild story using figurative language and exploiting nuances in word meaning for effect.

SUGGESTED WORKS

(E) indicates a CCSS exemplar text; (EA) indicates a text from a writer with other works identified as exemplars.

LITERARY TEXTS

Stories

- *The Call of the Wild* (Jack London)
- *Woodsong* (Gary Paulsen)
- *Far North* (Will Hobbs)
- *Incident at Hawk's Hill* (Allan W. Eckert)
- *Black Hearts in Battersea* (Joan Aiken)

Comparisons to *The Call of the Wild*
- *Touching Spirit Bear* (Ben Mikaelsen)
- *The Higher Power of Lucky* (Susan Patron)
- *Call It Courage* (Armstrong Sperry)
- *Hatchet* (Gary Paulsen)
- Other Will Hobbs survival tales, such as *Beardance*

Graphic Novel

- *The Call of the Wild* (Puffin Graphics, Jack London)

Poetry

- "The Song of Wandering Aengus" (William Butler Yeats) (E)

INFORMATIONAL TEXTS

Nonfiction

- *Into the Ice: The Story of Arctic Exploration* (Lynn Curlee)

- *SAS Survival Handbook, Revised Edition: For Any Climate, in Any Situation* (John "Lofty" Wiseman)

Biographies
- *Jack London: A Biography* (Daniel Dyer)
- *Guts* (Gary Paulsen)
- *Will Hobbs* (My Favorite Writer Series) (Megan Lappi)

ART, MUSIC, AND MEDIA

Art
- Théodore Géricault, *The Raft of the Medusa* (1818–1819)
- Winslow Homer, *The Gulf Stream* (1899)
- Frederic Edwin Church, *The Heart of the Andes* (1859)
- Albert Bierstadt, *The Rocky Mountains, Lander's Peak* (1863)
- Thomas Cole, *View from Mount Holyoke, Northampton, Massachusetts, after a Thunderstorm—The Oxbow* (1836)

Film
- Richard Gabai, dir., *Call of the Wild* (2009)
- Peter Svatek, dir., *The Call of the Wild: Dog of the Yukon* (1997)
- Mark Griffiths, dir., *A Cry in the Wild* (based on *Hatchet*) (1990)

SAMPLE ACTIVITIES AND ASSESSMENTS

1. INTRODUCTORY ACTIVITY

Read "The Song of Wandering Aengus" by William Butler Yeats. Talk with a classmate about what you think the poem means, both literally and figuratively. Write your ideas down in your journal or on an online document. You will revisit this poem at the end of the unit to see if your thoughts and ideas have changed. (RL.7.2, RL.7.4, SL.7.5)

2. NOTE TAKING ON CHARACTER DEVELOPMENT

As you read *The Call of the Wild,* take notes in your journal or on an online document about how the characters are affected by their environment. (Remember—characters that survive in the wild can be animals, too!) Be sure to note page numbers with relevant information or mark your text with sticky notes, so you can cite the text during class discussion. (RL.7.1, RL.7.2, L.7.5a,b,c)

- Which character are you studying?
- What is a typical day like for this character?
- What challenges did this character face?
- How did this character overcome these challenges?
- What is the "call of the wild"? How does it affect (Buck's) behavior throughout the novel?

  Prior to class discussion, your teacher may give you the opportunity to share your notes with a partner who read the same text.

3. NOTE TAKING AND CLASS DISCUSSION

Compare and contrast characters from the various novels read. Can you generalize about the types of character qualities that enable a person (or animal) to survive in the wild? After class discussion, create a two- or three-circle Venn diagram or summarize your thoughts in your journal or on the classroom blog to see how similar and different your thoughts are from those of your classmates. (SL.7.1, RL.7.3)

4. LITERATURE RESPONSE

Anthropomorphism is defined as giving human characteristics to animals or nonliving things (e.g., winds, rain, or the sun depicted as creatures with human motivations). The term derives from the combination of the Greek *anthropos,* meaning "human," and *morph,* meaning "shape" or "form." Find examples of anthropomorphism in the stories you have read, record them in your journal or on a class spreadsheet, and discuss how this additional "character" plays a role in the story. (RL.7.3, RL.7.6, L.7.5)

5. WRITING (ARGUMENT)

While reading *The Call of the Wild,* take notes in your journal about the roles of John Thornton and Judge Miller. Who, from the novel's point of view, is the better master? Write an argument in which you justify your opinion, citing specific evidence from the text. Enter your thoughts in the classroom blog so you can compare your argument with those of your classmates. (SL.7.4, RL.7.1, RL.7.3, W.7.1)

6. LITERATURE RESPONSE

Notice the use of flashback in *Hatchet* and how the past comes into Brian's present through his daydreams, night dreams, and flashbacks. Write a response to this question in your journal: How does Gary Paulsen incorporate the past into the present? Extend the activity by comparing two authors' use of flashbacks in two different works. (RL.7.3)

7. LITERATURE RESPONSE AND WRITING (ARGUMENT)

Is it important to read the original ("full") version of a novel? Read the graphic novel version of *The Call of the Wild* by Jack London and then write a convincing argument for reading the original version, citing similarities and differences between the versions read. You may talk through your ideas with a partner prior to writing your first draft. (RL.7.2, W.7.1, SL.7.4, L.7.1, L.7.2a,b, L.7.5)

8. RESEARCH ESSAY

After discussing the ethics of proper documentation of sources as a class, write a research essay about Jack London, Gary Paulsen, Will Hobbs, or another author of your choice who writes about survival in the wilderness. Describe at least three significant events in the author's life and explain their significance. Edit your writing for the grammar conventions studied so far this year. Read or watch online interviews with the authors (see Additional Resources) and try to arrange a teleconference conversation with him/her. Feel free to add multimedia elements, such as a digital slide presentation prior to presenting your research to the class. (W.7.7, RI.7.5, RI.7.8, SL.7.4, L.7.1, L.7.2a,b, L.7.3a)

9. MEDIA APPRECIATION

Compare the book *The Call of the Wild* to the movie version. Write your ideas down in your journal or mark your text with sticky notes. Be sure to cite specific similarities and differences between the versions. (RL.7.7)

10. WORD STUDY

[Continuing activity from the first three units.] Choose some words learned this unit and add these to your personal dictionary. Include a section on idioms and figures of speech. Develop groups by synonyms and antonyms. (L.7.4, L.7.5)

11. NARRATIVE ESSAY

Write your own survival-in-the-wilderness story, incorporating words, techniques, and styles from the novels read and discussed in class. Work with peers to strengthen writing in order to publish it on the class web page. Edit your writing for the grammar conventions studied so far this year before uploading it as a blog, podcast, movie, or other multimedia format of choice. (W.7.3, W.7.4, W.7.5, L.7.1, L.7.2a,b, L.7.3a)

12. CLASS DISCUSSION

Re-read the first poem read in this unit, "The Song of Wandering Aengus." After this unit of study, describe how your understanding of this poem has changed. What new insights have you gained? Add these insights on the shared online document created in Activity 1 (in a new column next to your initial thoughts). Memorize and/or recite the poem aloud while emphasizing different words. Record them using a video camera so you can see and hear the different phrasing. How does changing emphasis change the meaning of the sentences? Follow the performances with a class discussion about how this poem relates to the theme of this unit (survival in the wild). (RL.7.5, SL.7.6)

13. INFORMATIVE/EXPLANATORY ESSAY

Based on the novels read and discussed in class, write an informative/explanatory essay in response to the essential question: What similarities and differences exist among characters who survive in the wild? Cite at least three specific details from texts read. After your teacher reviews your first draft, work with a partner to strengthen your writing and edit it for the grammar conventions studied so far this year before final publication. Upload your essay to the classroom blog and consider posting your thoughts on a class wiki about survival in the wilderness. (W.7.9a,b, RI.7.8, RL.7.1, L.7.1,L.7.2a,b)

14. MECHANICS/GRAMMAR WALL

As a class, continue adding to the Mechanics/Grammar bulletin board started in Unit One. Remember— once skills are taught in a mini-lesson and listed on the bulletin board, you are expected to edit your work for these elements before publication. (L.7.1, L.7.2, L.7.3)

15. VOCABULARY/WORD WALL

As a class, continue adding to the Vocabulary Word Wall bulletin board where, throughout the year, you will add and sort words as you learn them in each unit of study. (L.7.4)

16. ART/CLASS DISCUSSION/WRITING

The works by Géricault and Homer are considered to be classic images of man's survival at sea. Study the works separately, beginning with the Géricault. Note the many ways in which the artist emphasized the high drama of the situation (e.g., the dramatic surf and sky, billowing sail, imposing wave). Observe that half of the men are reaching toward a barely visible ship on the horizon, while the rest slip slowly into the surf. Then turn to the Homer and identify similarities with the Géricault (e.g., the coming boat). Which work do you think documents a real event? Listen to the story of the *Medusa* shipwreck. Write a short story describing the events that you would imagine either led to or came after the scene in Homer's work. (SL.7.2, SL.7.4, SL.7.5, W.7.3)

17. ART/CLASS DISCUSSION

Look carefully at the paintings by Church, Bierstadt, and Cole. Each of these artists came from a common school of art called the Hudson River School. However, what differences can you see in their paintings? How did each artist choose to depict the wild? What aspects did each choose to highlight, and what did they choose to forgo in their depictions? (SL.7.1, SL.7.3, SL.7.4)

ADDITIONAL RESOURCES

- *Boys Read: Considering Courage in Novels* (ReadWriteThink) (RL.7.6)
- *Action Is Character: Exploring Character Traits with Adjectives* (ReadWriteThink) (RL.7.3)
- *Jack London's Call of the Wild: "Nature Faker"?* (National Endowment for the Humanities)
- *Anthropomorphic Poetry* (TeacherWeb)
- Interview with Gary Paulsen

TERMINOLOGY

Abridged	Flashbacks	Point of view
Anthropomorphism	Foreshadowing	

Grade Seven, Unit Four Sample Lesson Plan

"The Song of Wandering Aengus" by William Butler Yeats

In this series of two lessons, students read "The Song of Wandering Aengus" by William Butler Yeats, and they:

- Explore the speaker's tale (RL.7.2, RL.7.3, SL.7.4, SL.7.6, L.7.5)
- Identify the mythological origins of Aengus (RL.7.1, RI.7.1, SL.7.4)
- Listen to Donovan's rendition of the poem (RL.7.5, SL.7.2)
- Discuss the impact Donovan's interpretation has on the reader (L.7.5, SL.7.1, SL.7.6)

Summary

Lesson I: "The Song of Wandering Aengus"

- Probe the imagery in "The Song of Wandering Aengus" (RL.7.2, RL.7.3, RL.7.4, L.7.4, L.7.5, SL.7.4)
- Explore the speaker's mood (SL.7.2, SL.7.4, SL.7.6, L.7.5)
- Identify the mythological origins of Aengus (RI.7.1, RL.7.1, SL.7.1, SL.7.4, L.7.6)
- Probe the inspiration that Yeats found in the myth (RL.7.1, SL.7.1, SL.7.4)

Lesson II: "The Song of Wandering Aengus" and Donovan

- Listen to Donovan's rendition of "The Song of Wandering Aengus" (SL.7.2, L.7.5)
- Discuss Donovan's interpretation of the poem (RL.7.5, RL.7.7, SL.7.1, SL.7.2, SL.7.4, L.7.5)
- Recall earlier impressions of the poem (SL.7.1, SL.7.4)
- Discuss (in paragraph form) the impact that Donovan's interpretation has on the reader (W.7.2, SL.7.4, L.7.3, L.7.6)

Lesson I: "The Song of Wandering Aengus"

Objectives

- Probe the imagery in "The Song of Wandering Aengus" (RL.7.2, RL.7.3, RL.7.4, L.7.4, L.7.5, SL.7.4)
- Explore the speaker's mood (SL.7.2, SL.7.4, SL.7.6, L.7.5)
- Identify the mythological origins of Aengus (RI.7.1, RL.7.1, SL.7.1, SL.7.4, L.7.6)
- Probe the inspiration that Yeats found in the myth (RL.7.1, SL.7.1, SL.7.4)

Required Materials

☐ Class set of "The Song of Wandering Aengus" by W. B. Yeats
☐ Text describing the mythological origins of Aengus
☐ Computer with Internet access

Procedures

1. Lead-In:
Student volunteer reads "The Song of Wandering Aengus" aloud.

2. Step by Step:
   a. Students annotate the poem for its imagery.
   b. A discussion of the poem's imagery follows.
   c. Students probe how the imagery contributes to the poet's depiction of the speaker's mood.
   d. Teachers may either distribute texts that describe the life of Aengus, or allow the students to conduct research.
   e. With the new information, students probe the allusion to Aengus.

3. Closure:
Student volunteer rereads "The Song of Wandering Aengus" aloud.

Differentiation

Advanced

- Encourage students to create a modern-day interpretation of the poem. They must be able to justify how the modern version stays true to the original, while also changing style. Perhaps challenge them to create a movie similar in function to Donovan's.
- Give students an opportunity to bookmark the most helpful websites for other classmates to conduct their research. Collect the websites on a web portal.
- Select a student volunteer to read the poem at the end of class. Give the student an opportunity to practice reading dramatically, recorded with a video camera, so he/she can evaluate his/her performance and improve upon it.

Struggling

- Read the poem to students, or allow them to listen to a pre-recorded version on an MP3 player.
- Give students a worksheet of the poem they can write on or annotate, possibly even with sketches (nonlinguistic representations) to help aid memory and understanding. Alternatively, allow them to annotate by inserting their notes in a text document.
- Allow students to highlight examples of imagery. Lead a small-group discussion about why authors use imagery.
- Allow students to begin their research using the websites chosen by classmates (listed above).
- Record the student volunteer who reads the poem using a video camera so students can: (1) review and re-watch it as needed; and (2) practice reading along to aid in fluency and understanding.

Homework/Assessment
N/A

Science or Fiction?

This four-week unit of seventh grade examines the genre of science fiction and related science.

OVERVIEW

Like other genres studied to date, science fiction examines humanity, but often approaches characters and experiences in a futuristic context. Science fiction involves the imagining of ideas and technologies that haven't yet been invented; however, many of them may comport with our current understanding of science and technology. In addition to exploring classic and contemporary works of science fiction, students pair fictional stories with informational texts about science and astronomy. Student discussions trace the logic of various storylines, focusing on the believability of the stories read in class. This unit ends with the students' choice of writing an informative/ explanatory essay in response to the essential question: What makes science fiction believable?

FOCUS STANDARDS

These Focus Standards have been selected for the unit from the Common Core State Standards.

RL.7.1: Cite several pieces of textual evidence to support analysis of what the text says explicitly as well as inferences drawn from the text.

RI.7.9: Analyze how two or more authors writing about the same topic shape their presentations of key information by emphasizing different evidence or advancing different interpretations of facts.

W.7.2: Write informative/explanatory texts to examine a topic and convey ideas, concepts, and information through the selection, organization, and analysis of relevant content.

SL.7.5: Include multimedia components and visual displays in presentations to clarify claims and findings and emphasize salient points.

L.7.1: Demonstrate command of the conventions of Standard English grammar and usage when writing or speaking.

SUGGESTED STUDENT OBJECTIVES

- Compare and contrast the settings, characters, and unusual circumstances among science fiction stories and describe the unique nature of this genre.
- Analyze how a science fiction story evolves over the course of a text, and discuss how this is similar to and different from other novels read.
- Compare and contrast the ways in which two authors present information on the same topic (e.g., astronomy in *Beyond Jupiter* and *Summer Stargazing*).
- Conduct research on an astronaut or science fiction author of choice and present findings to the class in a multimedia format.
- Write a science fiction story.

SUGGESTED WORKS

(E) indicates a CCSS exemplar text; (EA) indicates a text from a writer with other works identified as exemplars.

LITERARY TEXTS

"Classic" Science Fiction

- *A Wrinkle in Time* (Madeleine L'Engle) (E)
- *Dune* (Frank Herbert)
- *The War of the Worlds* (H. G. Wells)
- *The Invisible Man* (H. G. Wells)
- *I, Robot* (Isaac Asimov)
- *Journey to the Center of the Earth* (Enriched Classics) (Jules Verne)

"Modern" Science Fiction

- *The Ear, the Eye, and the Arm* (Nancy Farmer)
- *My Favorite Science Fiction Story* (Martin H. Greenberg)
- *Eva* (Peter Dickinson)
- *The House of the Scorpion* (Nancy Farmer)
- *Fly by Night* (Frances Hardinge)
- *George's Cosmic Treasure Hunt* (Lucy and Stephen Hawking)
- *Among the Hidden* (Shadow Children Series, #1) (Margaret Peterson Haddix)
- *George's Secret Key to the Universe* (Lucy and Stephen Hawking)
- *The Hitchhiker's Guide to the Galaxy* (Douglas Adams)
- *Ender's Game* (Orson Scott Card)
- *The Collected Stories of Arthur C. Clarke* (Arthur C. Clarke)

Audiobooks

- *A Wrinkle in Time* (Madeleine L'Engle)

INFORMATIONAL TEXTS

- "Elementary Particles" from the *New Book of Popular Science* (E)
- "Space Probe" from *Astronomy & Space: From the Big Bang to the Big Crunch* (Phillis Engelbert) (E)
- *Almost Astronauts: 13 Women Who Dared to Dream* (Tanya Lee Stone)
- *Robo World: The Story of Robot Designer Cynthia Breazeal* (Women's Adventures in Science Series) (Jordan D. Brown)

Planets/Stars

- *Beyond Jupiter: The Story of Planetary Astronomer Heidi Hammel* (Women's Adventures in Science Series) (Fred Bortz)
- *Summer Stargazing: A Practical Guide for Recreational Astronomers* (Terence Dickinson)
- *Stephen Hawking: Cosmologist Who Gets a Big Bang Out of the Universe* (Mike Venezia)
- *Stars & Planets* (Carole Stott)
- *The Physics of Star Trek* (Lawrence M. Krauss)

ART, MUSIC, AND MEDIA

Music

- Gustav Holst, *The Planets* (1914 – 1916)

Media

- *War of the Worlds* (Orson Welles, *The Mercury Theater on Air,* October 30, 1938)

SAMPLE ACTIVITIES AND ASSESSMENTS

1. NOTE TAKING AND STORY ELEMENTS

As you read one of the science fiction novels, take notes in your journal or on a spreadsheet about the elements of the story that would classify it as science fiction. Be sure to note page numbers with relevant information so you can cite the text during class discussion.

- What is the setting of the novel?
- Who are the character(s) you are studying?
- What is familiar or believable about these characters?
- What is unusual about the characters' circumstances?
- What is the primary theme of the novel (i.e., good vs. evil)?

Prior to class discussion, your teacher may give you the opportunity to share your notes with a partner who read the same text. (RL.7.1, RL.7.2, RL.7.3)

2. CLASS DISCUSSION AND INFORMATIVE/EXPLANATORY WRITING

Compare and contrast settings and experiences from the various science fiction stories read. As you read one of the science fiction novels, take notes about the elements of the story that would classify it as science fiction. Be sure to note page numbers with relevant information so you can cite the text during class discussion. Then write a well-developed paper that explains what makes science fiction a unique genre. Include at least three characteristics of the genre and examples of each. Edit your writing for the grammar conventions studied so far this year. Upload your essay to the classroom blog so you can collaborate on this topic with your classmates. (SL.7.1a,b,c,d; RL.7.1, RL.7.3, L.7.1, L.7.2a,b, L.7.3a)

3. LITERATURE RESPONSE

While reading *A Wrinkle in Time* by Madeleine L'Engle, take notes in your journal in response to Meg's mother's words, "Just because we don't understand doesn't mean an explanation doesn't exist." How does this relate not only to the content of the book, but also to the scientific principles contained within? Defend your answers, citing specific information from the text. Enter your thoughts on the classroom blog so you can share ideas with your classmates. (RL.7.1, RL.7.4)

4. INFORMATIVE/EXPLANATORY WRITING

While reading *Eva* by Peter Dickinson, take notes in your journal about the author's comments on human beings' impact on the ecology of the earth. Did this book make you think more about this issue? Why or why not? Explain your answer in a well-developed paper that includes an engaging opening statement of your position, at least three clear reasons, and relevant evidence cited from the text. Edit your writing for the grammar conventions studied so far this year. (RL.7.1, RL.7.2, L.7.1, L.7.2 a,b, L.7.3a)

5. CLASS DISCUSSION

Why doesn't H. G. Wells give a name to his protagonist in *The War of the Worlds*? What is the significance of his anonymity? How does it add to the effectiveness of the story? Write your ideas in your journal and share ideas with a partner prior to class discussion. (SL.7.1, L.7.1)

6. RESEARCH PROJECT

Write a research essay about an astronaut or science fiction author of choice. Include at least three significant details about the person and cite at least three sources. Use both paraphrasing and direct quotations from research. (*Optional:* You may include multimedia components and visual displays, such as a digital slide presentation.) Edit your writing for the grammar conventions studied so far this year. Publish your research on the class web page, including proper endnote or footnote links to reference materials used, and present your report to the class. (W.7.7, W.7.2, W.7.4, W.7.5, W.7.6, W.7.8, SL.7.5, RI.7.1, RI.7.7, RI.7.10, L.7.1, L.7.3a, L.7.5c)

7. RESEARCH AND CLASS DISCUSSION

While conducting research on an astronaut or science fiction author of choice (see Activity 6), discuss with classmates the specific claims made by the writers of the texts you are consulting. Is the reasoning "sound" and the evidence "relevant and sufficient" to support the claims? Why or why not? If not, how could the writer have improved his/her argument? Enter your thoughts on the classroom blog so you can debate with your classmates. (RI.7.5, RI.7.8, SL.7.1, L.7.1)

8. ANALYSIS OF INFORMATIONAL TEXT AND INFORMATIVE/EXPLANATORY WRITING

Compare and contrast the ways in which the authors of *Beyond Jupiter* (biography) and *Summer Stargazing* (procedural text) discuss the topic of astronomy. How do the differences in approach affect the readers' understanding of the topic? (W.7.2, W.7.9)

9. MEDIA APPRECIATION AND PRESENTATION

After listening to the original 1938 radio broadcast of *The War of the Worlds,* discuss the following questions:

- Did the radio play hold your attention? Why or why not?
- Which techniques were effective in making the audio "come alive"?
- Were you invested in what happened to any of the characters? Why or why not?
- Does this remind you of any similar stories/broadcasts you have heard? (RL.7.7, SL.7.1)

Follow up by researching public reaction to the radio broadcast on the night before Halloween in 1938. What effect did the program have on listeners who tuned in late? What elements make the broadcast sound believable? Write your ideas in your journal (or on a shared spreadsheet) and share ideas with a partner prior to class discussion. Compile your own broadcast or other kind of multimedia presentation that exhibits the same elements. (SL.7.3, SL.7.4, SL.7.5)

10. MUSIC APPRECIATION

Each movement of *The Planets* by Gustav Holst is named after a planet of the solar system. All planets except Earth are represented. Discuss what makes the music for each planet unique. Take notes of your thoughts in your journal while listening to the music. (SL.7.1, L.7.1)

11. WORD STUDY

[Continuing activity from the first four units.] Choose some words learned this unit and add these to your personal dictionary. (L.7.4, L.7.5c)

12. NARRATIVE WRITING AND MULTIMEDIA PRESENTATION

Write your own science fiction story that answers the question, What if . . . ? Work with peers to edit and strengthen your story before presenting it to the class. Edit your writing for the grammar conventions studied so far this year. Publish it in multimedia format, such as a movie, or on the class web page. (SL.7.5, W.7.3, W.7.4, W.7.5, W.7.6, W.7.8, L.7.1, L.7.3a, L.7.5c)

13. INFORMATIVE/EXPLANATORY WRITING

Write an essay response to the essential question: What makes science fiction believable? Cite specific details from texts read. After your teacher reviews your first draft, work with a partner to strengthen your writing, and edit it for the grammar conventions studied so far this year before presenting it to the class. Publish it in written or multimedia format, such as a podcast, on the class web page. (RL.7.2, W.7.4, W.7.5, W.7.6, W.7.8, W.7.9a, W.7.9b, L.7.1, L.7.3a, L.7.5c)

14. MECHANICS/GRAMMAR WALL

As a class, continue adding to the Mechanics/Grammar bulletin board started in Unit One. Remember—once skills are taught in a mini-lesson and listed on the bulletin board, you are expected to edit your work for these elements before publication. (L.7.1, L.7.2, L.7.3)

15. VOCABULARY/WORD WALL

As a class, continue adding to the Vocabulary Word Wall bulletin board where, throughout the year, you will add and sort words as you learn them in each unit of study. (L.7.4)

ADDITIONAL RESOURCES

- *Finding the Science Behind Science Fiction Through Paired Readings* (ReadWriteThink) (RL.7.9)
- *Science-Fiction Author Ray Bradbury Was Born in 1920* (ReadWriteThink) (W.7.7)
- *Text Messages, Recommendations for Adolescent Readers Podcast: Episode 2—Teen Time Travel* (ReadWriteThink) (RL.7.9)
- *Star Wars Creator George Lucas Was Born in 1944* (ReadWriteThink) (RI.7.6)

TERMINOLOGY

Common settings for science fiction: in the future, alternate timelines, in outer space

Common themes for science fiction: time travel, alternate histories/societies, body and mind alterations

Fantasy versus science fiction

Grade Seven, Unit Five Sample Lesson Plan

A Wrinkle in Time by Madeleine L'Engle

In this series of five lessons, students read *A Wrinkle in Time* by Madeleine L'Engle, and they:

> Explore the genre of science fiction (RL7.6, RL.7.9, SL.7.1, SL.7.4, SL.7.6, L.7.4)
>
> Examine the adventures and the emotional evolution of Meg (RL.7.2, RL.7.3, RL.7.6, SL.7.4, L.7.5)
>
> Identify the components of the short story (RL.7.1, RL.7.4, W.7.7, SL.7.1, L.7.6)
>
> Compose science fiction stories (W.7.3, W.7.4, W.7.5, SL.7.6, L.7.1, L.7.2, L.7.3, L.7.5)

Summary

(The lessons begin following the independent reading of the novel.)

Lessons I/II: A Wrinkle in Time	Lesson III: Writing Science Fiction Stories
Explore the genre of science fiction (RL.7.6, RL.7.9, SL.7.1, SL.7.4, SL.7.6, L.7.4)	In groups, generate ideas for individual stories (W.7.5, SL.7.1)
Probe the roles of the key characters of the novel (RL.7.3, RL.7.6, SL.7.1, SL.7.4)	Outline the plot of the story (W.7.5, RL.7.2)
Note the qualities of these characters (RL.7.1, RL.7.3, SL.7.1, L.7.5)	Identify a conflict (W.7.5, RL.7.2, SL.7.1)
Retell the adventures of Meg, Charles Wallace, and Calvin O'Keefe (RL.7.3, RL.7.4, RL.7.6, SL.7.4, L.7.5)	Explore possible settings for the story (W.7.5, RL.7.2, SL.7.1)
Examine the changing settings of the novel (RL.7.3, RL.7.4, SL.7.1)	Explore the personalities of these characters (W.7.5, SL.7.1, L.7.5)
Identify the central conflict of the novel (RL.7.2, SL.7.4)	Begin writing the story (W.7.3, W.7.5, L.7.3)
Explore the lessons that Meg and her brother learn (RL.7.1, RL.7.6, SL.7.1)	

Lesson IV: Writing Science Fiction Stories

Resume writing (W.7.3, W.7.5, L.7.3)

Ponder the growth of the characters (W.7.5, SL.7.1, RL.7.3, RL.7.6)

Consider the lesson that the reader will learn from the story (W.7.5, SL.7.1, RL.7.2)

Identify the story's climax (W.7.5, SL.7.4, RL.7.3)

Offer a resolution (W.7.5, SL.7.1, SL.7.4, RL.7.3)

Lesson V: Revising the Short Stories

Reread the stories (W.7.5)

Identify possible weaknesses (W.7.4, SL.7.4, SL.7.6)

The conflict is unclear

The characters do not evolve

The dialogue is confusing

Revise essays (W.7.4, W.7.5, L.7.1, L.7.2, L.7.3, L.7.6)

Produce final drafts (a take-home assessment: 3–5 pp. long) (W.7.4, W.7.5, L.7.1, L.7.2, L.7.3, L.7.6)

Lesson III: Writing Science Fiction Stories

Objectives

In groups, generate ideas for individual stories (W.7.5, SL.7.1)

Outline the plot of the story (W.7.5, RL.7.2)

Identify a conflict (W.7.5, RL.7.2, SL.7.1)

Explore possible settings for the story (W.7.5, RL.7.2, SL.7.1)

Explore the personalities of these characters (W.7.5, SL.7.1, L.7.5)

Begin writing the story (W.7.3, W.7.5, L.7.3)

Required Materials

☐ Student notebooks

Procedures

1. Lead-In:
Introduce the opening activity; in small groups, the students will discuss ideas for writing short stories.

2. Step by Step:
   a. Students write brief descriptions in their notebooks of the plot of their stories. (The purpose of this step is to be sure that students keep their stories in focus.)
   b. An important component of a good story is a conflict. As students revisit their story summaries, they identify or strengthen the conflict.
   c. In their notebooks, students describe the setting of the story and consider why the setting is important. For example, if the story takes place in a mysterious forest, what would the forest look like and sound like?

d. A good way to create complex characters is to draw a chart. See the example shown in this lesson plan.

e. Students begin writing the stories.

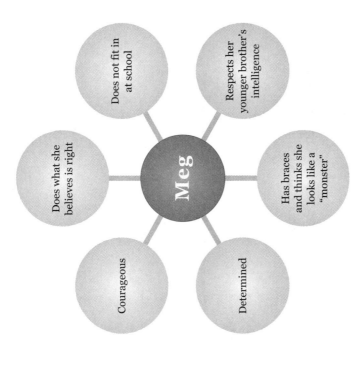

Meg

- Does not fit in at school
- Respects her younger brother's intelligence
- Has braces and thinks she looks like a "monster"
- Determined
- Courageous
- Does what she believes is right

3. Closure:
Explain the homework.

Differentiation

Advanced

- Students create more advanced stories with complex interaction among characters, setting, and plot.
- Students find a list of science fiction stories for their classmates that could be used to write modified endings (see last bullet below). Create an annotation (e.g., ReadWriteThink "Suggested Science Fiction").
- Students create a visual storyboard to show how their story elements work together. Students may start thinking about how to create a podcast or movie of their story once it is completed.
- Students create a website where all the stories can be posted once they are completed.

- Help students generate ideas for science fiction stories. If necessary, provide some student prompts.
- Provide students with as detailed a graphic organizer as they need (possibly a shared online template), which they can use to draft their stories. Include more or less scaffolding, as needed:

  - Who is your protagonist?
  - What does he/she want?
  - What happens to him/her? (In other words, what is the conflict?)
  - What does his/her world look like?
  - What background information does the reader need to know for this story to make sense?
  - About how long should this story be?

- Depending on what type of support students need, the graphic organizer may be something like the "Plot Alternatives Designer" found on the ReadWriteThink website.
- Model the writing of a story together in class, perhaps on a shared online document that all students could access at home.
- Allow students to write a shorter piece that may be a modified ending of a favorite science fiction story. More advanced students will generate a potential list of stories for their classmates.

Homework/Assessment

Continue working on the stories. Complete at least the first page.

Grade 7 ▶ *Unit 6*

Literature Reflects Life: Making Sense of Our World

In this final six-week unit of seventh grade, students conclude their year-long study of the human condition by examining how a variety of genres can address the human condition: fantasy, comedy, tragedy, the short story, and poetry.

ESSENTIAL QUESTION

Is literature always a reflection of life?

OVERVIEW

Although students read from various genres, writing and class discussions focus on how literature can help us make sense of our world. In particular, students will examine "point of view," analyzing how authors develop different points of view. The overall goal of this unit is for students to apply all the reading, writing, speaking, and listening strategies and skills they have learned up to this point in the year. The unit ends with an informative/explanatory essay in response to the essential question: Is literature always a reflection of life?

FOCUS STANDARDS

These Focus Standards have been selected for the unit from the Common Core State Standards.

RL.7.6: Analyze how an author develops and contrasts the points of view of different characters or narrators in a text.

W.7.1: Write arguments to support claims with clear reasons and relevant evidence.

SL.7.3: Delineate a speaker's argument and specific claims, evaluating the soundness of the reasoning and the relevance and sufficiency of the evidence.

L.7.3: Use knowledge of language and its conventions when writing, speaking, reading, or listening.

SUGGESTED STUDENT OBJECTIVES

- Describe how point of view is developed in a variety of genres—drama, short stories, and poetry.
- Explain the basic characteristics of comedy and tragedy.
- Compare novels with their theatrical and film versions.
- Identify a common theme in different novels and advance an argument about that theme.

SUGGESTED WORKS

(E) indicates a CCSS exemplar text; (EA) indicates a text from a writer with other works identified as exemplars.

LITERARY TEXTS

Stories

- *Home of the Brave* (Katherine Applegate)
- *A Girl Named Disaster* (Nancy Farmer)
- *Diary of a Wimpy Kid: The Last Straw* (Jeff Kinney)
- *Letters from a Nut* (Ted L. Nancy)
- *Cyrano* (Geraldine McCaughrean)
- *The Prince and the Pauper* (Mark Twain)
- *Dr. Jekyll and Mr. Hyde and Other Stories of the Supernatural* (Robert Louis Stevenson)

Fantasy

- *The Dark is Rising* (Susan Cooper) (E)
- *The Grey King* (Susan Cooper)
- *Peter Pan in Scarlet* (Geraldine McCaughrean)

Short Stories

- *Woman Hollering Creek: And Other Stories* (Sandra Cisneros) (EA)
- *Best Shorts: Favorite Stories for Sharing* (Avi)
- *Little Worlds: A Collection of Short Stories for the Middle School* (Peter Guthrie)
- *American Dragons: Twenty-Five Asian American Voices* (Lawrence Yep) (EA)

Poetry

- *Feel a Little Jumpy Around You: Paired Poems by Men & Women* (Naomi Shihab Nye and Paul B. Janeczko)

Drama

- *Cyrano de Bergerac* (Edmond Rostand)

INFORMATIONAL TEXTS

[None for this unit]

ART, MUSIC, AND MEDIA

Art

- Honoré Daumier, *André-Marie-Jean-Jacques Dupin Aîné* (1929/1930)
- Honoré Daumier, *Antoine-Maurice-Apollinaire, Comte D'Argout* (1929)
- Honoré Daumier, *Antoine Odier* (1929)
- Honoré Daumier, *Auguste Gady* (1929)
- Honoré Daumier, *Auguste-Hilarion, Comte de Kératry* (1929)

Film

- Fred Schepisi, dir., *Roxanne* (1987)

SAMPLE ACTIVITIES AND ASSESSMENTS

1. NOTE TAKING ON GENRE, SETTING, AND CHARACTERIZATION

As you read the novels and short stories from this unit, take notes about the story genre, setting, and characters in your journal or on a shared spreadsheet. Be sure to note page numbers with relevant information or mark the text with sticky notes so you can cite the text during class discussion.

- What is the genre of the novel?
- What is the setting?
- Who are the major character(s)?
- Who are the minor characters?
- What is the problem faced by the character(s)? How do he/she/they resolve the problem?
- What is the primary theme of the novel (i.e., good vs. evil)?

Prior to class discussion, your teacher may give you the opportunity to share your notes with a partner who read the same text. (RL.7.1, RL.7.2 RL.7.6, RL.7.10)

2. WRITING (ARGUMENT)

The human spirit can be defined as a combination of the traits that all human beings have in common. Select three of these traits that you think are present in the characters from the novels from this unit and discuss why you think these traits are essential to the human spirit. Why did you choose these traits? Justify your answer by citing specific information and examples from texts read, not only in this unit, but all year long. Edit your writing for the grammar conventions studied so far this year. Upload your essay to the classroom blog for your classmates to see and compare the traits you chose with those chosen by others. (W.7.1a,b,c,d,e; W.7.4, W.7.10, SL.7.3, L.7.1, L.7.2, L.7.3a, L.7.5, L.7.6)

3. WRITING (ARGUMENT)

While reading *The Dark is Rising* by Susan Cooper, take notes in your journal about Will's search for his destiny. Is his search organized or random? Choose a position and defend your answer in a well-developed paper that includes an engaging opening statement of your position, at least three clear reasons for your position and relevant evidence cited from the text. Edit your writing for the grammar conventions studied so far this year. After your teacher reviews your essay, post it to the class blog and ask your classmates to find weaknesses in your argument and help strengthen your position. (W.7.1, L.7.1, L.7.2, L.7.3, L.7.5, L.7.6)

4. WRITING (POETRY)

After reading *Peter Pan in Scarlet* by Geraldine McCaughrean, write a poem about Peter Pan and how he changed in this sequel from the original story. Choose poetic devices that exemplify his traits as a character, his experiences in the book, and/or his approach to life. You may talk through your ideas with a partner before writing your first draft, and ask this classmate to help you revise and edit the final draft. Memorize and recite your poem for the class. Record it using a video camera so you can evaluate your performance. (RL.7.5, SL.7.6, L.7.3, L.7.5, L.7.6)

5. WRITING (ARGUMENT)

Think about why beauty is so highly valued in our society while reading *Cyrano* by Geraldine McCaughrean. Take notes in your journal comparing Christian and Cyrano. Who is a better person? Why? Defend your answer in a well-developed paper that includes an engaging opening statement of your position, at least three clear reasons, and relevant evidence cited from the text. Edit your writing for the grammar conventions studied so far this year. After your teacher reviews your essay, post it to the class blog and ask your classmates to find weaknesses in your argument and help strengthen your position. (W.7.1, RL.7.6, L.7.1, L.7.2, L.7.3, L.7.5, L.7.6)

6. WRITING (ARGUMENT)

Is *Cyrano de Bergerac* a tragedy or comedy? Write your position on a sticky note, and your teacher will divide the class according to everyone's positions. Share ideas with classmates who are of the same opinion. Then write your own essay. Justify your answer by drawing on other stories read this year. Include at least three examples from the text that support your position. Be prepared to summarize and present your argument to the class. Ask your classmates to analyze your arguments for effectiveness. (W.7.1, W.7.4, W.7.10, SL.7.3, SL.7.4, L.7.3, L.7.5, L.7.6)

7. LITERATURE RESPONSE

While reading *The Prince and the Pauper* by Mark Twain, take notes in your journal about what makes Tom Candy and Edward Tudor unique. At the end, choose a character about whom to write a poem, using poetic devices that exemplify the character's traits and development throughout the story. Memorize and/or recite your poem for the class, and record it using a video camera so you can share it on the class website. (RL.7.2, RL.7.6)

8. CLASS DISCUSSION

In all comedy, there is an element of truth. Discuss some humorous stories, and specify how they provide insights into human character/existence. Write your ideas in your journal and share ideas with a partner prior to class discussion. (SL.7.1)

9. MEDIA APPRECIATION

Compare and contrast a written story with its filmed or theatrical version. Specifically examine the tools used to produce video, film, or theater (e.g., lighting, sound, color, camera angles) by comparing a written text (i.e., *Cyrano*) to its staged or multimedia version. (*Note:* Use select scenes from the 1987 movie *Roxanne*.) (RL.7.7)

10. INFORMATIVE/EXPLANATORY WRITING (AND WORD STUDY)

Select a genre studied this year and write an informative/explanatory essay in response to the essential question: Is literature always a reflection of life? Make sure to include elements that make it apparent to the reader which genre you chose, cite specific details from texts you've read, and use as many words as possible learned in Word Study this year. After your teacher reviews your first draft, work with a partner to edit and strengthen your writing before presenting it to the class. Edit your writing for the grammar conventions studied so far this year. Publish a well-developed paper in written or multimedia format on the class web page. (RL.7.10, W.7.1, W.7.4, W.7.5, W.7.6, W.7.8, W.7.9a,b, W.7.10, SL.7.3, L.7.1, L.7.2, L.7.3, L.7.5, L.7.6)

11. MECHANICS/GRAMMAR WALL

As a class, continue adding to the Mechanics/Grammar bulletin board started in Unit One. Remember— once skills are taught in a mini-lesson and listed on the bulletin board, you are expected to edit your work for these elements before publication. (L.7.1, L.7.2, L.7.3)

12. VOCABULARY/WORD WALL

As a class, continue adding to the Vocabulary Word Wall bulletin board where, throughout the year, you will add and sort words as you learn them in each unit of study. (L.7.4)

13. ART/CLASS DISCUSSION/WRITING

What emotions can you identify in the characters that Daumier has created? How has he shown these emotions artistically? What is different about these heads from other sculptures you have seen? What is the same? Describe what you see in a short paragraph, focusing on the visual aspects of the sculpture, then share your ideas with the class. Does everyone see the same visual elements in these sculptures? (SL.7.1, SL.7.3, SL.7.4, W.7.2)

14. ART/CLASS DISCUSSION/WRITING

Daumier made at least three dozen of these busts. Notice the level of detail, and appearance of monumentality, with which Daumier imbued these works. How tall do you think they are? None of these works is much taller than six inches. Select three works, rename the subjects, and assign the subject an occupation based on appearance. (SL.7.2, SL.7.4, SL.7.5, W.7.1, W.7.3)

ADDITIONAL RESOURCES

- *You Know the Movie Is Coming—Now What?* (ReadWriteThink) (RL.7.7)
- *Thoughtful Threads: Sparking Rich Online Discussions* (ReadWriteThink) (W.7.6)
- *Doodle Splash: Using Graphics to Discuss Literature* (ReadWriteThink) (SL.7.5)

TERMINOLOGY

Comedy	Irony: verbal,	Parody	Theme
Fantasy	situational, dramatic	Plot	Tragedy
Hyperbole	Oxymoron	Point of view	

Grade Seven, Unit Six Sample Lesson Plan

The Prince and the Pauper by Mark Twain

In this series of five lessons (that follow the students' independent reading of the novel) students read *The Prince and the Pauper* by Mark Twain, and they:

Investigate Mark Twain's use of the House of Tudor as background to the novel (RI.7.2, W.7.7, RL.7.3, RL.7.9, SL.7.1, SL.7.4, L.7.6)

Revisit the plot of *The Prince and the Pauper* (RL.7.1, RL.7.2, SL.7.1, SL.7.4, L.7.5, L.7.6)

Analyze the leading characters in the novel (RL.7.3, RL.7.6)

Probe Mark Twain's social criticism (RL.7.9, RI.7.6)

Summary

Lesson I: *The Prince and the Pauper* and the House of Tudor

Probe the historical background of the novel (RI.7.2, W.7.7, SL.7.1, SL.7.6)

Identify the lineage of the House of Tudor (RI.7.1, RI.7.3, SL.7.1, SL.7.4)

Explore Twain's choice of historical background (RL.7.9, SL.7.1, SL.7.4)

Lesson III: *The Prince and the Pauper*

Conduct close character analyses of the Prince and the pauper (RL.7.6, L.7.5, L.7.6, SL.7.1, SL.7.4)

Cite textual evidence to support analysis of the characters (RL.7.1, L.7.6, SL.7.1, SL.7.4)

Investigate the lessons that they learn about society (RL.7.1, RL.7.6, SL.7.1, SL.7.4)

Probe what the two learn about themselves (RL.7.1, RL.7.6, SL.7.1, SL.7.4, L.7.6)

Lesson II: *The Prince and the Pauper*

Investigate the events that lead up to Tom Canty's and Prince Edward's switch (RL.7.1, SL.7.1, SL.7.6)

Revisit the plot of *The Prince and the Pauper* (RL.7.2, SL.7.1, SL.7.4, L.7.5, L.7.6)

Probe the purpose of the parallel plots (RL.7.2, RL.7.6, SL.7.1, SL.7.4)

Lesson IV: Twain's Social Criticism

Investigate Twain's description of the life of the royal family (RL.7.4, RL.7.9, L.7.5, L.7.6, SL.7.1, SL.7.6)

Explore Twain's depiction of poverty (RL.7.1, SL.7.1, SL.7.6, L.7.5, L.7.6)

Examine the court cases in the novel (RL.7.1, RL.7.6, SL.7.1, SL.7.4, L.7.6)

Probe Twain's social critique (RL.7.9, RI.7.6, L.7.5, L.7.6, SL.7.1, SL.7.4, SL.7.6)

Lesson V: *The Prince and the Pauper*

Using the text, annotations, the chart, and other class notes, compose a five-paragraph essay in response to the following prompt: "How does the dramatic shift in the Prince's and the pauper's lives contribute to Twain's exploration of social injustice?" (W.7.2, RL.7.1)

Lesson III: The Prince and the Pauper

Objectives

Conduct a close character analysis of the Prince and the pauper (RL.7.6, L.7.5, L.7.6, SL.7.1, SL.7.4)

Cite textual evidence to support analysis of the characters (RL.7.1, L.7.6, SL.7.1, SL.7.4)

Investigate the lessons that they learn about society (RL.7.1, RL.7.6, SL.7.1, SL.7.4)

Probe what the two learn about themselves (RL.7.1, RL.7.6, SL.7.1, SL.7.4, L.7.6)

Required Materials

☐ Class set of *The Prince and the Pauper* by Mark Twain

☐ Class set of the chart below

Procedures

1. Lead-In:

Introduce the students to the chart below. Point to the example and tell the students that:
Each column must have ten examples that span the entire novel and the text must be cited.

2. Step by Step:

In pairs (or small groups) students collaboratively work on the chart below.

	Prince Edward	Tom Canty
Characteristics	During the first meeting between the Prince and the pauper, the Prince is kind. He says to Tom, "Thou lookest tired and hungry. Thou'st been treated ill. Come with me."	During the first meeting, Tom Canty is very open about his life. He tells the Prince that his grandmother has a "wicked heart."
Prince Edward and Tom Canty and Society		
Lessons that the Prince and the pauper learn about themselves		

3. Closure:
Share findings with a neighboring group.

Differentiation

Advanced

- Students should find five concrete examples from the text and give five examples that are based on inferences.
- Students should choose one more theme/event/plot to add to the chart. They should find up to ten examples to illustrate their choices, just as in the categories provided.
- Students may choose to extend the character analysis by creating an interactive poster or a comic using Internet tools, citing textual evidence for the items chosen to include.

Struggling

- Provide students with five to eight examples for them to sort into the appropriate boxes. Students must be able to justify why they put the examples in the boxes.
- Prepare students for this lesson by prompting them to mark their text with sticky notes while reading. That way, they can review sticky notes rather than reviewing the entire book. Alternatively, put the students into groups, divide the chapters among them, and tell them how many examples can be found in each chapter span. (For example, the group reviewing chapters two through eight should find three examples to put in the chart.) Students collect their information collaboratively on an online document in order to share their work.

Homework/Assessment
N/A

GRADE 8

In eighth grade, students begin to study complex psychological, philosophical, and moral themes in literature. They begin the year with two units on setting, the first on urban settings in America and the second on rural contexts. In these units, students consider relationships between setting and theme in literature and write their own stories set in cities and the countryside. From there, the units take various directions. One unit offers a historical perspective on America, while another looks at the relationship between art and artists. In the unit on drama, students read Shakespeare's *A Midsummer Night's Dream* and compare it with a film version of the play. The sixth unit focuses on the philosophical theme of "the greater good," beginning and ending with Robert Frost's "The Road Not Taken." Through class discussion, close reading, and writing, and through continued study of etymology, students deepen their understanding of all of these works and concepts. They continue to use graphic organizers to plan their writing. In their reports, research essays, and oral presentations, students draw on multiple sources, including literary, informational, and multimedia texts. In class discussions and literary responses, they pay close attention to figurative language and its effects. By the end of eighth grade, students should have a rich background in literature and literary nonfiction, with a grasp of the historical context and many nuances of the works they have read. They are ready for the rigors of high school.

Standards Checklist for Grade Eight

Standard	Unit 1	Unit 2	Unit 3	Unit 4	Unit 5	Unit 6	Standard	Unit 1	Unit 2	Unit 3	Unit 4	Unit 5	Unit 6
Reading—Literature							3c	A		A			A
1	A	A	A	A	A	A	3d	A		A			A
2	A	A	A	FA	A	A	3e	A		A			A
3			A	A	FA	A	4	A	A	A	A	A	A
4	A	A	A	A	A	A	5		A	A	A	A	A
5	A	FA	A	A	A	A	6		A	A	A	A	A
6		A	A	A	FA	A	7	A	A	FA	A	A	
7	A				FA	FA	Speaking and Listening						
8 n/a							1	F	FA	A	A	A	A
9			FA	A	A	A	1a	FA	A	A	A	A	A
10	A					A	1b	FA	A	A	A	A	A
Reading—Informational Text							1c		FA	A	A	A	A
1	FA	A	A	A	A	A	1d		FA	A	A	A	A
2	A	FA	A	A	A		2		A	FA			
3	A	A	FA	A	A		3			A	A	A	FA
4			A	A			4		A	A	FA	A	A
5	A	A		F			5		A		A	FA	A
6	FA	A	A	A	A	A	6	A	A	A	A		A
7	A	FA	A	A			Language						
8	A	A	A	FA		A	1	A	A	A	A	FA	A
9	A		FA	A			1a	A	A	A	A	A	A
10	A					A	1b	A	A	A	A	A	A
Writing							1c	A	A	A	A	A	A
1		FA		A	FA	A	2	A	A	A	A	A	A
1a		A			A	A	2a	A	A	A	A	A	A
1b		A			A	A	2b	A	A	A	A	A	A
1c		A			A	A	3	A	A	A	A	A	FA
1d		A			A	A	3a	A	A	A	A	A	A
1e		A			A	A	4	FA	FA	A	A	A	A
2	A		A	FA	A	A	4a	FA	A	A	A	A	A
2a	A		A	A	A	A	4b	A	FA	A	A	A	A
2b	A		A	A	A	A	4c	FA	A	A	A	A	A
2c	A		A	A	A	A	4d	A	FA	A	A	A	A
2d	A		A	A	A	A	5		A		FA		A
2e	A		A	A	A	A	5a		A		A		A
2f	A		A	A	A	A	5b		A		A		A
3	FA		A		FA		5c		A		A	A	A
3a	A		A		A		6			FA			A
3b	A		A		A								

F = Focus Standard; A = Activity/Assessment

Grade 8 ▶ *Unit 1*

Urban Settings in America: "It Happened in the City"

This six-week unit of eighth grade begins the year with reflections on the settings of stories and events—from poems and short stories to novels and nonfiction.

OVERVIEW

Students continue to explore characters and plots, but this unit takes a unique approach to examining how setting, directly or indirectly, affects these story elements. Students work on citing textual evidence that reveals the setting, analyze the effect of the setting on individuals and events, and write their own urban narrative. This unit ends with an informative/ explanatory essay in response to the essential question.

ESSENTIAL QUESTION

What does the urban setting contribute to these stories?

FOCUS STANDARDS

These Focus Standards have been selected for the unit from the Common Core State Standards.

RI.8.1: Cite the textual evidence that most strongly supports an analysis of what the text says explicitly as well as inferences drawn from the text.

RI.8.6: Determine an author's point of view or purpose in a text and analyze how the author acknowledges and responds to conflicting evidence or viewpoints.

W.8.3: Write narratives to develop real or imagined experiences or events using effective technique, relevant descriptive details, and well-structured event sequences.

SL.8.1: Engage effectively in a range of collaborative discussions (one-on-one, in groups, and teacher-led) with diverse partners on grade 8 topics, texts, and issues, building on others' ideas and expressing their own clearly.

SL.8.1(a): Come to discussions prepared, having read or researched material under study; explicitly draw on that preparation by referring to evidence on the topic, text, or issue to probe and reflect on ideas under discussion.

SL.8.1(b): Follow rules for collegial discussions and decision-making, track progress toward specific goals and deadlines, and define individual roles as needed.

L.8.4: Determine or clarify the meaning of unknown and multiple-meaning words or phrases based on grade 8 reading and content, choosing flexibly from a range of strategies.

L.8.4(a): Use context (e.g., the overall meaning of a sentence or paragraph; a word's position or function in a sentence) as a clue to the meaning of a word or phrase.

L.8.4(b): Use common, grade-appropriate Greek or Latin affixes and roots as clues to the meaning of a word (e.g., *precede, recede, secede*).

SUGGESTED STUDENT OBJECTIVES

- Compare and contrast story characters, plots, themes, and settings from works about urban America.
- Distinguish between explicit and implicit ways of describing the effect of setting on characters, plots, and themes.
- Analyze the ways in which the structure of a work affects how the setting is conveyed.
- Analyze different accounts of the same event.
- Write poetry (concrete or haiku) and perform it for classmates.
- Compare elements of the musical *Chicago* to other poetry and prose about the city of Chicago.
- Define related words and identify their parts of speech (e.g., *urban, urbanization, suburban; city, citify; metropolitan, metropolis*).

SUGGESTED WORKS

(E) indicates a CCSS exemplar text; (EA) indicates a text from a writer with other works identified as exemplars.

LITERARY TEXTS

Stories

- *The Great Fire* (Jim Murphy) (E)
- *The Catcher in the Rye* (J. D. Salinger)
- *KiKi Strike: Inside the Shadow City* (Kirsten Miller)
- *All of the Above* (Shelley Pearsall)
- *A Long Way from Chicago: A Novel in Stories* (Richard Peck)
- *The King of Dragons* (Carol Fenner)

Short Stories

(*Note:* These are used again in Unit Two.)

- *Nine Stories* (J. D. Salinger)
- *The Umbrella Man and Other Stories* (Roald Dahl) (EA)
- *America Street: A Multicultural Anthology of Stories* (Anne Mazer, ed.)
- *Bag in the Wind* (Ted Koozer)

Poetry

- "Chicago" (Carl Sandburg) (E)
- "O Captain! My Captain!" (Walt Whitman) (E)
- *Stone Bench in an Empty Park* (Paul Janeczko)
- *Technically, It's Not My Fault* (John Grandits)

Picture Books (as an Introduction to This Unit)

- *City by Numbers* (Stephen T. Johnson)
- *Bag in the Wind* (Ted Kooser)

INFORMATIONAL TEXTS

Nonfiction

- *The Building of Manhattan* (Donald Mackay) (E)
- *Skyscraper* (Lynn Curlee)
- *The New York Subways* (Great Building Feats Series) (Lesley DuTemple)
- *New York* (This Land is Your Land Series) (Ann Heinrichs)
- *September 11, 2001: Attack on New York City — Interviews and Accounts* (Wilborn Hampton)
- *September 11, 2001* (Cornerstones of Freedom, Second Series) (Andrew Santella)
- *Let's Roll! Ordinary People, Extraordinary Courage* (Lisa Beamer)
- "The Evolution of the Grocery Bag" (*American Scholar Magazine*, Autumn 2003) (Henry Petroski) (E)
- *America's Top 10 Cities* (Jenny E. Tesar)
- *An American Plague: The True and Terrifying Story of the Yellow Fever Epidemic of 1793* (Jim Murphy) (EA)

ART, MUSIC, AND MEDIA

Art

New York

- Edward Hopper, *Nighthawks* (1942)
- Piet Mondrian, *Broadway Boogie Woogie* (1942–1943)
- Joseph Stella, *Bridge* (1936)
- Jean Michel Basquiat, *Untitled* (1981)

Chicago

- Pablo Picasso, *Untitled* or "The Picasso" (1967)
- Anish Kapoor, *Cloud Gate* (2004–2006)
- Edward H. Bennett and Marcel F. Loyau, *Buckingham Fountain* (1927)

Music and Lyrics

- "Where Were You When the World Stopped Turning" (Alan Jackson)

Film

- Video footage from September 11, 2001

SAMPLE ACTIVITIES AND ASSESSMENTS

1. INTRODUCTORY ACTIVITY (FOR THE YEAR)

You will be reading a variety of literature and informational texts this year, including some genres that you may not have read before. On a shared spreadsheet, your teacher will give you a list of twenty genres (such as adventure, historical fiction, comedy, ancient history, science fiction, and fantasy) from which to select titles and to which you may add titles. Be sure to select titles, and topics, of enduring interest. One of your goals by the end of the year is to read books from at least four genres that are new to you. (RL.8.10, RI.8.10)

2. INTRODUCTORY ACTIVITY/CLASS DISCUSSION

Your teacher will read *Alphabet City* and *City by Numbers,* both by Stephen T. Johnson, to the class. What is the author's purpose in creating these texts? How can we use these books to begin looking at cities (urban settings) in a different way? What are the advantages and disadvantages to using picture books to examine setting? Write responses to these questions in your journal and share with a partner prior to class discussion. (RI.8.1, RI.8.5, RI.8.6, RI.8.7)

3. LITERARY GRAPHIC ORGANIZER

As you read one of the novels and/or short stories from this unit, take notes in your journal or on a spreadsheet about the story characters, plot, theme, and setting. As you take notes about these categories, think about how the setting affects the story. Be sure to note page numbers with relevant information that is explicitly stated or implied, so you can cite the text during class discussion.

- Who is/are the major character(s)?
- What is the problem faced by the character(s)? How does he/she/they resolve the problem?
- What is the theme of the novel? (i.e., good vs. evil, overcoming challenges, etc.)
- What is the effect of the setting(s) on the characters?
- Is the effect of the setting stated or implied?
- What unique words and phrases does the author use to describe the setting(s)?

Prior to class discussion, your teacher may give you the opportunity to share your notes with a partner who read the same text. (RL.8.1, RL.8.2, RL.8.4)

4. CLASS DISCUSSION

Compare and contrast settings, characters, plots, and themes of the various novels read. Can you make any generalizations about the effect the urban setting has on these stories? What are they? After class discussion, create a Venn diagram in your journal or with an online template that outlines the similarities and differences among the settings, characters, plots, and/or themes. Post your thoughts on the classroom blog in order to continue the conversation with your classmates. (SL.8.1a,b, RL.8.4)

5. INFORMATIVE/EXPLANATORY WRITING

(Use the research process learned and practiced in sixth and seventh grades when writing this essay.) Read at least three different informational texts about New York City, from books about the events of

September 11, 2001, or Ellis Island, to Manhattan architecture or the New York art world. Analyze how different texts make connections or distinctions among individuals, ideas, or events. Explain your findings in a well-developed essay. Cite at least three examples from each text to illustrate how their approaches to the topic are similar and different. Use a mixture of paraphrasing and direct quotations. Share ideas with a partner and revise your ideas, if desired. Edit your writing for gerunds, participles, infinitives, commas, ellipses, and dashes. Your teacher may ask you to upload your essay to the classroom blog. (RI.8.1, RI.8.3, RI.8.7, RI.8.9, SL.8.2, L.8.1a, L.8.2a)

6. NARRATIVE WRITING

While reading the short stories in this unit, explore your own style of writing. Compare and contrast the following aspects of the stories: Which author orients the reader to a story in a manner that is similar to your own? What sensory details do authors use that you like to use too? How does the author incorporate setting as an integral part of the story? Also, what new vocabulary words can you incorporate into your story? How will your story end? Write your own short story about a real or imagined experience that effectively explores the effect of an urban setting on characters and plot. (You may conduct brief research on a city of choice and incorporate facts about that city into your story, if you wish.) Edit your writing for gerunds, participles, infinitives, commas, ellipses, and dashes. Publish your story as a podcast or on a class blog and request feedback on your literary style from your classmates. (W.8.3, W.8.7, L.8.1a, L.8.2a)

7. NARRATIVE WRITING (AND MULTIMEDIA PRESENTATION)

Read haiku poems from *Stone Bench in an Empty Park* by Paul Janeczko and concrete poems from *Technically, It's Not My Fault* by John Grandits. Next, compare the portrayal of the grocery bag in *Bag in the Wind* by Ted Kooser to "The Evolution of the Grocery Bag" by Henry Petroski. How does the structure of each text affect the meaning? Write a concrete or haiku poem about a grocery bag and recite your poem accompanied by a visual/digital illustration. Edit your writing for gerunds, participles, infinitives, commas, ellipses, and dashes. Recite your poem for your classmates and record it using a video camera so you can evaluate your performance. (RL.8.2, RL.8.5, W.8.4, RI.8.2, SL.8.6)

8. CLASS DISCUSSION

Compare how different poems about the same item (i.e., the grocery bag) are unique in presentation, structure, and style. Which of these elements affects the meaning of the poem? Why? Write your thoughts in your journal and share with a partner prior to class discussion. Your teacher may ask you to respond to this prompt on the classroom blog and discuss your responses online with your classmates. (SL.8.1a,b)

9. MEDIA APPRECIATION/CLASS DISCUSSION

Compare and contrast the poem "Chicago" by Carl Sandburg and *The Great Fire* by Jim Murphy. These works are set in the same city. How is the urban setting portrayed in each? How does the structure of each contribute to its meaning? Write your thoughts in your journal and share with a partner prior to class discussion. (RI.8.1, RI.8.9, RL.8.5, RL.8.7)

10. CLASS DISCUSSION

It has been said that places have a character of their own. How is setting used as a "character"? Write your thoughts in your journal and share with a partner prior to class discussion. Be sure to cite specific information from the texts. You may also post responses to this prompt on a class blog in order to get feedback from others outside of your classroom. (SL.8.1a,b, RL.8.1, RI.8.1)

11. LITERATURE RESPONSE

What's in a name? Write a journal entry where you respond to this question based on a place read about in class, such as New York City or Chicago. Alternatively, create an ABC list describing a city of interest. An optional extension is to create a digital presentation of your ABC list. (W.8.9a,b, RL.8.1, RI.8.1)

12. WORD STUDY

Where do words come from? How does knowing their origin help us not only to spell the words, but also to understand their meaning? This is why we study etymology. Create a personal dictionary of terms found, learned, and used throughout this unit (e.g., *urban, urbanization, suburban, city, citify, metropolitan, metropolis*). This dictionary will be used all year long to explore the semantics (meanings) of words and their origins, especially those with Greek and Latin roots. (L.8.4a,b)

13. INFORMATIVE/EXPLANATORY WRITING

Write an informative/explanatory essay in response to the essential question: "What does the urban setting contribute to these stories?" Make sure to include words and phrases learned in this unit, including figurative and connotative language. After your teacher reviews your first draft, work with a partner to edit and strengthen your writing. Edit your writing for gerunds, participles, infinitives, commas, ellipses, and dashes. Be prepared to record your essay and upload it as a podcast on the class web page for this unit. (W.8.2, W.8.4, W.8.9a,b, SL.8.1a,b, L.8.1a, L.8.2a)

14. GRAMMAR AND USAGE

Your teacher will teach mini-lessons on the individual language standards. For example, he/she will explain verbals, and then will give you underlined words in a quotation to identify as a gerund, participle, or infinitive. For example:

- Happiness is having a large, <u>loving, caring</u>, close-knit family in another city. (George Burns) *(participle)*
- Happiness is <u>having</u> a large, loving, caring, close-knit family in another city. (George Burns) *(gerund)*
- I don't want <u>to achieve</u> immortality through my work. I want <u>to achieve</u> it through not dying. (Woody Allen) *(infinitive)*

   Select a piece of your own writing, circle the verbals, and see if you can identify whether they are gerunds, participles, or infinitives. (L.8.1a)

15. MECHANICS/GRAMMAR WALL

As a class, create a Mechanics/Grammar bulletin board where, throughout the year, you will add to a checklist of editing topics as they are taught through targeted mini-lessons. Once skills are taught in a mini-lesson and listed on the bulletin board, you are expected to edit your work for the elements before publication. (L.8.1, L.8.2, L.8.3)

16. VOCABULARY/WORD WALL

As a class, create a Vocabulary Word Wall bulletin board where, throughout the year, you will add and sort words as you learn them in each unit of study. (L.8.4)

17. ART/CLASS DISCUSSION

Edward Hopper's *Nighthawks* and Piet Mondrian's *Broadway Boogie Woogie*, which both depict New York City, were painted in the same year. Notice the dramatic difference in these artists' styles. The difference goes beyond realism versus abstraction. Discuss the painters' color palettes, the distance at which they placed the viewer, and the type of space in the work. Dwell on the extent to which each artist was focused on the people versus the place. Were they depicting the same time of day? (SL.8.1, SL.8.2, SL.8.4, SL.8.5)

18. ART/CLASS DISCUSSION

Compare *Cloud Gate* with the Picasso sculpture. Both public art sculptures are located in Chicago. Discuss the role(s) fine art can play in a public setting. What makes a public artwork successful? How is viewing art in public different from viewing it in a private setting? (SL.8.1, SL.8.2, SL.8.4, SL.8.5)

ADDITIONAL RESOURCES

- *Exploring Setting: Constructing Character, Point of View, Atmosphere, and Theme* (ReadWriteThink) (This lesson is geared toward grades 9–12, but may be adapted.) (RL.8.1)
- *Critical Media Literacy: Commercial Advertising* (ReadWriteThink) (RI.8.8)
- *Internalization of Vocabulary Through the Use of a Word Map* (ReadWriteThink) (RL.7.4, RI.7.4)
- *Improve Comprehension: A Word Game Using Root Words and Affixes* (ReadWriteThink) (RL.7.4, RI.7.4)
- *Flip-a-Chip: Examining Affixes and Roots to Build Vocabulary* (ReadWriteThink) (RL.7.4, RI.7.4)
- *You Can't Spell the Word Prefix Without a Prefix* (ReadWriteThink) (RL.7.4, RI.7.4)
- http://carl-sandburg.com/chicago.htm

TERMINOLOGY

Connotation	Literal versus figurative language	Setting
Explicit textual evidence		Theme
Implicit textual evidence		

Grade Eight, Unit One Sample Lesson Plan

"Chicago" by Carl Sandburg

In this series of two lessons, students read "Chicago" by Carl Sandburg, and they:

- Perform a close reading of the poem (RL.8.1, RL.8.2, RL.8.3)
- Explore Sandburg's use of poetic devices (RL.8.1, RL.8.4, SL.8.1, L.8.5)
- Analyze Sandburg's poem (RL.8.1, RL.8.4, L.8.4)
- Explore other Chicago poems (RL.8.1, RL.8.4, RL.8.5, SL.8.1, L.8.5)

Summary

Lesson I: "Chicago" by Carl Sandburg	Lesson II: Chicago Poems
Annotate "Chicago" for use of poetic devices (RL.8.4)	Select another Chicago poem (See Additional Resources) (RL.8.5)
Explicate the poem (RL.8.1, RL.8.2, RL.8.4)	Annotate the poem (RL.8.4)
Analyze the poem (RL.8.1, RL.8.3, RL.8.4, L.8.4, L.8.5, SL.8.1, SL.8.4)	Explicate the poem (RL.8.1, RL.8.2, RL.8.4)
Explore the theme of the poem (RL.8.2, SL.8.1, SL.8.4)	Analyze, in essay form, the poem's theme (RL.8.2, SL.8.1, SL.8.4)

Lesson I: "Chicago" by Carl Sandburg

Objectives

- Annotate "Chicago" for use of poetic devices (RL.8.4)
- Explicate the poem (RL.8.1, RL.8.2, RL.8.4)
- Analyze the poem (RL.8.1, RL.8.3, RL.8.4, L.8.4, L.8.5, SL.8.1, SL.8.4)
- Explore the theme of the poem (RL.8.2, SL.8.1, SL.8.4)

☐ Class set of "Chicago" by Carl Sandburg (The lines in the poem should be double-spaced, providing space for students' annotations.)

Procedures

1. Lead-In:
   A student volunteer reads the poem "Chicago" aloud.
2. Step by Step:
   a. Instruct the students to annotate the poem for the poet's use of poetic devices. If this practice is not familiar to the students, annotate the first stanza together with the whole class. Below is a sample of the first stanza annotated:

   The first two words give a violent impression; in particular, the word *butcher* is violent.
   Hog <u>Butcher</u> for the <u>World</u>: repeated use of capital letters: why?
   Tool <u>Maker</u>, Stacker of <u>Wheat</u>: "Maker" and "Stacker" are active nouns.
   Player with <u>Railroads</u> and the <u>Nation's</u> Freight <u>Handler</u>; Stormy, husky, brawling: the three adjectives seem to be "noisy."
   City of the <u>Big Shoulders</u>: here is a visual description . . . and personification

   b. Students annotate the poem.
   c. Using their annotations, the students (in a full class discussion) explicate the poem. The purpose of the explication is not analytical. It is simply to make sure that the students pay close attention to the tools that the poet uses as he expresses his feelings about the city of Chicago.
   d. Students are now ready for a more analytical discussion of the text. The teacher prompts may be:

   Why does the poet capitalize all these words?
   What is the image that the active nouns produce?
   What overall impression does the reader get from the first stanza?

   e. The above prompts lead to discussion of the theme of the poem: the poet's feelings for Chicago.
3. Closure:
   A student volunteer reads "Chicago" aloud.

Differentiation

Advanced

• Select student volunteers to practice reading the poem prior to this lesson, or while other students are working on annotations if he/she finishes annotating early. The students should practice reading dramatically, recorded with a video camera, so they can evaluate and improve upon their performances.

- Encourage students to read the poem with a variety of dramatic interpretations and choose the student with the most unique presentation to present to other advanced students. Students should evaluate the different interpretations and discuss how they work to enhance the poem or detract from it. These readings may be recorded with a video camera to share with other students, as time permits.
- Allow students to conduct online research of interpretations of this poem. They should critically analyze the posted information based on what they learned from class discussion.
- Encourage students to create a poem in the style of "Chicago" about their own city. They must be able to justify how their version stays true to the original while still changing the setting. Challenge students to create a movie or slide show that illustrates their new poem.

Struggling

- Be prepared with a list of guiding questions to support students in their annotations (e.g., What do you notice about the choice of words in the first phrase? Which line is an example of personification?). Students can mark their poem with sticky notes prior to class discussion.
- Give students a worksheet of the poem to write on during class discussion, possibly even with sketches (nonlinguistic representations) to help memory and understanding. Alternatively, allow them to annotate in a text document.
- Challenge students to create a movie or slide show that illustrates the literal and figurative meanings of the poem, as discussed in class, using photos of Chicago downloaded from the Internet.

Homework/Assessment
N/A

Grade 8 ▶ *Unit 2*

Rural Settings in North America: "It Happened in the Country"

This eight-week unit of eighth grade continues student reflections on the settings of stories and events—from poems and short stories to novels and nonfiction.

ESSENTIAL QUESTION

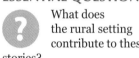 What does the rural setting contribute to these stories?

OVERVIEW

In this unit, students specifically refer back to Unit One, comparing and contrasting rural settings to urban ones. This unit expands beyond the borders of the United States into Canada and Mexico. Students examine how text structures contribute to meaning, identify and explain the characteristics of different genres, and begin writing arguments to support a point of view. This unit ends with an informative/explanatory essay response to the essential question: "What does the rural setting contribute to these stories?"

FOCUS STANDARDS

These Focus Standards have been selected for the unit from the Common Core State Standards.

RL.8.5: Compare and contrast the structure of two or more texts and analyze how the differing structure of each text contributes to its meaning and style.

RI.8.2: Determine a central idea of a text and analyze its development over the course of the text, including its relationship to supporting ideas; provide an objective summary of the text.

RI.8.7: Evaluate the advantages and disadvantages of using different mediums (e.g., print or digital text, video, multimedia) to present a particular topic or idea.

W.8.1: Write arguments to support claims with clear reasons and relevant evidence.

SL.8.1: Engage effectively in a range of collaborative discussions (one-on-one, in groups, and teacher-led) with diverse partners on grade 8 topics, texts, and issues, building on others' ideas and expressing their own clearly.

SL.8.1(c): Propel conversations by posing and responding to questions that probe reasoning and evidence; ensure a hearing for a full range of positions on a topic or issue; clarify, verify, or challenge ideas and conclusions; and promote divergent and creative perspectives.

SL.8.1(d): Respond thoughtfully to diverse perspectives; synthesize comments, claims, and evidence made on all sides of an issue; resolve contradictions when possible; and determine what additional information or research is required to deepen the investigation or complete the task.

L.8.4: Determine or clarify the meaning of unknown and multiple-meaning words or phrases based on grade 8 reading and content, choosing flexibly from a range of strategies.

L.8.4(c): Consult general and specialized reference materials (e.g., dictionaries, glossaries, thesauruses), both print and digital, to find the pronunciation of a word or determine or clarify its precise meaning or its part of speech.

L.8.4(d): Verify the preliminary determination of the meaning of a word or phrase (e.g., by checking the inferred meaning in context or in a dictionary).

SUGGESTED STUDENT OBJECTIVES

- Compare and contrast story characters, plots, themes, and settings in stories about rural North America.
- Evaluate the structure of various texts and discuss the effect of structure on their meaning.
- Write an argument, supported by clear reasons and evidence, about a memorable portrayal of rural North America.
- Recognize nuances in meaning among similar words (e.g., *rural, agrarian, agriculture, hamlet, village, country, countryside, rustic*).

SUGGESETED WORKS

(E) indicates a CCSS exemplar text; (EA) indicates a text from a writer with other works identified as exemplars.

LITERARY TEXTS

Stories

- *Travels with Charley: In Search of America* (John Steinbeck) (E)
- *This Land Was Made for You and Me: The Life and Songs of Woody Guthrie* (Elizabeth Partridge) (E)
- *The Adventures of Tom Sawyer* (Mark Twain) (E)
- *Roll of Thunder, Hear My Cry* (Mildred D. Taylor) (E)
- *The Land* (Mildred D. Taylor)
- *Of Mice and Men* (John Steinbeck)
- *The Last of the Mohicans* (James Fenimore Cooper)
- *Shane* (Jack Schaefer)
- *The Daybreakers (The Sacketts)* (Louis L'Amour)
- *Barrio Boy* (Ernesto Galarza)
- *The Incredible Journey* (Sheila Burnford)

Short Stories

(*Note:* These were also used in Unit One.)

- *Nine Stories* (J. D. Salinger)
- *The Umbrella Man and Other Stories* (Roald Dahl) (EA)
- *America Street: A Multicultural Anthology of Stories* (Anne Mazer, ed.)

Poetry

- "The Railway Train" (Emily Dickinson) (E)
- "Mending Wall" (Robert Frost) (EA)
- *Spoon River Anthology* (Edgar Lee Masters)
- *My America: A Poetry Atlas of the United States* (Lee Bennett Hopkins)

Picture Books (as an Introduction to This Unit)

- *A Mountain Alphabet* (Margriet Ruurs)
- *B is for Big Sky Country: A Montana Alphabet* (Sneed B. Collard III and Joanna Yardley)
- *P is for Piñata: A Mexico Alphabet* (Tony Johnston)

INFORMATIONAL TEXTS

Nonfiction

Rural United States

- *The Alamo* (Cornerstones of Freedom, Second Series) (Tom McGowen)
- *African-Americans in the Old West* (Cornerstones of Freedom Series) (Tom McGowen)
- *Trail of Tears* (Cornerstones of Freedom Series) (R. Conrad Stein)
- *Wild Horses I Have Known* (Hope Ryden)

American Science/Technical Subjects

- California Invasive Plant Council (Invasive Plant Inventory) (E)
- *Geeks: How Two Lost Boys Rode the Internet out of Idaho* (Jon Katz) (E)
- "The Marginal World" (1955) in *The Edge of the Sea* (Rachel Carson)

North America

- *Never Cry Wolf: The Amazing True Story of Life Among Arctic Wolves* (Farley Mowat)
- *One Hundred & One Beautiful Small Towns in Mexico* (Guillermo Garcia Oropeza and Cristobal Garcia Sanchez)

ART, MUSIC, AND MEDIA

Art

- Grant Wood, *American Gothic* (1930)
- Edward Hopper, *Gas* (1940)
- Edward Hopper, *Early Sunday Morning* (1930)
- Edward Hopper, *Cape Cod Evening* (1939)

SAMPLE ACTIVITIES AND ASSESSMENTS

1. INTRODUCTORY ACTIVITY/CLASS DISCUSSION

Your teacher will read *A Mountain Alphabet* by Margriet Ruurs or *P is for Piñata: A Mexico Alphabet* by Tony Johnston to the class. What was the author's purpose in creating this text? Contrast the way in which these authors present rural life to the way in which authors in the previous unit present urban life. What are the advantages and disadvantages to using picture books to examine setting? How is this portrayal similar to or different from information you find online? Write responses to these questions in your journal and share with a partner prior to class discussion. Consider creating your own ABC book or digital presentation while reading the stories in this unit, and you will find it can be as easy or as complex as you choose to make it. (RI.8.1, RI.8.2, RI.8.6, RI.8.7)

2. NOTE TAKING ON LITERARY ELEMENTS

As you read novels and/or short stories from this unit, take notes in your journal or on a spreadsheet about the story characters, plot, theme, and setting. As you take notes about these categories, think about how the setting affects the story, especially in comparison with the urban settings discussed in the previous unit. Be sure to note page numbers with relevant information or mark your book with sticky notes so you can cite the text during class discussion.

- Who is/are the major character(s)?
- What is the problem faced by the character(s)? How does he/she/they resolve the problem?
- What is the theme of the novel? (i.e., good vs. evil, overcoming challenges, etc.)
- What is the effect of the setting(s) on the characters?
- Is the effect of the setting stated or implied?
- What unique words and phrases are used to describe the setting(s)?

    Prior to class discussion, your teacher may give you the opportunity to share your notes with a partner who read the same text. (RL.8.1, RL.8.2, RL.8.4, RL.8.5)

3. RESEARCH PROJECT (EXTENSION)

Use the research process to research the setting for a novel that you are reading. For example, if you are reading *The Adventures of Tom Sawyer,* you can research Missouri in the 1830s and explain to the class what the area was like at that time. Paraphrase or cite from at least three sources, using the standard bibliographic format preferred by your teacher. You may want to present your findings in a multimedia format. (W.8.7)

4. CLASS DISCUSSION

Compare and contrast the settings of the various novels read in this unit; compare these works as a group with those that have urban settings (from the previous unit). Can you make any generalizations about the effect that the rural setting has on these stories? After class discussion, create a Venn diagram in your journal (or by using an online template) that outlines the similarities and differences. Post your thoughts on the classroom blog in order to continue the conversation with your classmates started in the first unit. (SL.8.1, RL.8.4)

5. INFORMATIONAL/LITERATURE TEXT RESPONSE COMPARISON

Read and compare the portrayals of Canada in *Never Cry Wolf: The Amazing True Story of Life Among Arctic Wolves* by Farley Mowat and in *The Incredible Journey* by Sheila Burnford. Develop a multimedia presentation that explores the visual similarities and differences. (RI.8.1, RI.8.2, RL.8.2, RL.8.5, L.8.1a,b, L.8.2a,b)

6. LITERARY RESPONSE

Travels with Charley is considered a "travelogue." How does the structure contribute to the meaning in a way that is different from the way poetic structures shape meaning in poetry? Talk about your ideas with a partner. Then, in your journal, describe how Steinbeck uses point of view and other literary devices to convey his thoughts and feelings about America. Cite specific examples and page numbers from the text. Your teacher may ask you to post your thoughts on the classroom blog in order to get feedback from your classmates. (RL.8.1, RL.8.2, RL.8.4, RL.8.5, RL.8.6, L.8.1a,b, L.8.2a,b)

7. INFORMATIONAL TEXT RESPONSE

What "power of nature" does Carson find in "The Marginal World"? How does the structure contribute to the meaning? Talk about your ideas with a partner. Then, in your journal or on the classroom blog, discuss the phrase "the shore has a dual nature" in your explanation and cite additional support from the text. (RI.8.1, RI.8.2, RI.8.3, RI.8.4, RI.8.5, RI.8.6, L.8.1a,b, L.8.2a,b)

8. INFORMATIVE/EXPLANATORY WRITING

Respond to this line from the poem "Mending Wall" by Robert Frost: "Good fences make good neighbors." Why does this surface contradiction make sense, not only in the context of the poem, but also in daily life? How does the structure contribute to the meaning? After discussing it as a class, write a well-developed essay, citing at least three specific examples. Edit your writing, especially for active and passive voice and the use of ellipses to indicate an omission. Share with a partner prior to class discussion. Your teacher may ask you to upload your essay to the classroom blog. (RL.8.1, RL.8.2, RL.8.4, RL.8.5, SL.8.1, SL.8.3, L.8.1a,b, L.8.2a,b)

9. POETRY ANALYSIS/RECITATION

After reading selections from *My America: A Poetry Atlas of the United States* by Lee Bennett Hopkins, select your favorite poem. How does the structure of poetry contribute to its meaning in a different way than the structure of prose does? What does the poem reveal about life in America? Write responses to these questions in your journal and share with a partner. Memorize and recite your favorite poem for your classmates. Record it using a video camera so you can evaluate your performance. (RL.8.5, SL.8.6)

10. WRITING (ARGUMENT)

What has been the most memorable portrayal of rural America that you have read? What made it memorable to you? Did your familiarity with urban settings (by contrast) help or hinder the powerful effect of the piece you chose? Write a well-developed paper that includes an engaging opening statement of your position, at least three clear reasons, and relevant evidence cited from the text. (If needed, you may conduct brief research on your rural area choice and incorporate those facts into your argument.) Edit your writing for active and passive voice and ellipses to indicate an omission. Publish your story on a class blog and request feedback on the strength of your argument from your classmates and others outside your class. (W.8.1, W.8.5, W.8.6, W.8.7, L.8.1a,b, L.8.2a,b)

11. ART AND INFORMATIVE/EXPLANATORY WRITING

How is rural life in America portrayed in Wood's famous painting *American Gothic*? Notice the symmetry of the elements in the painting and the frontality of the figures. What does this imply? Who is looking at you and who is not? Why do you believe that Wood made these choices? How does the structure of art affect meaning in ways similar to and different from writing? Write responses to these questions in your journal and share with a partner prior to class discussion. (RL.8.5, SL.8.1)

12. WORD STUDY (1)

[Continuing activity from the first unit.] Where do words come from? How does knowing their origin help us not only to spell the words, but also to understand their meaning? Add words found, learned, and used throughout this unit to your personal dictionary (e.g., *rural, agrarian, agriculture, hamlet, village, country, countryside, rustic*). This dictionary will be used all year to explore the semantics (meanings) of words and their origins. (L.8.4)

13. CLASS DISCUSSION/WORD STUDY (2)

Discuss the etymology of the word *suburban*. In your experience, what elements of urban and rural settings qualify as "suburban"? Discuss similarities and differences found in suburban settings. Your teacher may ask you to create an online concept map connecting *urban, rural, and suburban*. (SL.8.1, L.8.4)

14. INFORMATIVE/EXPLANATORY ESSAY

Write an informative/explanatory essay in response to the essential question: What does the rural setting contribute to these stories? Make sure to include words and phrases learned as part of word study, including figurative and connotative language. After your teacher reviews your first draft, work with a partner to strengthen your writing and edit it, especially for active and passive voice and for the use of ellipses to indicate an omission. Be prepared to record your essay and upload it as a podcast (or other multimedia format of your choice) on the class web page for this unit. (W.8.4, W.8.9a,b, SL.8.1, L.8.1a,b, L.8.2a,b)

15. GRAMMAR AND USAGE

Edit a newspaper article or magazine article (or a classmate's essay) by changing passive to active voice when possible. Discuss with your partner how these changes affect the tone and/or meaning of the text. (L.8.3)

16. MECHANICS/GRAMMAR WALL

As a class, continue adding to the Mechanics/Grammar bulletin board started in Unit One. Remember—once skills are taught in a mini-lesson and listed on the bulletin board, you are expected to edit your work for these elements before publication. (L.8.1, L.8.2, L.8.3)

17. MECHANICS

Your teacher will teach mini-lessons on the individual language standards. For example, your teacher will give you a set of paragraphs that do not contain commas. Working with a partner, you will insert commas when necessary. (L.8.2b)

18. VOCABULARY/WORD WALL

As a class, create a Vocabulary Word Wall bulletin board where, throughout the year, you will add and sort words as you learn them in each unit of study. (L.8.4)

19. ART/CLASS DISCUSSION

Examine the Hopper paintings. What is different in these rural works versus the urban paintings viewed in the previous unit? Do you see a source of light in Hopper's paintings? Where? Why do you think he included the elements that he did—or left certain elements out? What role do the people play in these works? (SL.8.1, SL.8.2, SL.8.4, SL.8.5)

ADDITIONAL RESOURCES

- *Exploring Setting: Constructing Character, Point of View, Atmosphere, and Theme* (This unit is geared toward grades 9–12, but may be adapted.) (ReadWriteThink) (RL.8.1)
- *Critical Media Literacy: Commercial Advertising* (ReadWriteThink) (RI.8.8)
- *Cowboys* (Discovery Channel, Discovery Education Lesson Plans Library) (RL.8.5)
- Robert Frost reads "Mending Wall"

TERMINOLOGY

Explicit textual evidence	Implicit textual evidence	Text structures
Genre	Setting	Travelogue

Grade Eight, Unit Two Sample Lesson Plan

"The Railway Train" by Emily Dickinson

In this series of two lessons, students read "The Railway Train" by Emily Dickinson, and they:

Conduct close reading of the poem (RL.8.1, RL.8.2, RL.8.4, L.8.5, SL.8.6)

Explicate the poem (RL.8.1, RL.8.2, RL.8.4, W.8.1, W.8.4, SL.8.1, SL.8.4)

Summary

Lesson I: Preparing to Write About "The Railway Train"	Lesson II: Writing About Poetry
Perform close reading of "The Railway Train" (RL.8.1, RL.8.2, RL.8.4, SL.8.6)	Revisit "The Railway Train" (RL.8.1, RL.8.2, RL.8.4, SL.8.1)
Identify new vocabulary words (RL.8.1, RL.8.4, L.8.4, L.8.5, SL.8.6)	Examine and discuss notes from Lesson I (RL.8.1, RL.8.2, RL.8.4, SL.8.1, SL.8.6)
Note the presence of alliteration (RL.8.1, RL.8.4, L.8.4, L.8.5, SL.8.1)	Explore "The Courage That My Mother Had" by Edna St. Vincent Millay (RL.8.2, SL.8.1, SL.8.4, L.8.4, L.8.5)
Examine the use of personification (RL.8.1, RL.8.4, L.8.3)	Critically examine the sample paragraph explicating "The Courage That My Mother Had" (RL.8.2, SL.8.1, SL.8.4, L.8.6)
Explore the use of metaphors in the poem (RL.8.1, RL.8.4, L.8.5)	Explicate "The Railway Train" (RL.8.1, RL.8.2, RL.8.4, W.8.1, W.8.4, SL.8.1, SL.8.4)
Look at the use of allusions (RL.8.1, RL.8.4, L.8.5)	

Lesson II: Writing About Poetry

Objectives

Revisit "The Railway Train" (RL.8.1, RL.8.2, RL.8.4, SL.8.1)

Examine and discuss notes from Lesson I (RL.8.1, RL.8.2, RL.8.4, SL.8.1, SL.8.6)

Explore "The Courage That My Mother Had" by Edna St. Vincent Millay (RL.8.2, SL.8.1, SL.8.4, L.8.4, L.8.5)

Critically examine the sample paragraph explicating "The Courage That My Mother Had" (RL.8.2, SL.8.1, SL.8.4, L.8.6)

Explicate "The Railway Train" (RL.8.1, RL.8.2, RL.8.4, W.8.1, W.8.4, SL.8.1, SL.8.4)

□ Class set of "The Railway Train," by Emily Dickinson

□ Class set of "The Courage That My Mother Had" by Edna St. Vincent Millay

□ Class set of a sample paragraph: "Explication of the First Stanza of 'The Courage That My Mother Had'"

□ Class set of writing guidelines for explicating a stanza

Procedures

1. Lead-In:

Silently reread "The Railway Train," by Emily Dickinson.

2. Step by Step:

   a. A class discussion of the findings from Lesson I follows.

   b. Students read "The Courage That My Mother Had," by Edna St. Vincent Millay*:

The Courage That My Mother Had

The courage that my mother had
Went with her, and is with her still:
Rock from New England quarried;
Now granite in a granite hill

The golden brooch my mother wore
She left behind for me to wear;
I have no thing I treasure more:
Yet, it is something I could spare.

Oh, if instead she'd left to me
The thing she took into the grave!—
That courage like a rock, which she
Has no more need of, and I have.

   c. Students read the sample paragraph:

Explication of the First Stanza of "The Courage That My Mother Had" by Edna St. Vincent Millay

In "The Courage That My Mother Had," Edna St. Vincent Millay pays tribute to her mother's courage. The first line of the poem seems to be important since it is a repetition of its title "The Courage That My Mother Had." Millay uses the past tense, suggesting that the mother is no longer around. The first three words of the second line, "Went with her," refer to the courage that she had. The active use of the verb "went" hints at an independent power that the poet attributes to her mother's courage. Millay then notes that this courage is "with her still." The use of the word *still* may suggest more than just a simple meaning that her courage is with her now. "Still" can also indicate rest, quiet, or tranquility; these available interpretations add to the reader's vision of her courage. In the next two lines, through the use of a metaphor, Millay describes her mother: "Rock from New England quarried;/ Now granite in a granite hill." These lines no longer describe the courage, but rather the mother. The use of "rock" as the metaphor depicts her strength. Millay also tells us that her mother is from New England; she says that her mother *is* the rock that is chiseled from that area. The next line is an extension of the metaphor. Her mother is not only a rock from New England, now she *is* "granite in a granite hill."

d. Students discuss the paragraph. They note the following:

The poet and poem are identified

A topic is established

A close reading, using short quotations, follows

The paragraph is deliberately developed

Simple present tense is used

3. Closure:
Distribute and explain the homework.

Differentiation

Advanced

• Prior to this lesson, select student volunteers to read the poems for classmates (on an MP3 player, below). Give the students an opportunity to practice reading dramatically, recorded with a video camera, so they can evaluate and improve upon their performances.

• Encourage students to find other examples of alliteration, personification, metaphor, and allusion used by authors.

• Encourage students to create a modern-day interpretation of one of the poems from this unit. They must be able to justify how the modern version stays true to the original while also changing style. Perhaps challenge them to create a movie.

Struggling

• Read the poems to the students or allow them to listen (or re-listen) to prerecorded versions.

• Give students paper copies of the poems that they can write on, possibly even with sketches (nonlinguistic representations) to help memory and understanding. Students can circle vocabulary words and highlight examples of alliteration, personification, metaphor, and allusion. Alternatively, allow them to annotate in a text document. Perhaps pre-create a key for this to facilitate student work.

• Lead a small group discussion about why authors use the techniques of alliteration, personification, metaphor, and allusion.

• Distribute a paper copy of the "'Explication of the First Stanza of 'The Courage That My Mother Had'" so they can highlight or mark *where*:

• The poet and poem are identified

• The topic is established

• The paragraph is deliberately developed

• The simple present tense is used

Alternatively, students can do this in a text document using highlighting and comments features. After analyzing this explication, allow some students to begin homework while you read and start the homework with other students.

Homework/Assessment

In a well-organized paragraph, explicate a stanza of your choice from "The Railway Train" by Emily Dickinson.

Writing Guidelines

Clearly establish the topic of the paragraph and contextualize it.

Organize the sequence of ideas according to the purpose of the paragraph.

Present a clear, thorough, explication of the stanza of your choice.

Cite the text using short quotes that are integrated into your narrative.

Avoid grammatical errors.

Use present simple tense.

Grade 8 ▶ *Unit 3*

Looking Back on America

This eight-week unit of eighth grade continues with reflections on the settings of stories and events, this time from a historical perspective.

OVERVIEW

Students read works of historical fiction and discuss how authors' perspectives might produce accounts of historical events that differ from what we know happened. Students work collaboratively to reconcile different authors' points of view and discuss why these differences occur. Students read "Paul Revere's Ride" by Henry Wadsworth Longfellow and study the actual events of that night to consider the effect that poetry can have on historical memory. An in-depth research project accompanied by a multimedia presentation is a highlight of this unit, because these creative processes integrate essential skills and meaningful content. This unit ends with an informative/explanatory essay in response to the essential question.

FOCUS STANDARDS

These Focus Standards have been selected for the unit from the Common Core State Standards.

RL.8.9: Analyze how a modern work of fiction draws on themes, patterns of events, or character types from myths, traditional stories, or religious works such as the Bible, including describing how the material is rendered new.

RI.8.3: Analyze how a text makes connections among and distinctions between individuals, ideas, or events (e.g., through comparisons, analogies, or categories).

RI.8.9: Analyze a case in which two or more texts provide conflicting information on the same topic and identify where the texts disagree on matters of fact or interpretation.

W.8.7: Conduct short research projects to answer a question (including a self-generated question), drawing on several sources and generating additional related, focused questions that allow for multiple avenues of exploration.

SL.8.5: Integrate multimedia and visual displays into presentations to clarify information, strengthen claims and evidence, and add interest.

L.8.3: Use knowledge of language and its conventions when writing, speaking, reading, or listening.

SUGGESTED STUDENT OBJECTIVES

- Compare and contrast story characters, plots, themes, and settings from stories about American history.
- Analyze how historical fiction draws on themes, patterns of events, or character types from myths or traditional stories.
- Determine the author's point of view in two texts about the same topic and discuss the effect it has on the work.
- Conduct an in-depth research project on a historical event of choice, followed by a multimedia report that includes insights from historical fiction.

SUGGESTED WORKS

(E) indicates a CCSS exemplar text; (EA) indicates a text from a writer with other works identified as exemplars.

LITERARY TEXTS

Stories

- *Cast Two Shadows: The American Revolution in the South* (Great Episodes) (Ann Rinaldi)
- *Johnny Tremain* (Esther Forbes)
- *Code Talker: A Novel About the Navajo Marines of World War Two* (Joseph Bruchac)
- *The Year of the Hangman* (Gary Blackwood)

Poetry

- "Paul Revere's Ride" (Henry Wadsworth Longfellow) (E)
- "I, Too, Sing America" (Langston Hughes) (E)
- "I Know Why the Caged Bird Sings" (Maya Angelou)
- *Hour of Freedom: American History in Poetry* (Milton Meltzer)

INFORMATIONAL TEXTS

Nonfiction

- Preamble to the United States Constitution (1787) (E)
- First Amendment to the United States Constitution (1791) (E)
- 1812, February 3: Adams to Jefferson (John Adams) (E)
- *The Words We Live By: Your Annotated Guide to the Constitution* (Linda R. Monk) (E)
- *Freedom Walkers: The Story of the Montgomery Bus Boycott* (Russell Freedman) (E)
- *The American Revolutionaries: A History in Their Own Words 1750–1800* (Milton Meltzer)

- Paul Revere's Ride (David Hackett Fischer)
- *Lincoln: A Photobiography* (Russell Freedman)
- *We Shall Not Be Moved: The Women's Factory Strike of 1909* (Joan Dash)
- *Day of Infamy, 60th Anniversary: The Classic Account of the Bombing of Pearl Harbor* (Walter Lord) (EA)
- *George vs. George: The American Revolution As Seen from Both Sides* (Rosalyn Schanzer)
- *Good Women of a Well-Blessed Land: Women's Lives in Colonial America* (Brandon Marie Miller)
- *The Boys' War: Confederate and Union Soldiers Talk About the Civil War* (Jim Murphy) (EA)

Biographies

- *George Washington, Spymaster: How the Americans Outspied the British and Won the Revolutionary War* (Thomas B. Allen)
- *Tell All the Children Our Story: Memories and Mementos of Being Young and Black in America* (Tonya Bolden)
- *America's Paul Revere* (Esther Forbes and Lynd Ward)

Picture Books (as an Introduction to This Unit)

- *We the People* (Peter Spier)

ART, MUSIC, AND MEDIA

Art

- Grant Wood, *The Midnight Ride* (1931)
- Emanuel Leutze, *Washington Crossing the Delaware* (1851)
- John Trumbell, *Declaration of Independence* (1819)
- James Rosenquist, *F-111* (1933)
- Robert Rauschenberg, *Retroactive 1* (1964)

SAMPLE ACTIVITIES AND ASSESSMENTS

1. LITERARY GRAPHIC ORGANIZER

As you read historical fiction from this unit, take notes in your journal or on a spreadsheet about the characters, plot, themes, patterns of events, and setting. As you take notes about these categories, continue to think about how the historical setting affects the story. Be sure to note page numbers with relevant information or mark your text with sticky notes so you can cite the text during class discussion.

- Who is/are the major character(s)?
- Do they remind you of any character types from myths or other traditional stories? How?
- What is the problem faced by the character(s)? How does he/she/they resolve the problem?
- What is the theme of the novel? (i.e., good vs. evil, overcoming challenges, etc.)
- What is the effect of the historical setting(s) on the characters, plot, or theme?
- Are there any recognizable patterns of events? What are they, and what do they remind you of?

    Prior to class discussion, your teacher may give you the opportunity to share your notes with a partner who read the same text. (RL.8.1, RL.8.2, RL.8.5, RL.8.9)

2. CLASS DISCUSSION

Compare and contrast the effect of historical settings on characters, plots, and themes in the various novels read. Can you make any generalizations about the effect historical setting has on these stories? After class discussion, create a Venn diagram in your journal (or in an online template) that outlines the similarities and differences among the settings, characters, plots, and/or themes. Post your thoughts on the classroom blog in order to continue the conversation with your classmates. (SL.8.1, RL.8.9)

3. CLASS DISCUSSION AND INFORMATIONAL TEXT RESPONSE

Read the Preamble to the United States Constitution silently and reread it with the class. As a class, discuss how new the idea of freedom described in the Preamble was at the time it was written. Then, in small groups:

- Discuss why you think the framers included a Preamble for the Constitution
- Note the words that are new to you (perhaps *ordain, tranquility,* or *posterity*) and discuss what you think they mean
- Confirm the meanings of the words by using a dictionary
- Discuss how carefully you think the framers of the Constitution chose these words
- (On chart paper) work together to diagram the sentence.
- Note the multiple verbs and their direct objects
- What kind of phrase is the introductory phrase?

  For homework, memorize the Preamble and be prepared to recite it for fellow classmates. (RI.8.1, RI.8.2, RI.8.4, RI.8.7, RI.8.9, W.8.2, L.8.1, L.8.3, SL.8.6)

4. INFORMATIVE/EXPLANATORY WRITING

Read John Adams's letter to Thomas Jefferson of February 3, 1812, and note the translation of the Latin phrase he includes. Discuss in small groups:

- Whether you think Adams believes the new union will survive
- On what does Adams think the preservation of the union depends?

  Reconvene as a class to discuss the small groups' opinions. For homework, write a one- to three-paragraph argument in which you discuss your opinion on whether Adams thinks the new nation will survive. (*Note:* Another letter or excerpt may be used at teacher's discretion. See the Additional Resources section for a link to more options.) (RI.8.2, RI.8.4, RI.8.6, W.8.1, SL.8.1)

5. INFORMATIVE/EXPLANATORY WRITING

Compare the two sides of the American Revolution as presented in *George vs. George: The American Revolution As Seen from Both Sides* by Rosalyn Schanzer. In your journal, describe how events are perceived differently depending on your point of view. What specific lines or incidents in the book helped you to learn more about the revolution? Then, write a well-developed paper, citing at least three specific examples from the text that answers this question. Edit your writing for form and use of verbs in the indicative, imperative, interrogative, conditional, and subjunctive moods, as well as for spelling. (RL.8.1, RL.8.2, RL.8.3, RL.8.6, L.8.1, L.8.2, L.8.3)

6. POETRY RESPONSE/CLASS DISCUSSION

Respond to this line from the poem "Paul Revere's Ride" by Henry Wadsworth Longfellow: "The fate of a nation was riding that night." What is the literal versus figurative meaning of this line? Discuss how literature can give a different view of history than informational texts. Why are we so drawn to poetry? Write responses to these questions in your journal and share with a partner prior to class discussion. (RL.8.1, RL.8.2, RL.8.4, RL.8.5, SL.8.1, SL.8.3, L.8.3)

7. DRAMATIZATION/FLUENCY

After reading "I Know Why the Caged Bird Sings" by Maya Angelou, discuss the meaning of this poem as it relates to life in America. How does the structure of poetry contribute to its meaning in a different manner than prose? Does the caged bird remind you of any character types from other stories read? Decide how to share lines or stanzas with a classmate, and perform a dramatic reading of this poem for your classmates. Record your performance using a video camera so you can evaluate your performance. (RL.8.5, RL.8.9, SL.8.6, L.8.3)

8. RESEARCH, INFORMATIVE/EXPLANATORY WRITING, AND MULTIMEDIA PRESENTATION

Focusing on the connections among individuals, ideas, and events, choose an event from America's past to research. In order to find multiple perspectives on the event, draw on several sources, including a variety of literary, informational, primary, secondary, and multimedia texts. Write an informative/explanatory essay and, as you draft your essay, work with classmates to strengthen its quality. Be sure to cite your sources accurately using the standard bibliographic format preferred by your teacher. Prior to publishing, integrate multimedia and/or visual displays into your report to clarify information and strengthen your claims with evidence. Edit your writing for form and use of verbs in the indicative, imperative, interrogative, conditional, and subjunctive moods, as well as for spelling and punctuation when paraphrasing and including direct quotations. Present your report to the class and upload it to a class web page for this unit. (RL.8.6, RI.8.3, RI.8.6, RI.8.7, RI.8.8, W.8.2, W.8.5, W.8.6, W.8.7, SL.8.4, SL.8.5, L.8.1a,b,c; L.8.2, L.8.3)

9. ART/CLASS DISCUSSION

Before the advent of photography, painters would document, interpret, and record important events in paintings. The artists who created these works were not usually present during the event they depicted. View the works by Wood, Leutze, and Trumbell. What did each of these artists record? To what extent do the artists seem to be trying to document the event literally, or to capture its essence? How do works such as these help us to appreciate the events they depict? (SL.8.1, SL.8.2, SL.8.4, SL.8.5)

10. ART/CLASS DISCUSSION

View Rauschenberg's and Rosenquist's works. Can you tell which events both artists wanted to highlight? Do you believe there is any social commentary present in these works? How are these different from documentary works, like the first three examined? (SL.8.1, SL.8.2, SL.8.4, SL.8.5)

11. WORD STUDY

[Continuing the activity from the second unit.] Add the words we've found, learned, and used throughout this unit to your personal dictionary (e.g., from "Paul Revere's Ride": *moorings, muster, barrack, grenadiers, belfry,* and *encampment*). This dictionary will be used all year long to explore the semantics (meanings) of words and their origins. (L.8.4)

12. INFORMATIVE/EXPLANATORY WRITING

Write an informative/explanatory essay in response to the essential question: How does learning history through literature differ from learning through informational text? Make sure to include words and phrases you have learned as part of word study, including figurative and connotative language, and refer to literature and informational texts you have read. After your teacher reviews your first draft, work with a partner to strengthen your writing and edit it for the use of verbs in the indicative, imperative, interrogative, conditional, and subjunctive moods, as well as for spelling. Be prepared to record your essay and upload it as a podcast, or other multimedia format of your choice, on the class web page for this unit. (W.8.4, W.8.9a,b, SL.8.1, SL.8.4, L.8.1, L.8.2, L.8.3)

13. GRAMMAR AND USAGE

Your teacher will teach mini-lessons on the individual language standards. For example, he/she will teach the class about verbs in the (a) indicative, (b) imperative, (c) interrogative, (d) conditional, and (e) subjunctive mood, and you will alter a given sentence so that each new sentence exemplifies the use of each mood. For example,

a. I want to be an astronaut.
b. Be an astronaut!
c. Do you want to be an astronaut?
d. If you don't like science, you might not like being an astronaut.
e. If I were you, I would become an astronaut.

Select a piece of your own writing, find the verbs and identify whether they are in the indicative, imperative, interrogative, conditional, or subjunctive mood. (L.8.1c)

14. MECHANICS/GRAMMAR WALL

As a class, continue adding to the Mechanics/Grammar bulletin board started in Unit One. Remember—once skills are taught in a mini-lesson and listed on the bulletin board, you are expected to edit your work for these elements before publication. (L.8.1, L.8.2, L.8.3)

15. VOCABULARY/WORD WALL

As a class, create a Vocabulary Word Wall bulletin board where, throughout the year, you will add and sort words as you learn them in each unit of study. (L.8.4)

ADDITIONAL RESOURCES

- *The Real Midnight Ride* (KidsandHistory.Com) (RI.8.9)
- *Pocahontas Married John Rolfe on This Date in 1614* (ReadWriteThink) (RI.8.9)
- *Battling for Liberty: Tecumseh's and Patrick Henry's Language of Resistance* (ReadWriteThink) (SL.8.3)
- *It's Independence Day! Or is it?* (ReadWriteThink) (W.8.7)
- *The History Behind Song Lyrics* (ReadWriteThink) (RI.8.7)
- *Esther Forbes, Author of* Johnny Tremain, *Was Born in 1891* (ReadWriteThink) (W.8.3)
- *Picturing America: Grant Wood's* Midnight Ride of Paul Revere, *1931* (National Endowment for the Humanities)
- *The Paul Revere House* (Paul Revere Memorial Association)
- *The True Story of Paul Revere's Ride* (Archiving Early America)

- *15 Historical Events that Fascinate Us* (Frikoo.Com)
- *From the Correspondence of John Adams and Thomas Jefferson* (National Humanities Center)
- http://www.education.ne.gov/SS/DOCUMENTS/PreambleChoralReading.doc

TERMINOLOGY

Character types	Patterns of events	Preconceived notion
Historical fiction	Point of view	

Grade Eight, Unit Three Sample Lesson Plan

Preamble and First Amendment to the Constitution of the United States

In this interdisciplinary series of seven lessons, students read the Preamble and the First Amendment to the Constitution of the United States, and they:

Explore the historical origins of the Constitution and the Bill of Rights (RI. 8.2, SL.8.1b,c, SL.8.2, SL.8.4)

Familiarize themselves with the Constitutional Convention and its delegates (RI.8.1, RI.8.3, RI.8.6)

Examine the content of the Preamble to the Constitution (RI.8.2, RI.8.4, RI.8.5, SL.8.1b,c, SL.8.2, SL.8.4)

Assess the importance of the First Amendment to the Constitution (RI.8.2, RI.8.5, SL.8.1, SL.8.4)

Debate a First Amendment case (SL.8.1, SL.8.4)

Reflect on and understand the importance of the First Amendment (W.8.2)

Summary

Lesson I: Historical Background to the Constitutional Convention	Lesson II: The Constitutional Convention
Revisit the Declaration of Independence	Identify the principal founding fathers – the architects of the Constitution
Recall the emergence of the Articles of Confederation	Explore (select excerpts from) "Notes of Debates in the Federal Convention of 1787" by James Madison (RI.8.1, RI.8.3, RI.8.6)
Explore the criticism of the Articles of Confederation	Examine the philosophical points of view among the founders (RI.8.6)
	Evaluate the contribution of the debates to the drafting of the Constitution (SL.8.1b,c, SL.8.2, SL.8.4)

Lesson III: The Preamble to the Constitution

Consider the historical significance of the words: "We the people of the United States ..." (RI.8.2)

Identify the declared purpose of the document ("in order ...") (RI.8.2)

Note the goals for the republic enumerated in the preamble (RI.8.4)

Evaluate the impact of a single sentence — the Preamble to the Constitution — on the new nation (RI.8.2, RI.8.4, RI.8.5, SL.8.1b,c, SL.8.2, SL.8.4)

Lesson IV: The Origins of the Bill of Rights

Identify the historical origins of the Bill of Rights

Consider the historical impact of the following words: "A bill of rights is what the people are entitled to against every government on earth, general or particular; and what no just government should refuse, or rest on inferences." (Thomas Jefferson to James Madison, 1787) (RI.8.2, SL.8.1b,c, SL.8.2, SL.8.4)

Lesson V: The First Amendment

Evaluate the impact of Thomas Jefferson's words regarding the First Amendment: "I do not like ... the omission of a bill of rights providing clearly and without the aid of sophisms for freedom of religion, freedom of the press ..." (RI.8.2)

Closely examine the rights guaranteed in the First Amendment (RI.8.2, RI.8.5)

Identify the impact of the First Amendment on the individual in American society (SL.8.1, SL.8.4)

Lesson VI: Preparing to Debate the Case of Judge Roy Moore

Identify the facts in the 2003 case of Roy Moore, Chief Justice of the Supreme Court of Alabama

Prepare to support or oppose Judge Moore's decision to install a monument of the Ten Commandments in the rotunda of Alabama's state judicial building (W.8.1, W.8.2)

Examine the role that the First Amendment plays in the position of both sides

Lesson VII: The First Amendment in Action—Debating the Case of Judge Roy Moore

Debate the case of Judge Moore (SL.8.1, SL.8.4)

Discuss the merits of debates in a democratic society (SL.8.1a, SL.8.7.1b)

Reflect on and understand the importance of the First Amendment (W.8.2)

Lesson VI: Preparing to Debate the Case of Judge Roy Moore

Objectives

Identify the facts in the 2003 case of Roy Moore, Chief Justice of the Supreme Court of Alabama

Prepare to support or oppose Judge Moore's decision to install a monument of the Ten Commandments in the rotunda of Alabama's state judicial building (W.8.1, W.8.2)

Examine the role that the First Amendment plays in the position of both sides

Required Materials

☐ Handouts relating the details of Judge Moore's case

☐ Access to the Internet

Procedures

1. Lead-In:
   Students will learn about the 2003 case involving Judge Roy Moore of Alabama. (Either offer a brief lecture here, introducing the basic facts, or distribute a handout providing details of the case.)

2. Step by Step:
   a. Students will split into two groups: one group will gather material that will defend Judge Moore's position, while the other side will gather material to oppose his actions.
   b. Students will break into three subgroups (six in total).
   c. Each of the subgroups will be responsible for a single argument and three facts in support of that argument.

3. Closure:
   Once students complete the research, each side will produce a three-page document that presents and defends its views. The position papers will include: (1) an introductory paragraph that declares their positions, (2) arguments and supporting facts, and (3) a conclusion that recaps the role that the First Amendment plays in American society. Students should incorporate simple visual aids as necessary to help support their claims.

Differentiation

Advanced

- Pre-assess (all) students for their knowledge of the case of Judge Roy Moore. If students are already familiar with the case, have them find additional materials to help deepen their understanding of the case (e.g., reading the Constitution of the State of Alabama, Judge Roy Moore's book, *So Help Me God: The Ten Commandments, Judicial Tyranny, and the Battle for Religious Freedom*, or news coverage of the case from a variety of perspectives).

- Students can share what they learned about the case with students in different classes and create an online poll to see how the community feels about this case and its outcome (e.g., using Internet tools).

Struggling

- Pre-assess (all) students for their knowledge of the case of Judge Roy Moore. Consider pre-teaching key ideas to students on the day prior (for example, giving them the handout of the lecture to read).
- Read the Preamble to the Constitution as a Reader's Theater where each line is amplified. Discuss the meaning of the amplification in addition to practice reading fluently. (See Additional Resources.)
- Work with a small group to collaboratively outline the facts of the case, and then divide into two groups to choose a position to defend. Groups write the introductory paragraph together on a shared online document or using a digital projector. As partners research facts to support their argument, they can refer back to the initial paragraph to ensure the facts support the introduction.

Homework/Assessment

N/A

Lesson VII: The First Amendment in Action—Debating the Case of Judge Roy Moore

Objectives

Debate the case of Judge Moore (SL.8.1, SL.8.4)

Discuss the merits of debates in a democratic society (SL.8.1a, SL.8.7.1b)

Reflect on and understand the importance of the First Amendment (W.8.2)

Required Materials

- ☐ Handouts relating the details of Judge Moore's case
- ☐ Position papers

Procedures

1. Lead-In:
   Prepare for debate.
2. Step by Step:
   a. Student volunteers read the position papers.
   b. During the presentations, students take notes in order to prepare rebuttals to the other side's point of view.
   c. In groups, students prepare to discuss the positions of the case based on the notes they have just taken.
   d. A debate follows.
3. Closure:
   Reflective discussion gives students the opportunity to consider the merits of debate and the importance of supporting a position with evidence.

Differentiation

Advanced

- Students can share what they learned about the case with students in different classes, and create an online poll to see how the community (the rest of the grade level, other students in the school) feels about this case and its outcome (e.g., using Internet tools).

Struggling

- During position paper presentations, provide students with a graphic organizer (T-chart) upon which to note the facts that support opposing positions of the case.
- Before students write their reflective essays, facilitate a small-group discussion so students can talk through the analysis of the debate, make connections to the First Amendment, and outline their ideas on index cards, sticky notes, or in a shared spreadsheet.

Homework/Assessment

Students write a brief (two pages long) reflective essay discussing the debate and emphasizing the importance of the First Amendment. Their essays must:

- Have an introduction that includes a thesis statement
- Contain an analysis — not a summary — of the debate
- Cite specific examples from the debate
- Follow a logical, step-by-step progression of the thesis
- Use Standard English grammar

Grade 8 ▶ *Unit 4*

Authors and Artists

This fourth four-week unit of eighth grade examines the similarities and differences between literary authors and artists.

ESSENTIAL QUESTION

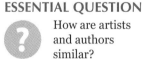

How are artists and authors similar?

OVERVIEW

In this unit, students step back and consider the motivations of authors and artists alike: What inspires artists? Are their inspirations similar or different? How is the process of creating a painting or sculpture similar to and different from the process of writing a story or poem? Students read books written about artists and study artwork found in museums across America. Students work with classmates to discern the unspoken meaning in literature and art. Students also discuss illustrations and other forms of commercial art, looking for differences and similarities in fine and commercial art, in terms of both its motivation and its presentation. They write an informative/explanatory essay about an artist of interest. The unit ends with an informative/explanatory essay in response to the essential question.

FOCUS STANDARDS

These Focus Standards have been selected for the unit from the Common Core State Standards.

RL.8.2: Determine a theme or central idea of a text and analyze its development over the course of the text, including its relationship to the characters, setting, and plot; provide an objective summary of the text.

RI.8.5: Analyze in detail the structure of a specific paragraph in a text, including the role of particular sentences in developing and refining a key concept.

RI.8.8: Delineate and evaluate the argument and specific claims in a text, assessing whether the reasoning is sound and the evidence is relevant and sufficient; recognize when irrelevant evidence is introduced.

W.8.2: Write informative/explanatory texts to examine a topic and convey ideas, concepts, and information through the selection, organization, and analysis of relevant content.

SL.8.2: Analyze the purpose of information presented in diverse media and formats (e.g., visually, quantitatively, orally) and evaluate the motives (e.g., social, commercial, political) behind its presentation.

L.8.5: Demonstrate understanding of figurative language, word relationships, and nuances in word meanings.

L.8.5(b): Use the relationship between particular words to better understand each of the words.

L.8.5(c): Distinguish among the connotations (associations) of words with similar denotations (definitions) (e.g., *bullheaded, willful, firm, persistent, resolute*).

SUGGESTED STUDENT OBJECTIVES

- Determine an author's point of view in a text, compare it with an artist's perspective in a work of art, and discuss the effect that perspective has on the work.
- Compare and contrast authors' and artists' motivations for creativity.
- Conduct research on an artist of choice; define and refine a research question as research proceeds.
- Determine the meaning of words and phrases as they are used to describe authors and artists, including figurative and technical vocabulary.

SUGGESTED WORKS

(E) indicates a CCSS exemplar text; (EA) indicates a text from a writer with other works identified as exemplars.

LITERARY TEXTS

Stories

- *From the Mixed-Up Files of Mrs. Basil E. Frankweiler* (E. L. Konigsburg)
- *Leaving Eldorado* (Joann Mazzio)
- *Talking With Tebe: Clementine Hunter, Memory Artist* (Mary E. Lyons)
- *A Portrait of the Artist as a Young Man* (James Joyce)

Poetry

- *Is This Forever, or What? Poems & Paintings from Texas* (Naomi Shihab Nye)

INFORMATIONAL TEXTS

Nonfiction

- *A Short Walk Around the Pyramids & Through the World of Art* (Philip M. Isaacson) (E)
- *Smithsonian Q&A: American Art and Artists—The Ultimate Question and Answer Book* (Tricia Wright)

Biography

- *Vincent van Gogh: Portrait of an Artist* (Jan Greenberg and Sandra Jordan) (E)
- *Norman Rockwell: Storyteller with a Brush* (Beverly Gherman)
- *Sparky: The Life and Art of Charles Schulz* (Beverly Gherman)
- *Andy Warhol, Prince of Pop* (Jan Greenberg and Sandra Jordan)

- *A Caldecott Celebration: Seven Artists and their Paths to the Caldecott Medal* (Leonard S. Marcus)
- *Marc Chagall* (Artists in Their Time Series) (Jude Welton)
- *Mary Cassatt: Portrait of an American Impressionist* (Tom Streissguth)
- *Artist to Artist: 23 Major Illustrators Talk to Children About Their Art* (Eric Carle, Mitsumasa Anno, and Quentin Blake)
- *Vincent van Gogh: Sunflowers and Swirly Stars* (Smart About Art Series) (Brad Bucks and Joan Holub)
- *Henri Matisse: Drawing with Scissors* (Smart About Art Series) (Jane O'Connor and Keesia Johnson)
- *Pablo Picasso: Breaking All the Rules* (Smart About Art Series) (True Kelley)
- *The Lives of the Artists* (Giorgio Vasari) (excerpt on Michelangelo or Leonardo)
- *Maya Angelou* (Just the Facts Biographies) (L. Patricia Kite)
- *Invincible Louisa: The Story of the Author of Little Women* (Cornelia Meigs)
- *Margaret Wise Brown: Awakened by the Moon* (Leonard S. Marcus)
- *Mark Twain* (Just the Facts Biographies) (Susan Bivin Aller)
- *Bram Stoker: The Man Who Wrote Dracula* (Great Life Stories) (Steven Otfinoski)
- *Aung San Suu Kyi: Fearless Voice of Burma* (Whitney Stewart)

Pictorial History

- *Buffalo Hunt* (Russell Freedman) (EA)
- *The Buffalo and the Indians: A Shared Destiny* (Dorothy Hinshaw Patent)

Picture Books (as an Introduction to This Unit)

- *Museum ABC* (The Metropolitan Museum of Art)
- *Museum Shapes* (The Metropolitan Museum of Art)

ART, MUSIC, AND MEDIA

Art

- Édouard Manet, *Dead Toreador* (1864)
- Andrea Mantegna, *Lamentation over the Dead Christ* (1480)
- Michelangelo Merisi da Caravaggio, *Supper at Emmaus* (1601)
- Paul Cézanne, *The Card Players* (1890–1892)
- Paolo Uccello, *Niccolo Mauruzi da Tolentino at the Battle of San Romano* (1438–1440)
- Hieronymus Bosch, *The Garden of Earthly Delights* (1503–1504)
- Chuck Close, *Fanny/Fingerpainting* (1985)
- Sylvia Plimack Mangold, *The Linden Tree* (1988)

SAMPLE ACTIVITIES AND ASSESSMENTS

1. INTRODUCTORY ACTIVITY/CLASS DISCUSSION

Read *Museum ABC* or *Museum Shapes* with the class. What is the author's purpose in creating these texts? How do these books provide a different way of looking at art and artists? How is this presentation similar to or different from information you find online? Consider creating, as a class, an ABC book or digital presentation about the art and artists studied in this unit. (RI.8.1, RI.8.6, RI.8.7)

2. ART/CLASS DISCUSSION

Examine and discuss the variety of perspectives used by the artists in the artworks (e.g., worm's-eye view, sitting at the table, far away, or up close). Identify the perspective in each work. How does the perspective affect the viewer's relationship to the work? For instance, in the works by Caravaggio and Cézanne, does it seem as if there is a spot left for the viewer at the table? How does this differ from the perspective in Bosch's work? What about Close's? How do these artists use perspective to draw viewers in? Write responses to these questions in your journal and share with a partner prior to class discussion. Discuss how this compares to authors' use of perspective in the characters they create. (SL.8.1, W.8.1, W.8.2)

3. NOTE TAKING ON BIOGRAPHIES

As you read biographies of authors and artists, take notes in your journal or on a spreadsheet about the creator's motivation for creativity. As you take notes about these categories, think about the similarities and differences between authors and artists. Be sure to note page numbers with relevant information so you can go back and cite the text during class discussion.

- Who is the focus of the biography?
- When did the author or artist first know that he/she was a creative person?
- How did the time in which the author or artist lived, or his/her physical location (i.e., urban or rural), affect his/her work?
- What unique words and phrases are used to describe the artist?

    Prior to class discussion, your teacher may give you the opportunity to share your notes with a partner who read the same text. (RI.8.1, RI.8.2, RI.8.3, RI.8.8, RL.8.1, RL.8.2, RL.8.3, RL.8.4)

4. CLASS DISCUSSION

Compare and contrast the lives of authors and artists using the information from your notes. Can you make any generalizations about how authors and artists are similar? What are they? After class discussion, create a Venn diagram in your journal or in an online template that outlines the similarities and differences among the lives of the artists. Post your thoughts on the classroom blog in order to continue the conversation with your classmates. (SL.8.1, RL.8.4)

5. RESEARCH PROJECT/BIO-POEM

Read a variety of informational texts, in print and online, about authors and artists, and choose one that interests you. Write a bio-poem about this person that includes important facts you think your classmates should know. Include audio or visual displays in your presentation, such as digital slides or a movie, as appropriate. Before turning in your poem, edit your writing for the grammar conventions studied so far this year. (RI.8.1, RI.8.8, RI.8.9, W.8.7, L.8.1a,b,c; L.8.2, L.8.3)

6. RESEARCH AND INFORMATIVE/EXPLANATORY WRITING

Look at the websites listed earlier and read through *A Short Walk Around the Pyramids & Through the World of Art* by Philip M. Isaacson in order to select an artist whose work you enjoy. Choose at least two different biographies about this artist to read. As you read the biographies, determine the figurative, connotative, and technical meanings of words and phrases as they are used to describe the artist and his/her work. Supplement this reading with additional research about the artist, his/her artistic style, preferred subjects, and where his/her art is exhibited. Possibly try to arrange a web interview with the artist. Work with classmates to strengthen your writing through planning, revising, and editing your essay. Edit your writing for the grammar conventions studied so far this year. Your teacher may give you the option of adding a multimedia component to your research report—either by creating a digital slide presentation to highlight key points, or by reading your essay set to music and images from your country of choice. Present both to the class. (RI.8.1, RI.8.2, RI.8.3, RI.8.4, RI.8.5, RI.8.8, W.8.2, W.8.5, W.8.6, W.8.7, L.8.1a,b,c; L.8.2, L.8.3)

7. INFORMATIVE/EXPLANATORY WRITING

Read and compare the use of humor in *From the Mixed-Up Files of Mrs. Basil E. Frankweiler* by E. L. Konigsburg to the use of humor in *Vincent Van Gogh: Sunflowers and Swirly Stars* by Brad Bucks and Joan Holub. How does the use of humor engage the reader? How do artists use humor in their art to engage the observer? Write a well-developed response to these questions, citing at least three specific examples from the texts. Share with a partner prior to class discussion. Edit your writing for the grammar conventions studied so far this year. (RI.8.1, RI.8.2, RI.8.3, RI.8.5, RL.8.2, RL.8.6, L.8.1a,b,c; L.8.2, L.8.3)

8. INFORMATIVE/EXPLANATORY WRITING

From the Mixed-Up Files of Mrs. Basil E. Frankweiler takes place in an art museum. How does the setting contribute to this story? Why? How are the characters' motivations (Claudia, Jamie, Mrs. Frankweiler) similar and different? Write a well-developed response to these questions, citing at least three specific examples from the text. Edit your writing for the grammar conventions studied so far this year. Share with a partner prior to class discussion. Enter your response on the classroom blog to encourage additional dialogue about this topic with your classmates. (RL.8.1, RL.8.2, RL.8.6, L.8.1a,b,c; L.8.2, L.8.3)

9. LITERARY RESPONSE

How do Maude's circumstances in *Leaving Eldorado* by Joann Mazzio hinder her dreams of becoming an artist? How do these circumstances motivate her? Does this story remind you of others read? Why? Write responses to these questions in your journal or on the classroom blog, citing specific examples and page numbers from the text. (RL.8.1, RL.8.6, RL.8.9)

10. LITERARY RESPONSE

How does James Joyce's stream-of-consciousness style in *A Portrait of the Artist as a Young Man* help you understand the character's motivations? Write responses to these questions in your journal, citing specific examples and page numbers from the text. (RL.8.1, RL.8.6, RL.8.9)

11. CLASS DISCUSSION

Look at a variety of art: fine art, illustrations, ads, pictorial histories, and so on. Evaluate the motives (e.g., social, commercial, or political) behind each presentation. How does the motivation affect the message? Why? Write responses to these questions in your journal and share with a partner prior to class discussion. Your teacher may ask you to upload images of the art onto a shared spreadsheet. Each class member will add either audio or text that articulates his/her thoughts regarding the artist's motivation. (SL.8.1, SL.8.2)

12. RECITATION/FLUENCY

After reading selections from *Is This Forever, or What? Poems & Paintings from Texas* by Naomi Shihab Nye, select your favorite poem. How does the structure of the poem selected contribute to its meaning and style? How does the point of view of the author create effects such as suspense or humor?

Share your insights with a partner and then recite your favorite poem for your classmates. Record your performance using a video camera so you can evaluate it. (RL.8.5, SL.8.6)

13. WORD STUDY

[Continuing activity from the third unit.] Add words found, learned, and used throughout this unit to your personal dictionary (e.g., from *From the Mixed-Up Files of Mrs. Basil E. Frankweiler: inconspicuous, impostor,* and *stowaway;* elements of art and principles of design: color, line, proportion, shape, space, unity, balance, form, texture, and rhythm). This unit focuses on distinguishing among the connotations of these words as they are used by artists. This dictionary will be used all year long to explore the semantics (meanings) of words and their origins. (L.8.4, L.8.5b,c)

14. ART/CLASS DISCUSSION

If the elements and principles of art and design are the building blocks for artists, what are the building blocks for writers? Write responses to these questions in your journal and share with a partner prior to class discussion. Be prepared to defend your position with examples. Your teacher may invite you and your classmates to discuss the question on the classroom blog. (SL.8.1, SL.8.4)

15. INFORMATIVE/EXPLANATORY WRITING

As you reflect on everything read, written, and discussed in this unit, write an informative/explanatory essay in response to the essential question: How are artists and authors similar? Make sure to include words and phrases learned as part of word study, including connotative language. After your teacher reviews your first draft, work with a partner to strengthen your writing and edit it for the grammar conventions studied so far this year. Be prepared to record your essay and upload it as a podcast or other multimedia format on the class web page for this unit. (W.8.4, W.8.9a,b, SL.8.1, L.8.1a,b,c; L.8.2, L.8.3, L.8.5b,c)

16. MECHANICS/GRAMMAR WALL

As a class, continue adding to the Mechanics/Grammar bulletin board started in Unit One. Remember—once skills are taught in a mini-lesson and listed on the bulletin board, you are expected to edit your work for these elements before publication. (L.8.1, L.8.2, L.8.3)

17. VOCABULARY/WORD WALL

As a class, continue adding to the Vocabulary Word Wall bulletin board where, throughout the year, you will add and sort words as you learn them in each unit of study. (L.8.4)

ADDITIONAL RESOURCES

- *Artist Pablo Picasso Was Born on This Day in 1881* (ReadWriteThink) (RI.8.2)
- WebQuest *From the Mixed-Up Files of Mrs. Basil E. Frankweiler*
- *Looking at Art: Seeing Questions* (Incredible @rt Department)
- *How to Look at Art* (Kinder Art)
- *Most Famous World Art Museums* (ExploringAbroad.Com)
- *Art Museums in the USA* (ExploringAbroad.Com)
- *10 Breathtaking Pencil and Ink Works of Art* (Frikoo.Com)
- *Extreme Engineering: 15 of Man's Most Impressive Construction Projects* (Frikoo.Com)

TERMINOLOGY

Biography	Irony	Perspective	Style
Humor	Mood	Point of view	Tone

Grade Eight, Unit Four Sample Lesson Plan

Vincent van Gogh: Portrait of an Artist by Jan Greenberg and Sandra Jordan

In this series of ten lessons, students read *Vincent van Gogh: Portrait of an Artist* by Jan Greenberg and Sandra Jordan, and they:

- Explore the details of Vincent van Gogh's life (RI.8.1, RI.8.2, SL.8.1, SL.8.4)
- Investigate influences on van Gogh's style of painting (RI.8.2, RI.8.7, SL.8.1, SL.8.4, L.8.6)
- Study select paintings by van Gogh (W.8.7, SL.8.1, SL.8.4, L.8.6)
- Examine the content of select letters by van Gogh (RL.8.2, RL.8.4, SL.8.1, SL.8.4, L.8.6)
- Exhibit independent study results (SL.8.5, SL.8.6)

Summary

Lesson I: "A Brabant Boy, 1853–1875"	Lesson II: "Vincent in England, 1876–1877" and "The Missionary, 1879–1880"
Identify van Gogh's birthplace on a world map (RI.8.1, SL.6.6)	Record van Gogh's early struggles (RI.8.1, RI.8.2, RI.8.3, L.8.6)
Investigate biographical details about young van Gogh's life (RI.8.1, RI.8.2, RI.8.7, SL.8.1, SL.8.4, L.8.6)	Explore van Gogh's initial exploration of drawing (RI.8.1, RI.8.2, SL.8.1, SL.8.4, L.8.6)
Note the members of van Gogh's family (RI.8.1, SL.8.1)	Critically examine the drawing, *Square in Ramsgate* (1876) (RI.8.7, W.8.7, SL.8.1, SL.8.4, L.8.6)
	Document preliminary impressions of van Gogh's character (RI.8.6, L.8.6)

Lesson IV: "A Country Bumpkin in Paris, 1886–1887" and "Vincent and Friends, 1887–1888"

Note the influence of Impressionist painting and other sources—such as Japanese woodcuts—on van Gogh's work (W.8.7, W.8.8, RI.8.3, SL.8.1)

Explore van Gogh's relationships with the "bohemian artists' community of Paris" (RI.8.1, RI.8.2, SL.8.1, SL.8.4)

Examine the artistic vision of the Impressionist movement (W.8.7, RI.8.2, RI.8.7, SL.8.1, L.8.6)

Investigate the origins of the name "Impressionism" (W.8.7)

Explore the background of leading Impressionist artists (W.8.7, RI.8.1, RI.8.2, SL.8.1, SL.8.4, L.8.6)

View works by artists van Gogh met in Paris (RI.8.7, SL.8.5)

Lesson VI: "St.-Remy: The Asylum, 1889–1890," "Auvers-sur-Oise: The Last Refuge, 1890," and "Postscript"

Explore van Gogh's illness (RI.8.1, RI.8.3, SL.8.1, SL.8.4, L.8.6)

Examine the content of van Gogh's letter to Theo from May 4, 1890 (RL.8.2, RL.8.4)

Probe van Gogh's death and examine the painting *Wheatfield with Crows* (RI.8.1, RI.8.2, SL.8.1, SL.8.4)

Note the contribution of Jo, Theo's wife, to posterity (RI.8.1, RI.8.2, SL.8.1)

Lesson III: "In Love, 1881–1883" and "Vincent the Dog, 1883–1885"

Explore van Gogh's growing passion for drawing following the reading of this passage by Greenberg and Jordan: "Since he first picked up a pencil in the Borinage, he had focused on drawing, persuaded that it was the foundation of everything. Now, after several years of strenuous effort, he felt the time had come to start painting, and his letters gloried in his newfound pleasure." (p. 36) (RI.8.1, RI.8.2, RI.8.4, SL.8.1, L.8.6)

Examine the biographical significance of van Gogh's letters (RI.8.6)

Explore the content of van Gogh's letter to Theo dated April 30, 1885 (RL.8.2, RL.8.4, SL.8.1, SL.8.4, L.8.6)

View *The Potato Eaters* and discuss why the painting is considered "one of the great paintings of the nineteenth century" (p. 45) (RI.8.7, W.8.7, SL.8.1, SL.8.5)

Lesson V: "Vincent in Arles, 1888–1889" and "Arles: 'A High Yellow Note,' 1888–1889"

Explore the details of van Gogh's letter to Émile Bernard from June 18, 1888 (available online) (RL.8.2, RL.8.4, SL.8.1, SL.8.4, L.8.6)

Study paintings by van Gogh (e.g., *Bedroom in Arles*, *The Starry Night*, *The Night Café*, *Still Life with Sunflowers*) (RI.8.7, W.8.7)

Probe the authors' comment that the "artist, who had written earlier that his brush strokes had no system, was producing works in a style that would forever be unique to him, even those canvases without his now famous signature, the single name Vincent" (p. 69) (RI.8.1, RL.8.4, SL.8.1, SL.8.4, L.8.5)

Examine van Gogh's years in Arles and his friendship with Paul Gauguin (RI.8.1, RI.8.3, RI.8.7, SL.8.1, SL.8.4)

Note van Gogh's illness and examine *Self-Portrait with Bandaged Ear* (RI.8.1, SL.8.1)

Lessons VII–IX: The Paintings and the Letters of van Gogh

View self-portraits by van Gogh (W.8.7, RI.8.7, SL.8.1, SL.8.5)

Survey the letters of van Gogh (RL.8.2, RL.8.4, SL.8.4, L.8.6)

Select a letter and a painting from the same period in van Gogh's life (available online) (RL.8.2, RL.8.4)

Explore the content of the letter (RL.8.2, RL.8.4, SL.8.1, SL.8.4, L.8.6)

Examine the painting (W.8.7, RI.8.7, SL.8.1, SL.8.5)

Express impressions of both letter and painting in paragraph form (W.8.2, SL.8.1, SL.8.4, L.8.6)

Edit the paragraph (W.8.2, L.8.1, L.8.2)

Prepare the painting, the letter, and the paragraph for presentation (L.8.3)

Lesson X: The Exhibit

View the exhibit of van Gogh's paintings and letters

Examine classmates' impressions (SL.8.1, SL.8.5)

Explore shared experiences (SL.8.1, SL.8.4, L.8.6)

Lesson IV: "A Country Bumpkin in Paris, 1886–1887" and "Vincent and Friends, 1887–1888"

Objectives

Note the influence of Impressionist painting and other sources — such as Japanese woodcuts — on van Gogh's work (W.8.7, W.8.8, RI.8.3, SL.8.1)

Explore van Gogh's relationships with the "bohemian artists' community of Paris" (RI.8.1, RI.8.2, SL.8.1, SL.8.4)

Examine the artistic vision of the Impressionist movement (W.8.7, RI.8.2, RI.8.7, SL.8.1, L.8.6)

Investigate the origins of the name "Impressionism" (W.8.7)

Explore the background of leading Impressionist artists (W.8.7, RI.8.1, RI.8.2, SL.8.1, SL.8.4, L.8.6)

View works by artists van Gogh met in Paris (RI.8.7, W.8.7, SL.8.1, SL.8.5)

Required Materials

☐ Computers with Internet access

☐ Library

☐ *Vincent van Gogh: Portrait of an Artist,* by Jan Greenberg and Sandra Jordan

Procedures

1. Lead-In:
Read "A Country Bumpkin in Paris, 1886–1887," and "Vincent and Friends, 1887–1888," aloud.

2. Step by Step:

a. In class discussion, students recall details about van Gogh's days in Paris and his relationship with the Impressionist artists. They note the authors' description of the influence that Claude Monet, Camille Pissarro, and Paul Signac had on van Gogh.

b. In small groups, using online sources or the library, students explore the artistic vision of the Impressionist movement. They note the origin of the artistic movement's name (Claude Monet's painting, *Impression, Sunrise*). There are many good online sources; here are a few recommended sites:

"'Impressionism: Art and Modernity'" (The Metropolitan Museum of Art); "Tour: Impressionism" (National Gallery of Art)

c. Assign a specific artist to each group. The students are responsible for identifying key biographical information about the artist. They explore the artist's role in the Impressionist movement. They also prepare a five-minute multimedia presentation where they share their findings with the rest of the class. The list is likely to include:

Frédéric Bazille: 1841–1870

Émile Bernard: 1868–1941

Paul Cézanne: 1839–1906

Edgar Degas: 1834–1917

Paul Gauguin: 1848–1903

Armand Guillaumin: 1841–1927

Édouard Manet: 1832–1883

Claude Monet: 1840–1926

Camille Pissarro: 1830–1903

Pierre-Auguste Renoir: 1841–1919

Georges Seurat: 1859–1891

Paul Signac: 1863–1935

Henri de Toulouse-Lautrec: 1864–1901

d. Presentations of findings.

3. Closure:

Students revisit Greenberg and Jordan's assertion that the artists van Gogh met in Paris influenced his work. (Perhaps display some paintings that illustrate the influence that they discuss.)

Differentiation

Advanced

- Research the Post-Impressionist movement. Learn what distinguished it from Impressionism and locate van Gogh's place in each movement.
- Give students an opportunity to bookmark the most helpful websites for other classmates to conduct their research. Collect the websites on a web portal.

- Encourage students to develop a page for the class website where presentations can be uploaded and viewed by others after class presentations.
- Encourage students to research some lesser-known Impressionist artists to increase the number of artists studied. Students should analyze and evaluate why their artist may be less well-known than van Gogh.

Struggling

- Have a print version of the text available for students to write upon, or mark with sticky notes prior to class discussion. If students need to listen to the passage read multiple times, have an audio version available for individual students.
- Have a four-column graphic organizer available for students where they can note the influence of Claude Monet, Camille Pissarro, and Paul Signac on van Gogh. Students should also note how van Gogh's paintings differed from those artists' paintings.
- Allow students to begin their research using the websites chosen by classmates (listed above).
- Provide students with a graphic organizer to help structure research and presentations.
- Students may videotape themselves in a run-through of the presentation using a video camera in order to evaluate what works and what needs improvement.

Homework/Assessment
N/A

Dramatically Speaking

This four-week unit of eighth grade continues an examination of the arts, focusing on the dramatic performance of plays, speeches, and poems.

? How is reading a speech, poem, or script for a play different from performing it?

OVERVIEW

In this unit, students read plays such as *Sorry, Wrong Number* and compare them to a Shakespeare play or a film with similar themes. They read and listen to famous speeches by Franklin Delano Roosevelt and Barbara Jordan. They read and perform poetry by Nikki Giovanni, Pablo Neruda, and T. S. Eliot. While exploring the different genres, students analyze lines of dialogue, scenes, or words that are critical to the development of the story or message. They analyze how the use of flashback can create a sense of suspense in the reader/listener. They pay special attention to diction, and how connotation may be enhanced through tone and inflection. Students must also choose a genre that they prefer and defend that choice, strengthening their skills at writing arguments. Finally, this unit ends with an informative/explanatory essay in response to the essential question.

FOCUS STANDARDS

These Focus Standards have been selected for the unit from the Common Core State Standards.

RL.8.3: Analyze how particular lines of dialogue or incidents in a story or drama propel the action, reveal aspects of a character, or provoke a decision.

RL.8.6: Analyze how differences in the points of view of the characters and the audience or reader (e.g., created through the use of dramatic irony) create such effects as suspense or humor.

RL.8.7: Analyze the extent to which a filmed or live production of a story or drama stays faithful to or departs from the text or script, evaluating the choices made by the director or actors.

W.8.1: Critique and write arguments to support claims with clear reasons and relevant evidence.

SL.8.3: Delineate a speaker's argument and specific claims, evaluating the soundness of the reasoning and relevance and sufficiency of the evidence and identifying when irrelevant evidence is introduced.

L.8.5: Demonstrate understanding of figurative language, word relationships, and nuances in word meanings.

L.8.5(a): Interpret figures of speech (e.g., verbal irony, puns) in context.

L.8.5(b): Use the relationship between particular words to better understand each of the words.

SUGGESTED STUDENT OBJECTIVES

- Read and discuss a variety of dramatic fiction and nonfiction about plays, playwrights, public speakers, and poets.
- Analyze how particular lines of dialogue in *Sorry, Wrong Number* propel the action and reveal aspects of a character.
- Compare and contrast characters, plots, themes, settings, and literary techniques used in plays and films.
- Analyze the extent to which a filmed or radio production of *Sorry, Wrong Number* stays faithful to or departs from the text or script, evaluating the choices made by the director or actors.
- Conduct research on a playwright or public speaker of choice.
- Discuss how creating a sound argument is essential to engaging listeners in a speech.
- Perform for classmates in a variety of styles (e.g., drama, poetry, or speeches).
- Participate in group discussions and critically evaluate classmates' arguments.

SUGGESTED WORKS

(E) indicates a CCSS exemplar text; (EA) indicates a text from a writer with other works identified as exemplars.

LITERARY TEXTS

Stories
- *King of Shadows* (Susan Cooper) (EA)

Poetry
- "A Poem for My Librarian, Mrs. Long" in *Acolytes: Poems* (Nikki Giovanni) (E)
- *The Book of Questions* (Pablo Neruda) (E)
- "Macavity" (T. S. Eliot)

Drama
- *Sorry, Wrong Number* (Lucille Fletcher) (E)
- *A Midsummer Night's Dream* (William Shakespeare)
- *Zora Neale Hurston: Collected Plays* (Zora Neale Hurston)
- *Famous Americans: 22 Short Plays for the Classroom, Grades 4–8* (Liza Schafer, editor)
- *A Raisin in the Sun* (Lorraine Hansberry)

INFORMATIONAL TEXTS

Biographies

- *The Play's the Thing: A Story About William Shakespeare* (Creative Minds Biographies) (Ruth Turk)
- *Hitchcock on Hitchcock: Selected Writings and Interviews* (Alfred Hitchcock)
- *Franklin Delano Roosevelt* (Russell Freedman)
- *Who Was Ronald Reagan?* (Joyce Milton)
- *Barbara Jordan: Voice of Democracy (Book Report Biography)* (Lisa Renee Rhodes)
- *Memoirs* (Pablo Neruda)
- *Sorrow's Kitchen: The Life and Folklore of Zora Neale Hurston* (Great Achievers Series) (Mary E. Lyons)

Literary Criticism

- "Shakespeare's Plays: Comedy" (Debora B. Schwartz)
- "Midsummer Night's Dream" (D. J. Snider)

Speeches

- "The Banking Crisis" (First Fireside Chat, Franklin Delano Roosevelt) (March 12, 1933)
- "A Time for Choosing" (Ronald Reagan) (October 27, 1964)
- Keynote Address to the Democratic National Convention (Barbara Jordan) (July 12, 1976)

ART, MUSIC, AND MEDIA

Music and Lyrics

- "Macavity," from *Cats* (Andrew Lloyd Webber)

Film

- Anatole Litvak, dir., *Sorry, Wrong Number* (1948)
- Alfred Hitchcock, dir., *Dial M for Murder* (1954)
- Michael Hoffman, dir., *A Midsummer Night's Dream* (1999)
- David Mallet, dir., *Cats* (1998, PBS Great Performances)
- Daniel Petrie, dir., *A Raisin in the Sun* (1961)
- Mirra Bank, dir., *Spirit to Spirit: Nikki Giovanni* (1988)

SAMPLE ACTIVITIES AND ASSESSMENTS

1. LITERARY GRAPHIC ORGANIZER

As you read the plays (and view the films) in this unit, take notes in your journal or on a spreadsheet about particular lines of dialogue or incidents that propel the action, reveal aspects of a character, or provoke a decision. Be sure to note page numbers with relevant information so you can cite the text during class discussion.

- What is the setting of the play?
- Who are the major and minor characters?

- What is the theme of the play?
- What problems are faced by the character(s)? How does he/she overcome this challenge?
- Which lines of dialogue or events were pivotal to the play? Why?
- Describe the use of literary techniques, such as flashback, in the play. How do these reveal the point of view of the character and create suspense?

Prior to class discussion, your teacher may give you the opportunity to share your notes with a partner who read the same text. (RL.8.1, RL.8.2, RL.8.3, RL.8.6, RL.8.7)

2. CLASS DISCUSSION

Compare and contrast the plots, settings, themes, characters, and literary techniques used. Can you begin to make any generalizations about how films and plays have different effects on viewers from the effects literature has on readers? What are they? Evaluate the claims made by your classmates and evaluate the soundness of reasoning they use in discussion. After class discussion, create a Venn diagram in your journal or by using an online template that outlines the similarities and differences among the techniques used. Post your thoughts on the classroom blog in order to continue the conversation with your classmates. (SL.8.1, SL.8.3, RL.8.6)

3. WRITING (ARGUMENT)

Why have Shakespeare's plays, such as *A Midsummer Night's Dream,* stood the test of time? Why do we study these plays today? Talk through your ideas with a partner. Then, write an argument in support of studying Shakespeare in eighth grade, including citations from selections read. You may choose to make connections between the plays and other novels, plays, poems, or films. Post your thoughts on a class blog in order to continue the conversation with others outside of your classroom. (W.8.1, W.8.4, SL.8.1, RL.8.6, RL.8.9)

4. DRAMATIZATION/CLASS DISCUSSION

Read the script of *Sorry, Wrong Number* with your classmates. Discuss how the use of flashbacks adds suspense to the tone of the play. Then listen to the radio drama version and/or view the film version and compare these to the written version. Analyze the extent to which a filmed or live production of a story or drama stays faithful to or departs from the text or script, evaluating the choices made by the director or actors. Write responses to these questions in your journal and share with a partner prior to class discussion. (RL.8.3, RL.8.5, RL.8.6, RL.8.7, SL.8.6)

5. RESEARCH AND INFORMATIVE/EXPLANATORY WRITING

How are playwrights or public speakers similar to and different from other authors? Conduct research about a playwright or public speaker whose work you have read. As you read about his/her life, try to determine the author's purpose for writing the text you read. How is the purpose of the text related to its point of view? Write an informative/explanatory essay in which you explain how point of view is established. Work with classmates to strengthen your writing through planning, revising, and editing your report. Edit your writing for shifts in verb mood and voice. Publish your report about playwrights or public speakers on a class wiki. (RI.8.1, RI.8.2, RI.8.3, RI.8.6, W.8.2, W.8.5, W.8.6, W.8.7, L.8.1, L.8.2, L.8.3, L.8.5a,b,c)

6. LITERARY RESPONSE

Select two political speeches, such as those by Barbara Jordan and Ronald Reagan. Read them closely. How are they similar? How are they different? What perspectives do they bring to their speeches? How do these speakers inspire listeners? What is important for us to learn from these speeches, and why is it important to continue reading them from generation to generation? Share ideas with a partner and then write your own response in your journal or on the classroom blog. (RL.8.2, RL.8.4, RL.8.5, RL.8.6, SL.8.1)

7. RESPONSE TO LITERARY NONFICTION

Create a T-chart or Venn diagram in your journal where you compare two speeches, such as the "Fireside Chat" by Franklin Delano Roosevelt and Barbara Jordan's keynote address at the 1976 Democratic National Convention. Delineate each speaker's arguments and specific claims, evaluate the soundness of the reasoning, and make a judgment about the relevance and sufficiency of the evidence. Point out any particular words that you understand better because of how they were used in context. Write a response to this question in your journal or on the classroom blog: "What is the difference between reading the speech and hearing it/seeing it performed live?" (SL.8.1a,b,c,d; SL.8.3, L.8.5a,b,c; RL.8.5)

8. CLASS DISCUSSION

How is the delivery of spoken messages in plays and speeches similar and different? When would you choose to give a speech? When would you choose to embed a speech (monologue) in a drama? What are the similarities and differences between performing in a play and delivering a speech? Write responses to these questions in your journal or on the classroom blog, citing specific examples and page numbers from the texts read and speeches heard. (RL.8.1, RL.8.5, SL.8.1)

9. DRAMATIZATION/FLUENCY

Choose your favorite selection from *Acolytes: Poems* by Nikki Giovanni or from *The Book of Questions* by Pablo Neruda. Talk with a classmate about the meaning of the poem chosen. Practice reading it, changing the words emphasized and inflection used. Memorize and/or recite the poem for your class, choosing two different interpretations. Be sure you can articulate how the different interpretations change the tone and mood of the poem. Record yourself using a video camera, not only so you can evaluate your performance, but also so you can see the different interpretations for yourself. Use these experiences to help you articulate how different recitations may change the way listeners interpret the poem. (RL.8.2, RL.8.3, SL.8.6)

10. POETRY RESPONSE

Compare and contrast the T. S. Eliot poem "Macavity" to the character of the same name in the Andrew Lloyd Webber musical *Cats*. How are they similar and different? Write a response in your journal, citing specific examples from the poem and musical to justify your thinking. Share links within the classroom blog to performances available online so that your classmates understand your perspective. (RL.8.1, RL.8.6, RL.8.9)

11. WORD STUDY

[Continue this activity from the fourth unit.] Add words found, learned, and used throughout this unit to your personal dictionary (i.e., *dialogue, monologue, staging,* etc.). This unit will especially focus on vocabulary unique to plays. This dictionary will be used all year long to explore the semantics (meanings) of words and their origins. (L.8.4, L.8.5a,b,c)

12. CLASS DISCUSSION/MEDIA APPRECIATION

How is the plot and use of suspense similar and different between *Sorry, Wrong Number* and *Dial M for Murder*? Write responses to these questions in your journal and share with a partner prior to class or classroom blog discussion. (RL.8.6, SL.8.1a,b,c,d)

13. INFORMATIVE/EXPLANATORY (OR ARGUMENT) WRITING

Reflecting on your experiences reading and performing in this unit, write an informative/explanatory essay in response to the essential question: How is reading a speech, poem, or script for a play different from actually performing dramatically? Write a well-developed paper that includes at least four examples from a poem, speech, or play read. (Alternatively, write an argument in which you explain which you prefer and why. Include examples, as described above.) After your teacher reviews your first draft, work with a partner to edit and strengthen your writing. Edit your writing for shifts in verb mood and voice. Be prepared to record your essay and upload it as a podcast or other multimedia format of choice on the class web page in order to facilitate sharing with your classmates. (W.8.1, W.8.4, W.8.9a,b, SL.8.1, L.8.1, L.8.2, L.8.3, L.8.5)

14. MECHANICS/GRAMMAR WALL

As a class, continue adding to the Mechanics/Grammar bulletin board started in Unit One. Remember— once skills are taught in a mini-lesson and listed on the bulletin board, you are expected to edit your work for these elements before publication. (L.8.1d)

15. VOCABULARY/WORD WALL

As a class, create a Vocabulary Word Wall bulletin board where, throughout the year, you will add and sort words as you learn them in each unit of study. (L.8.4)

ADDITIONAL RESOURCES

- Grade Eight: *A Model Unit for Teaching Drama in Context* (Saskatchewan Education) (RL.8.9)
- *Looking at Plays* (Saskatchewan Education) (RL.8.5)
- *Entering History: Nikki Giovanni and Martin Luther King Jr.* (ReadWriteThink) (SL.8.3)
- *A Playwriting Project for Eighth Grade Theater Students* (Yale-New Haven Teachers Institute)
- *Scribbling Women* (Northeastern University)
- *Story Arts Online* (Heather Forest)
- *Speeches by Famous Women* (FamousQuotes.Me.UK)
- *Famous Presidential Speeches* (FamousQuotes.Me.UK)
- *Classic Movie Scripts* (Aellea.Com)

TERMINOLOGY

Dialogue	Film noir	Screenplay
Diction	Flashback	Script
Drama	Monologue	Staging

Grade Eight, Unit Five Sample Lesson Plan

A Midsummer Night's Dream by William Shakespeare

In this series of ten lessons, students read *A Midsummer Night's Dream* by William Shakespeare, and they:

Identify the classic structure of the comedy (RL.8.2, RL.8.5, RL.8.9, SL.8.1, SL.8.4, L.8.5)

Explore the dramatic structure of the comedy (RL.8.3, RL.8.5, RL.8.6, L.8.5, SL.8.1)

Rehearse and perform select scenes from the comedy (SL.8.6)

Summary

Lessons I–II: A Midsummer Night's Dream

Listen to a reading of the comedy (available online at LibriVox) (L.8.3, L.8.5, L.8.6)

Identify the characters of the comedy (RL.8.2, SL.8.1, SL.8.4)

Create a character map (RL.8.6)

Lessons V–IX: Rehearsing Scenes

Identify scenes to perform (SL.8.1b)

(In groups) note the setting of the scenes (SL.8.1)

(In groups) explore the dramatic context of the scenes (RL.8.3, RL.8.6, SL.8.1, L.8.5)

Assign roles to group members (SL.8.1b)

(In groups) identify the dramatic impact of the scene (SL.8.1, RL.8.1, RL.8.3, RL.8.6)

(In groups) rehearse the assigned scene (SL.8.6)

Lessons III–IV: A Dramatic Structure

Identify the classic structure of the comedy (RL.8.2, RL.8.5, RL.8.9, SL.8.1, SL.8.4, L.8.5)

Examine the three worlds that the comedy depicts (RL.8.3, RL.8.5, RL.8.6, L.8.5, SL.8.1, L.8.6)

Note the dramatic structure of the comedy (RL.8.5, L.8.5)

Lesson X: Performing Scenes

Perform the scenes (SL.8.6)

Note the dramatic impact of the performances (SL.8.4)

Share impressions (SL.8.1)

Lesson III–IV: A Dramatic Structure

Objectives

Identify the classic structure of the comedy (RL.8.2, RL.8.5, RL.8.9, SL.8.1, SL.8.4, L.8.5)

Examine the three worlds that the comedy depicts (RL.8.3, RL.8.5, RL.8.6, L.8.5, SL.8.1, L.8.6)

Note the dramatic structure of the comedy (RL.8.5, L.8.5)

Required Materials

☐ Class set of *A Midsummer Night's Dream* by William Shakespeare

☐ Class set of "Shakespeare's Plays: Comedy" by Dr. Debora Schwartz, California Polytechnic State University

Procedures

1. Lead-In:
Distribute Schwartz's description of the comedy.

2. Step by Step:
   a. Students discuss the five parts of the classic comedy that Schwartz identifies:
      1. A situation with tensions or implicit conflict
      2. Implicit conflict is developed
      3. Conflict reaches height; frequently an impasse
      4. Conflict begins to resolve
      5. Problem is resolved; knots are untied
   b. Students apply the five parts of the classic comedy to the five acts of *A Midsummer Night's Dream*. For example, in Act I, the reader learns about the conflict: Hermia, Egeus's daughter, loves Lysander, but her father, who has absolute authority, orders her to marry Demetrius.
   c. This step is optional, but recommended. Inspired by the critical essay "Midsummer Night's Dream," by D. J. Snider (available on Jstor.com), lead a class discussion about the three "phases or divisions" of the play. Snider refers to the "Real World," represented by the Duke and the laws of Athens; secondly, the "Fairy World" is in the woods outside of Athens; and finally the "Representation in Art" is the "return from the Fairyland to the world of reality." (p. 167)
   This type of analysis broadens the earlier discussion. The conflict emerges because Athens has unbending laws that Hermia and Lysander do not accept. Therefore, they move away from the "Real World." In the forest, the laws of Athens do not count. Use a series of prompts, inspired by Snider's essay, that will emphasize the dramatic tension between the two worlds. Such analytical discussion contributes to the understanding of the dramatic structure of the whole play.

3. Closure:
Introduce the next activity—performances of select scenes from the comedy.

Differentiation

Advanced

- Students should conduct online research and find other interpretations of "the classic comedy." Students should critically evaluate what is found online, based on Schwartz's work.
- Students will create an online concept map based on the word *comedy*.
- Encourage students to create a modern-day interpretation of a select comedic scene from *A Midsummer Night's Dream*. Students must be able to justify how the modern version stays true to the original, while also changing style. Perhaps challenge them to create a movie with "pop-up bubbles" that explain the comedic elements, as defined by Schwartz.
- Give students an opportunity to bookmark helpful websites for other classmates to learn more about Shakespeare and the history behind the writing of *A Midsummer Night's Dream*. Collect the websites on a web portal.

Struggling

- Provide students with a handout on which they can graphically (non-linguistically) interpret the five parts of the classic comedy, as presented by Schwartz, and how they relate to each other.
- Encourage students to mark the five elements of the comedy in their text with sticky notes. First, students should try this on their own before participating in a guided group discussion. Alternatively, divide the students into groups; they can work with partners to find one element together to mark. Students share their findings with the group.
- If students need assistance understanding what they are reading, they can watch select scenes on DVD or a handheld device and read along. Seeing Shakespeare's plays performed often aids in comprehension of the text.

Homework/Assessment

Begin to explore scenes for performance.

Grade 8 ▶ *Unit 6*

"The Road Not Taken"

This final six-week unit of eighth grade encourages students to explore their strengths by reading about strong characters who ventured against conventional wisdom in search of the greater good.

ESSENTIAL QUESTION

Can literature help us to define the greater good?

OVERVIEW

The stage is set by Robert Frost's poem "The Road Not Taken." Although students read from classic and contemporary literature, writing and class discussions focus on how literature helps us define the tension between the needs of the individual and the greater good of society. The goal of this unit is for students not only to apply the reading, writing, speaking, and listening strategies and skills they have learned up to this point in the year, but also to analyze how authors use allegory, symbolism, and satire to affect the reader. Students will revisit "The Road Not Taken" as the unit concludes, in order to see how this unit led to deeper understanding of the poem. This unit ends with an essay in response to the essential question. (The essay is followed with a choice for students: write their own narrative or create their own multimedia presentation that demonstrates what they learned this year.)

FOCUS STANDARDS

These Focus Standards have been selected for the unit from the Common Core State Standards.

RL.8.7: Analyze the extent to which a filmed or live production of a story or drama stays faithful to or departs from the text or script, evaluating the choices made by the director or actors.

W.8.3: Write narratives to develop real or imagined experiences or events using effective technique, relevant descriptive details, and well-structured event sequences.

SL.8.4: Present claims and findings, emphasizing salient points in a focused, coherent manner with relevant evidence, sound valid reasoning, and well-chosen details; use appropriate eye contact, adequate volume, and clear pronunciation.

L.8.3: Use knowledge of language and its conventions when writing, speaking, reading, or listening.

L.8.3(a): Use verbs in the active and passive voice and in the conditional and subjunctive mood to achieve particular effects (e.g., emphasizing the actor or the action; expressing uncertainty or describing a state contrary to fact).

SUGGESTED STUDENT OBJECTIVES

- Read and discuss a variety of novels that reveal, explicitly or implicitly, "the greater good."
- Experiment with performing poetry in variety of styles and discuss how these changes affect its interpretation.
- Compare and contrast characters, plots, themes, settings, and literary techniques used in the stories read.
- Analyze how particular lines of dialogue in literature propel the action and reveal aspects of a character.
- Analyze how writing styles and literary techniques, such as symbolism or satire, are used and how their use affects meaning and reader engagement.
- Write a variety of responses to literature and informational text.
- Analyze the extent to which a filmed version of a story stays faithful to or departs from the text, evaluating the choices made by the director or actors.
- Create a multimedia presentation on "the greater good," where the message is either explicitly stated or implied.

SUGGESTED WORKS

(E) indicates a CCSS exemplar text; (EA) indicates a text from a writer with other works identified as exemplars.

LITERARY TEXTS

Stories

- *Little Women* (Louisa May Alcott) (E)
- *I, Juan de Pareja* (Elizabeth Borton de Trevino)
- *Lord of the Flies* (William Golding)
- *The Old Man and the Sea* (Ernest Hemingway)
- *Gulliver's Travels* (Jonathan Swift)
- *The Sea-Wolf* (Oxford World's Classics Edition) (Jack London)
- *Rebecca* (Daphne du Maurier)
- *American Dragons: Twenty-Five Asian American Voices* (Laurence Yep) (EA)
- *The Color of My Words* (Lynn Joseph)
- *Children of the River* (Linda Crew)
- *Amos Fortune, Free Man* (Elizabeth Yates)
- *The Outsiders* (S. E. Hinton)
- *Stargirl* (Jerry Spinelli)

Poetry

- "The Road Not Taken" (Robert Frost) (E)
- "Nothing Gold Can Stay" (Robert Frost) (E)
- *Things I Have to Tell You: Poems and Writing by Teenage Girls* (Betsy Franco)
- *Night Is Gone, Day Is Still Coming: Stories and Poems by American Indian Teens and Young Adults* (Annette Piña Ochoa, Betsy Franco, and Traci L. Gourdine)

INFORMATIONAL TEXTS

Nonfiction

- "Trek 7, The Fractal Pond Race" (from *Math Trek: Adventures in the Math Zone*) (Ivars Peterson and Nancy Henderson) (E)

Literary Criticism

- "Robert Frost, Poet of Action" (James McBride Dabbs)

ART, MUSIC, AND MEDIA

Art

- Diego Velázquez, *Juan de Pareja* (1650)
- Artemisia Gentileschi, *Self-Portrait as the Allegory of Painting* (1638–1639)

Film

- Mervyn LeRoy, dir., *Little Women* (1949)
- Gillian Armstrong, dir., *Little Women* (1994)
- John Sturges, dir., *The Old Man and the Sea* (1958)
- Jud Taylor, dir., *The Old Man and the Sea* (1990)
- Charles Sturridge, dir., *Gulliver's Travels* (1996)
- Michael Curtiz, dir., *The Sea Wolf* (1941)

SAMPLE ACTIVITIES AND ASSESSMENTS

1. INTRODUCTORY ACTIVITY

Read "The Road Not Taken" by Robert Frost. Talk with a classmate about what you think the poem means, both literally and figuratively. Write your ideas down in your journal or on a spreadsheet. We will revisit this poem at the end of the unit to see if our thoughts and ideas have changed. (RL.8.2, RL.8.4, SL.8.5)

2. LITERARY GRAPHIC ORGANIZER

As you read the novels (and view the films) in this unit, take notes in your journal or on a spreadsheet about particular lines of dialogue or incidents that propel the action, reveal aspects of a character, or suggest the greater good. Be sure to note page numbers with relevant information so you can cite the text during class discussion.

- What is the setting of the novel?
- Who are the major and minor characters?

- What problems or challenges does(do) the character(s) face? How does he/she overcome these challenges?
- Which lines of dialogue or events are pivotal to the novel? Why?
- What elements were changed between the novel and the film version?
- What traditional, mythical, or Biblical references are made in the novel?
- What elements of the greater good are revealed, implicitly or explicitly, in the novel?

Prior to class discussion, your teacher may give you the opportunity to share your notes with a partner who read the same text. (RL.8.1, RL.8.2, RL.8.3, RL.8.7, RL.8.9, RL.8.10)

3. CLASS DISCUSSION

Compare and contrast settings, themes, and characters, and how these story elements help us to define the greater good. Evaluate the claims made by your classmates and evaluate the soundness of reasoning they use in discussion. Can you begin to make any generalizations about what is the greater good? Your teacher may encourage you to continue the class discussion on the classroom blog throughout the course of this unit. (SL.8.1, SL.8.3, RL.8.9)

4. INFORMATIONAL TEXT RESPONSE

After reading "Trek 7, The Fractal Pond Race" from *Math Trek: Adventures in the Math Zone* by Ivars Peterson and Nancy Henderson, respond to the following question in your journal: How did Benoit Mandelbrot follow "The Road Not Taken" in his approach to fractals? What can we learn from him? Post your response on the classroom blog to encourage conversation among your classmates. (RI.8.1, RI.8.6, RI.8.8, RI.8.10, W.8.4, W.8.9b, L.8.1, L.8.2, L.8.3, L.8.5)

5. LITERARY RESPONSE/CLASS DISCUSSION

After reading *Little Women* by Louisa May Alcott:

- Discuss the role of the setting in *Little Women*. Why does Alcott put such an important historical event into the background of her story?
- Why does Alcott alternate between stories about each of the four March sisters throughout *Little Women*? Why is this literary technique effective?

Write responses to these questions in your journal or on the classroom blog and share with a partner prior to class discussion. (SL.8.1, RL.8.2, RL.8.4, RL.8.6, RL.8.10)

6. INFORMATIVE/EXPLANATORY WRITING AND PRESENTATION

Compare the societal discriminations that the Logan family experienced in *Roll of Thunder, Hear My Cry* by Mildred Taylor (read in Unit Two) to the gender discrimination described in *Little Women* by Louisa May Alcott. How are the characters' experiences similar yet different? Write a well-developed speech that includes an engaging opening statement describing your position and at least three examples cited from the texts. Edit your writing for the grammar conventions studied this year. Present your speech to the class and record it using a video camera so you can evaluate your performance. (RL.8.1, RL.8.2, RL.8.3, RL.8.10, W.8.1, W.8.4, L.8.1, L.8.2, L.8.3, L.8.5)

7. ART/LITERARY RESPONSE

How does the writing style (from the first-person point of view) in *I, Juan de Pareja* by Elizabeth Borton de Trevino affect your connection to the protagonist, de Pareja? How is de Pareja's struggle to paint (because Spanish slaves at the time were forbidden to practice the arts) simultaneously fascinating, suspenseful, and inspiring? View Diego Velázquez's portrait of Juan de Pareja. How does looking at this painting expand your knowledge of its subject? Write responses to these questions and other self-generated questions in your journal. (RL.8.2, RL.8.3, RL.8.6, RL.8.10, W.8.9a)

8. ART/CLASS DISCUSSION

Velázquez painted his assistant, Juan de Pareja, who was also a painter. Velázquez is believed to have painted de Pareja in preparation for a portrait he was soon to paint of Pope Innocent X. Does this strike you as a mere preparatory work? Has Velázquez given de Pareja an assistant's bearing or a more regal one? (SL.8.1, SL.8.2, SL.8.4, SL.8.5)

9. ART/CLASS DISCUSSION

Gentileschi was the first female artist to be admitted to the prestigious Accademia delle Arti del Disegno in Florence, Italy, yet she struggled to break into the art world. Compare Gentileschi's self-portrait to Velázquez's portrayal of de Pareja. How are the portraits depicted? What artistic elements engage the viewer? Note that the paintings are nearly contemporaneous. How do the works compare? (SL.8.1, SL.8.2, SL.8.4, SL.8.5)

10. INFORMATIVE/EXPLANATORY WRITING

Compare the allegorical nature of *Lord of the Flies* by William Golding to Ernest Hemingway's *The Old Man and the Sea* in your journal. What important symbols are used in each novel? How is the use of symbolism integral to these novels? Begin by outlining your ideas using a Venn diagram in your journal or using an online template. Write an informative/explanatory essay comparing and contrasting the similarities and differences in these novels, citing specific page numbers for explicit and implicit text references. Share your essay with a partner, and discuss as a class. Your teacher may ask you to upload your essay to the classroom blog in order to encourage an electronic conversation with your classmates. (W.8.2, W.8.4, SL.8.1, RL.8.4, RL.8.5, RL.8.9)

11. LITERARY RESPONSE

Respond to the following questions in your journal or on a spreadsheet:

- How does Swift use language to express satire in *Gulliver's Travels*?
- How does Swift's writing style change as the story evolves?
- How do the characters' physical characteristics reflect their inner feelings?
- How does *Gulliver's Travels* explore the idea of utopia?
- How is the idea of utopia related to "the greater good"? (RL.8.4, RL.8.6, RL.8.9, W.8.4, W.8.9a, L.8.5a,b,c)

12. LITERARY RESPONSE

Compare the characters of Hump and Larsen from *The Sea-Wolf* by Jack London. How do their perspectives on life differ? Are there any similarities between the two characters? Write your responses to these questions in your journal. (RL.8.1, RL.8.3, RL.8.6, RL.8.10)

13. LITERARY RESPONSE

In your journal, respond to the following prompts about *Rebecca* by Daphne du Maurier:

- What effect does the nameless heroine have on how we read the novel? What does this anonymity symbolize?

- What is the role of Manderley in the novel? How does setting contribute to the plot? To the tone? To the suspenseful nature?
- What would be "the greater good" learned from *Rebecca*? (RL.8.2, RL.8.4, RL.8.6)

14. DRAMATIZATION/CLASS DISCUSSION

Read one of the novels from this unit. Then view select scenes from the film version and compare them to the scenes as written. Analyze the extent to which a filmed or live production of a story or drama stays faithful to or departs from the text, evaluating the choices made by the director or actors. Write responses to these questions in your journal and share with a partner prior to class discussion. (RL.8.5, RL.8.7, SL.8.6)

15. CLASS DISCUSSION AND RECITATION

Re-read the first poem read in this unit, "The Road Not Taken." After this unit of study, describe how your understanding of this poem has changed. What new insights have you gained? After class discussion, practice reading the poem aloud, emphasizing different words. How does changing emphasis change the meaning? Highlight the words and phrases you want to emphasize. Memorize and recite it for your class. How is your interpretation similar to and different from others? (RL.8.2, RL.8.4, SL.8.6)

16. WRITING (NARRATIVE AND ARGUMENT) AND MULTIMEDIA PRESENTATION

Reflecting on your experiences reading novels and viewing related films in this unit, as well as literature read all year, write an argument in response to the essential question: Can literature help us to define the greater good? Include at least three examples from texts to support your position, explaining why they help define "the greater good." You may also choose to write a narrative that reveals your definition of the greater good or develop a multimedia presentation in which your definition is revealed and explained. In your narrative or presentation, include references to specific examples of what you learned from novels read and films viewed about characters, the effect of settings, and pivotal lines of dialogue. Incorporate a variety of words learned this year. Edit your writing for the grammar conventions studied this year. Publish your essay, story, or multimedia presentation as your culminating project for eighth grade. (W.8.3, W.8.5, W.8.6, W.8.8, W.8.9a,b, W.8.10, SL.8.4, SL.8.5, L.8.1, L.8.2, L.8.3, L.8.5, L.8.6)

17. MECHANICS/GRAMMAR WALL

As a class, continue adding to the Mechanics/Grammar bulletin board started in Unit One. Remember—once skills are taught in a mini-lesson and listed on the bulletin board, you are expected to edit your work for these elements before publication. (L.8.1, L.8.2, L.8.3)

18. VOCABULARY/WORD WALL

As a class, create a Vocabulary Word Wall bulletin board where, throughout the year, you will add and sort words as they are learned within each unit of study. (L.8.4)

ADDITIONAL RESOURCES

- *Learning the Lines* (My Favorite Poem Project, Boston University) (RL.8.5)
- *Louisa May Alcott was Born in 1832* (ReadWriteThink) (This unit is geared toward grades 9–12, but may be adapted.) (W.8.3)
- *From Dr. Seuss to Jonathan Swift: Exploring the History behind the Satire* (ReadWriteThink) (This is a unit for grades 9–12, but may be adapted.) (RL.8.6)

- *Blogtopia: Blogging About Your Own Utopia* (ReadWriteThink) (This is a unit for grades 9–12, but may be adapted.) (W.8.6)
- Full Texts of Classic Literature (SparkNotes)
- Lesson Plans: Robert Frost's "The Road Not Taken" (Bright Hub)
- *Lord of the Flies* lesson plans (Discovery Channel, Discovery Education Lesson Plans Library)
- *Understanding The Old Man and the Sea: A Student Casebook to Issues, Sources, and Historical Documents* (Patricia Dunlavy Valenti)
- Robert Frost Reads "The Road Not Taken"

TERMINOLOGY

Allegory	Satirey	Symbolism
Hero/heroine	Strength of character	Style

Grade Eight, Unit Six Sample Lesson Plan

"The Road Not Taken" by Robert Frost

In this series of two lessons, students read "The Road Not Taken" by Robert Frost, and they:

Examine the speaker's message in "The Road Not Taken" (RL.8.1, RL.8.2, SL.8.1, L.8.3)

Explore the challenge of interpreting "The Road Not Taken" (RL.8.1, RL.8.2, RL.8.2, RL.8.4, W.8.2a, W.2b,d,e; SL.8.1)

Summary

Lesson I: Reading "The Road Not Taken" by Robert Frost

Examine the form of "The Road Not Taken" (RL.8.1, SL.8.1, L.8.3)

Identify the rhyming scheme (RL.8.1, SL.8.1)

Note the rhyming scheme's influence on the reader (RL.8.1, SL.8.1, L.8.3)

Visualize the poem's setting (RL.8.1)

Explore the speaker's situation and decision (RL.8.1, SL.8.1)

Lesson II: The Challenge of Interpreting "The Road Not Taken"

Explore James McBride Dabbs's claim that Robert Frost is "a poet of action" (RL.8.1, RL.8.4, SL.8.1)

Revisit the speaker's decision (RL.8.1, RL.8.2, SL.8.1)

Discuss the implication of the contrast between lines 10/11 and line 19 (RL.8.1, RL.8.2, SL.8.1, L.8.3)

Examine the speaker's point of view in the final stanza (RL.8.1, RL.8.2, SL.8.1)

Investigate the challenge of interpreting "The Road Not Taken" (RL.8.1, RL.8.2, W.8.2a, W.2b,d,e; SL.8.1)

Lesson II: The Challenge of Interpreting "The Road Not Taken"

Objectives

Explore James McBride Dabbs's claim that Robert Frost is "a poet of action" (RL.8.1, RL.8.4, SL.8.1)

Revisit the speaker's decision (RL.8.1, RL.8.2, SL.8.1)

Discuss the implication of the contrast between lines 10/11 and line 19 (RL.8.1, RL.8.2, SL.8.1, L.8.3)

Examine the speaker's point of view in the final stanza (RL.8.1, RL.8.2, SL.8.1)

Investigate the challenge of interpreting "The Road Not Taken" (RL.8.1, RL.8.2, W.8.2a, W.2b,d,e; SL.8.1)

Required Materials

☐ Copies of "The Road Not Taken," by Robert Frost

☐ Excerpts from James McBride Dabbs's essay, "Robert Frost, Poet of Action"

Procedures

1. Lead-In:

Students read excerpts from Dabbs's essay:

> At his best in his lyrics, Robert Frost, in my opinion, will be remembered because he is, even there, a poet of action. These will endure as finished pictures of things done. They have the classic completeness of actions planned, executed, understood. And they reveal modern man, complete in his incompleteness.... Well, what is life? I am willing to take my stand with Aristotle—though perhaps I extend somewhat his meaning—that "life consists in an action''; not in mere physical movement with its sensuous accompaniment, but in the expression in time and space of a man. Robert Frost, I think, expresses life so conceived.

> James McBride Dabbs, "Robert Frost, Poet of Action," *The English Journal*, Vol. 25, No. 6 (1936): 443–451.

2. Step by Step:

    a. Tell the students to read quietly the excerpts from Dabbs's essay.

    b. In the context of "The Road Not Taken," students discuss the idea that Robert Frost is "a poet of action."

    c. Probe the speaker's decision.

    d. Discuss the contrast between lines 10/11 and line 19.

    - Were the roads the same?

    - Is the speaker's decision random or deliberate?

    - What is the effect of this discussion on the claim that Frost was "a poet of action"?

    e. Students explore the challenge of interpreting "The Road Not Taken."

3. Closure:

    Reread the poem.

Differentiation

Advanced

- Students will explore the phrase "a poet of action" on a cube (i.e., by finding other examples of poets who could be described in a similar manner and representing them/their work on the faces of the cube).

- Encourage students to read the poem with a variety of dramatic interpretations and choose the most unique to present to other students. Students should evaluate the different interpretations and discuss how they work to enhance the poem, or detract from it. These readings may be recorded with a video camera to share with other students as time permits.

- Encourage students to create a modern-day interpretation of the poem. They must be able to justify how the modern version stays true to the original while also changing style. Perhaps challenge them to create a movie or digital slide show.
- Encourage students to find other poems and references inspired by "The Road Not Taken." Students should be able to explain how the reference is made. Alternatively, students can read other early poems by Robert Frost and compare and contrast their meaning and style to the one studied in this lesson.

Struggling:

- Reread the poem to students, or allow them to listen to a pre-recorded version.
- Students will discuss the Dabbs excerpt with a partner or in a small group with the teacher.
- Students will explore the phrase "a poet of action" on a cube in order to make this abstract concept more concrete (i.e., describe it, contrast it with "poet," associate it with a "finished picture," apply it to a poet's work, analyze the words — root words/origin, argue for or against it).
- Students create a T-chart or Venn diagram that contrasts the differences between lines 10/11 and line 19.
- Record the student volunteer who reads the poem using a video camera so students can (1) review it as needed, and (2) practice reading along to aid in fluency and understanding.
- Provide the students with a graphic organizer on which they can draft the elements of the homework in a small group or with a partner prior to finishing it at home. Alternatively, have them write their ideas on index cards and then organize them at home.
- Contrast two ways of reading the poem — reading where you pause at the end of each line and where you simply honor the punctuation. Discuss how this nuance changes the interpretation or meaning.

Homework/Assessment

Compose a well-organized and brief essay in which you discuss the challenge of interpreting Robert Frost's "The Road Not Taken."

Writing Guidelines

- Clearly establish the topic of the essay and contextualize it.
- Organize the sequence of ideas according to the purpose of the paragraph.
- Cite the text using short quotations.
- Use Standard English form.
- Avoid grammatical and mechanical errors.
- Use present simple tense.

ABOUT COMMON CORE

Common Core is a nonprofit 501(c)3 organization formed in 2007 to advocate for a content-rich liberal arts education for all students in America's K–12 schools. We believe that a student who graduates from high school without an understanding of culture, the arts, history, literature, civics, and language has been left behind. To improve education in America, we promote programs, policies, and initiatives at the local, state, and federal levels that provide students with challenging, rigorous instruction in the full range of liberal arts and sciences. We also undertake research and projects, such as the Common Core Curriculum Mapping Project, which aim to provide educators with tools that will help students to become strong readers and learners. Go to www.commoncore.org for more information. Despite the coincidence of name, Common Core and the Common Core State Standards are not affiliated.

Common Core has been led by Lynne Munson, as president and executive director, since its founding. From 2001 to 2005, Munson was deputy chairman of the National Endowment for the Humanities. In that post, Munson conceived of and designed Picturing America. The most successful public humanities project in NEH history, Picturing America put more than 75,000 sets of fine art images and teaching guides into libraries, K–12 classrooms, and Head Start centers. From 1993 to 2001, Munson was a research fellow at the American Enterprise Institute, where she wrote *Exhibitionism: Art in an Era of Intolerance.* Munson has written on contemporary cultural and educational issues for numerous national publications, including the *New York Times, The Wall Street Journal, USA Today, Educational Leadership,* and *American Educator.* She has appeared on CNN, FoxNews, CNBC, C-SPAN, and NPR.

Joy Hakim, author, *A History of the US* and *The Story of Science*

Bill Honig, president, Consortium on Reading Excellence (CORE); former California superintendent of public instruction

Carol Jago, director, California Reading and Literature Project at UCLA; former president, National Council of Teachers of English (NCTE)

Juan Rangel, chief executive officer, United Neighborhood Organization (UNO)

ACKNOWLEDGMENTS

Common Core and I, personally, have many people to thank for their support of and contribution to this mapping project. The Bill & Melinda Gates Foundation's support of these Maps was central to their creation. Jamie McKee and Melissa Chabran deserve our deepest thanks. Dane Linn from the National Governors Association encouraged this project all along. David Coleman and Sue Pimentel of the Common Core State Standards ELA writing team have become wonderful colleagues in the course of this work. Our expert advisors—David Driscoll, Toni Cortese, and Russ Whitehurst— provided crucial guidance. And Checker Finn, Pat Riccards, and Andy Rotherham each offered well-timed counsel that was always on target. Wiley's Kate Bradford is an engaged and enthusiastic editor.

We are tremendously thankful to the American Federation of Teachers members, Milken educators, National Alliance of Black School Educators representatives, and the many other teachers and administrators who reviewed our Maps with care, thoroughness, and honesty. I am grateful for the wise guidance and unwavering encouragement of Common Core's trustees. Extra thanks to trustees Pat Forgione, Jason Griffiths, Carol Jago, and again to Toni, who each played a key role in this work. I'm grateful to research assistant Stephanie Porowski, her predecessor James Elias, as well as interns Meagan Estep and Denise Wilkins, each of whose investigatory skills is surpassed only by their ability to keep track of the nearly 200 documents that comprise these Maps. Thanks to Ed Alton for converting our Maps into a navigable—and now interactive—digital feast. And to Shannon Last, Laura Bornfreund, and Kathleen Porter-Magee for perfecting our every last word. Diana Senechal, Melissa Mejias, and Leslie Skelton each made important contributions to our high school Maps. Many thanks to Jack Horak, Ed Spinella, Christine Miller, Donald Holland, and particularly to Stephen Griffith, for keeping our increasingly complex affairs in order.

We've made many new friends as a result of this work as calls and e-mails have poured in from nearly every state. Very special thanks to Buddy Auman and Teresa Chance of the Northwest Arkansas Educational Cooperative, who have helped us to see our Maps in action. Julie Duffield from WestEd introduced us to twenty-first-century outreach. Donna Perrigo, Karen Delbridge, Linda Diamond, Joe Pizzo, Julie Joslin, and Laura Bednar have helped to spread word of our Maps in Arizona, Wyoming, California, New Jersey, North Carolina, and Arkansas. Many others from those states—and from New York, Florida, Ohio, Pennsylvania, and Utah, in particular—deserve our gratitude.

Lastly, the teachers who wrote the Maps deserve the utmost thanks. Each of our lead writers brought deep dedication, along with years of experience, to the project: Sheila Byrd Carmichael, our project coordinator and lead writer of the high school Maps, is an expert on education standards and former leader of the American Diploma Project; Ruthie Stern, who, in addition to her work on the high school Maps, led the writing of the seventy-six sample lesson plans, is a longtime New York City Public Schools teacher and a professor at Columbia Teachers College; Lorraine Griffith, lead writer for the elementary grades, is a fifth-grade teacher in Asheville, North Carolina, coauthor of numerous books on reading, and a Common Core trustee; Cyndi Wells, lead writer for the middle grades, is a teacher and fine arts facilitator in Charlottesville, Virginia, and our project's jack-of-all-trades; and Louisa Moats, author of our pacing guide for reading foundations, is a writer of the CCSS in reading and a true leader in her field. These women stuck with this project as it grew, wonderfully, beyond what any of us originally had imagined. They did all of this despite the challenges of the school schedules, motherhood, book deadlines, family vacations, and much else. It was an honor for me to have the opportunity to work alongside these teachers as they drew on their wealth of knowledge and experience to forge what we hope are tools that their peers nationwide will enjoy.

Lynne Munson
President and Executive Director, Common Core
Washington, D.C.
September 2011

INDEX OF SUGGESTED WORKS

This index lists the creators and titles of works included in the Maps. To search for other information (for example, ideas, places, events) please go to the online version of the Maps at http://commoncore.org/maps/ and use the search function.